FARTHER
THAN
ANY
MAN

Also by Martin Dugard

Surviving the Toughest Race on Earth
Knockdown: The Harrowing True Account of a
    Yacht Race Turned Deadly

FARTHER THAN ANY MAN

The Rise and Fall of CAPTAIN JAMES COOK

Martin Dugard

ALLEN&UNWIN

First published in Australia in 2001
First published in the United States in 2001 by Pocket books,
a division of Simon & Schuster, Inc.

Allen & Unwin
83 Alexander Street
Crows Nest NSW 2065
Australia
Phone: (61 2) 8425 0100
Fax: (61 2) 9906 2218
Email: info@allenandunwin.com
Web: www.allenandunwin.com

National Library of Australia
Cataloguing-in-Publication entry:

Dugard, Martin.

Farther than any man: the rise and fall of Captain James
Cook.

ISBN 1 86508 631 2.

1. Cook, James, 1728–1779—Journeys. 2. Voyages around
the world. 3. Explorers—England—Biography. 4. Oceania
—Discovery and exploration. I. Title.

910.92

Printed by Griffin Press, South Australia

10 9 8 7 6 5 4 3 2 1

For Devin, Connor, and Liam

You call it luck. I call it destiny.

    —Adventurer Daniel Dravot, in Rudyard
    Kipling's *The Man Who Would Be King,*
    on becoming a god

ACKNOWLEDGMENTS

The special genius of Jason Kaufman made this book possible.

Thanks also to Phil Kennington, Graem Sims, Harry Lumb, Steve Madden, Mary and John Harney, Mark Burnett, Jeff Probst, Craig Piligian, Scott Waxman, Gordon Wright, Austin Murphy, and Dean Austin Lewis.

Farewell to Monique Dugard Lewis and Marc Dugard—you did not go gently.

Love to Calene, Devin, Connor, and Liam.

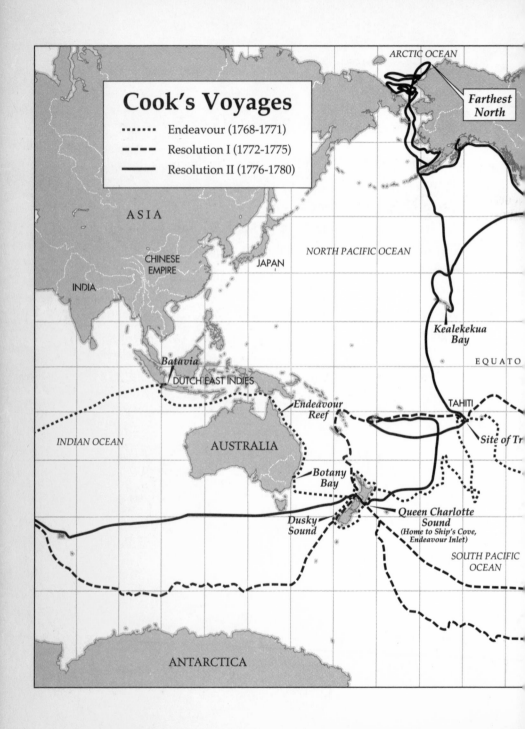

Cook's Voyages

········· Endeavour (1768-1771)

– – – Resolution I (1772-1775)

——— Resolution II (1776-1780)

ARCTIC OCEAN

Farthest North

ASIA

CHINESE EMPIRE

INDIA

JAPAN

NORTH PACIFIC OCEAN

Kealekekua Bay

EQUATO

Batavia

DUTCH EAST INDIES

TAHITI

Endeavour Reef

INDIAN OCEAN

AUSTRALIA

Site of Tr

Botany Bay

Dusky Sound

Queen Charlotte Sound
(Home to Ship's Cove, Endeavour Inlet)

SOUTH PACIFIC OCEAN

ANTARCTICA

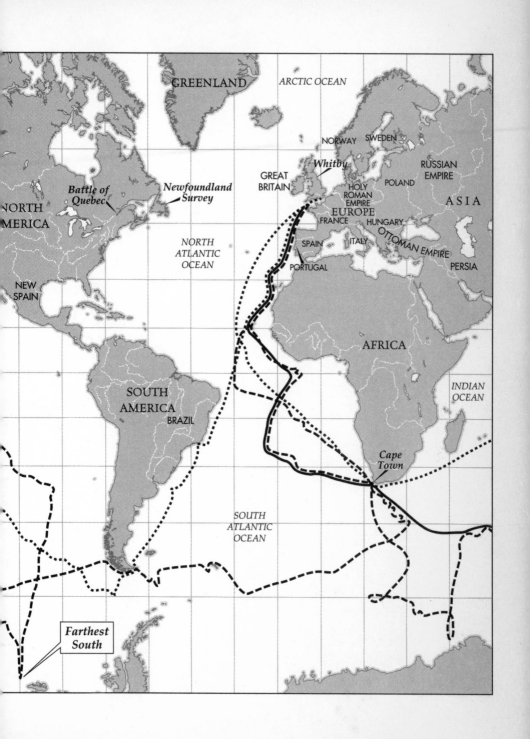

CONTENTS

Prologue: Newport, Rhode Island   1

PART ONE: Land of Hopes and Dreams   7

CHAPTER 1: Land of Hopes and Dreams   9
CHAPTER 2: Adam Raised Cain   15
CHAPTER 3: In the Navy   32
CHAPTER 4: Politics   42

PART TWO: *Endeavour*: Living on the Edge
of the World   55

CHAPTER 5: The Great *Endeavour*   57
CHAPTER 6: Rio   68
CHAPTER 7: The Promised Land   84
CHAPTER 8: Rendezvous   94
CHAPTER 9: Coasting on the Edge of the World   106
CHAPTER 10: Trapped   119

PART THREE: First *Resolution*: Farther Than
Any Man   139

CHAPTER 11: Local Hero   141
CHAPTER 12: Ice   157
CHAPTER 13: Cannibals   181
CHAPTER 14: The Forbidden Lands   204
CHAPTER 15: Homeward Bound   212

PART FOUR: Last *Resolution*   219

CHAPTER 16: Fame   221
CHAPTER 17: The Call of Adventure   229
CHAPTER 18: Rum, Sodomy, and the Lash   244
CHAPTER 19: North   266
CHAPTER 20: Lono   270

            Epilogue: Captain Cook, Hawaii   281

Newport, Rhode Island

I've come here, to this natural harbor fronting New England's intra-coastal waterway, to begin my search for the real James Cook. I want to clear away the tangle of myth and hero worship that has elevated this relentless, passionate loner into the realm of historic sainthood. My goal is to better understand him and the motivations that led him to wander away from home and safety for years at a time. It was a wandering that became an addiction, then a bewilderment, and ultimately, a death sentence.

In learning about Cook I hope to learn more about myself, for I am slowly becoming addicted to adventurous wandering, too. The drive is enigmatic, contradictory to my deep love for my wife and three young children, and has made me fixate on a hard question: Why do people who are otherwise deeply content feel the need to risk all—family, career, and even life—to pursue adventure?

The question predates Cook, but feels fresh in an era when the societal craving to scale sheer rock faces, sail the globe, or merely cling to an inflatable raft as it bucks through Class V white water has rendered adventure almost status quo. There is nothing, however, status quo about the horrific consequences of that moment the rope breaks, a rogue wave hits at midnight, or the raft flips, and whatever illusion of immortality the adventurer had clung to for reassurance is exposed as myth. Death is part and parcel of adventure.

The question's easy answer is that adventurers have death wishes; we're all aching to go out in the twenty-first century's version of dying with our boots on. But I know that's not the case. Adventure's great irony is that adventurers hold life in higher esteem than the general populace. By pushing limits and confronting fears, life becomes sweeter, more easily savored moment by moment. The other answer, of course, is an addiction to adrenaline. But any adventurer will tell you that's false, because the only time adrenaline enters into the picture is when things go very wrong. Only the foolhardy get hooked on adrenaline.

I suspect the answer lies with James Cook, the original adventurer. Prior to Cook, the term adventure was synonymous with gambling. The Latin origin of the word is advenire, meaning "about to happen." A gambler would yell "Adventure!" for help at the roulette wheel, much the same way a modern gambler might cry "Come on, seven!" Gambling was rife in all levels of English society, but to be an "adventurer" was to be of the lowest caste— a man without responsibility or care, abiding by the rules of a parallel society. Quite often adventurer was hurled as an insult.

Then Jonathan Swift wrote Gulliver's Travels. Swift spun adventure on its head, using the word to imply bravery and edge-of-the-envelope daring. The book was a smash, and adventure's new meaning filtered into the public's collective frontal lobe. Men of distinction and daring became glad to hear their names associated with adventure. But it was Cook, sailing the globe forty years after Gulliver's publication, who became synonymous with the word. He imbued it with courage and class.

Adventure wasn't just risk-taking to Cook, but a form of labor that bordered on art. "He carried out work that was so all-encompassing," the great French explorer La Pérouse noted of Cook's daring, "that there was little for his successors to do but admire it."

Over the past two centuries, however, Cook has faded to a historical line drawing. Australians beatify the man (perhaps because Cook is the primary reason they don't speak French), native cultures vilify him, corporations longing to sound worldly take his name. Admirers ignore his shortcomings and paint him as a humble saint. Those with a vague awareness of Cook sum him up as a cartoon figure—a musty, fusty British sailor in a white-powdered wig, spyglass in hand, thundering orders with the gravitas of Charles Laughton. But few identify him with hard-core adventure.

Adding to the confusion is the alliterative way Cook's name and rank trip off the tongue like a trademark—Coca-Cola, Kentucky Fried Chicken, Captain Cook. That catchy collection of consonants has trivialized the man, but is also a major reason Cook has not disappeared from the public consciousness as have more phonetically challengingly named explorers such as Abel Tasman or Pedro Fernandes de Queirós. Captain Cook became Sir James Matthew Barrie's Captain Hook of Peter Pan in 1904 and Gene Roddenberry's Captain Kirk of Star Trek in 1966. Cook's ambition "to go as far as I think it possible for man to go" even became the starship Enterprise's mission "to boldly go where no man has gone before."

It's worth noting that the alliteration is misleading. In his fifty years on earth, Cook held the rank of captain just four years. The rank does not define the man.

A more thorough insight comes from the personality-typing theories Carl Jung would set forth a century and a half after Cook's death. Based on actions, relationships, and written words, Jung would label people like Cook an INTJ (Introvert, Intuitive, Thinker, Judger). The INTJs' mental strength makes them exceptionally independent. They are passionate and warm-hearted but, because of their introversion, can come across as aloof. They have a critical mind that questions everything. They disdain authority if it seems illogical. They daydream constantly, and their drive to transfer those dreams into reality can even come across as eccentric to those who don't share the vision.

Cook, then, was quirky, bold, caring, and proud—and had a vision of the world that is only now being realized. It was Cook who began knitting earth's cultures one island at a time. Two centuries after Cook, the Internet finished the task, creating a global village. It's sweet irony that Tuvalu, the modern name for the first collection of South Sea islands Cook ever laid eyes on, has overcome its remote global locale by basing its entire economy on the Internet.

I park my rental car at Newport's transportation center. It's October, not yet 8 A.M. I've got the place to myself. The sunlight is pale, a pastel backdrop for the autumn reds and yellows bursting in colorful exclamation about the horizon. I walk toward the ocean on this blustery morning, twisting my body into the blow until I am aerodynamic, letting the wind slip over and around me without smashing me hard in the teeth.

I stop a moment along the waterfront and stare out to sea. It's hard to imagine men willingly setting forth for multiyear journeys atop that unpredictable, unforgiving, indomitable tempest whose color ranges from sky blue to pea green to opaque black.

Then I continue down historic Washington Street, parallel to the waterfront, toward the Newport Bridge and the waterfront military facility housing the Naval War College. The houses along Washington Street are painted in primary colors. They are old—Revolutionary War old—and I feel as though I've stepped back into Cook's era. Many have plaques stating the name and occupation of the house's owner two centuries ago, when the British ran the town, imprisoning the colonial rebels (whom they considered wayward British citizens, and thus under their domain) and dating the girls of Newport.

The smell of dead, wet leaves and the salty taste from breathing the Atlantic air relax me. I turn my face into the wind, letting it slap my cheeks and smash my teeth, liking how alive I feel. The sensation will be fleeting, and as soon as I find my way back to the rental or find a Starbucks, I'll prefer comfort over cold. But for now I like this biophilia—this innate hunger to connect with nature.

I stumble down to the shoreline behind the Naval War College. The waterfront is lined with rocks, along with a small collection of new beer cans. The steel span of the Newport Bridge rises to my left. I reach down and touch the cold, green Atlantic, then fix my eyes on a patch of water a hundred yards offshore. Research shows that thirty feet beneath that spot lie the remains of HM Bark Endeavour—the first ship Cook brazenly sailed around the globe. Sunken and out of sight, she is a powerful connection to what once was. Standing so close makes a fine symbolic beginning to my adventure, but it doesn't begin to answer my question.

I return down Washington Street, wind at my back, emboldened to continue the search for Cook. I will go to London next, to a thoroughfare known as Mile End Road.

PART ONE

Land of Hopes and Dreams

CHAPTER I

Land of Hopes and Dreams

August 1768

T he summer had been one of the hottest on record. The Friday-night air was muggy, or "close" as Londoners liked to say, when James and Elizabeth Cook spent their last night together before *Endeavour's* departure. Through the open bedroom window of their cramped brick row house, the mingled aromas of fermenting juniper from the gin distillery next door and the open sewers of Mile End Road below wafted past the thin curtains. He was thirty-nine, stoic and six foot plus, with shoulders squared from leaning hard into many a rope. She was twenty-six, a pretty, extroverted former shop girl hours away from losing her husband, lover, companion, confidant, and soul mate for three years—maybe forever.

Seventy miles away, HM Bark *Endeavour* waited for Cook at the mouth of the English Channel, in the port of Deal. The week before she had been eased from the clutter of Deptford Yard and guided down the Thames by a river pilot. In the morning Cook would travel to Deal by coach. There he would discharge the pilot and begin a voyage around the world.

The bedroom is a private place, and what went on between the two of them that night of August 5, 1768, can only be conjecture. But James and Elizabeth, married six years, were devoted to one another. Their courtship had been whirlwind, with mere weeks elapsing from meeting to marriage. And while he'd spent six months each year charting North America, James was never unfaithful in his travels.

Elizabeth, for her part, was unswerving in the belief that her self-assured sailor was destined for greatness. They endured the separations, knowing that each hard-won assignment was another rung up the competitive ladder of Royal Navy career advancement. Silently, smugly, they ached for those passionate, frantic nights of homecoming. Their three children—boys James and Nathaniel, and baby Elizabeth—had all been born either forty weeks after the start of a voyage or forty weeks after Cook had returned home. Now Elizabeth alone would care for them.

On this last night, James and Elizabeth might have dreamed of the time between their next meeting, but they probably avoided discussing the most pressing concern of all: that his profession was one of the most perilous on earth, and even veteran sailors such as Cook weren't immune to the sea's dangers. Whether by shipwreck, fire, cannibals, mutiny, shipboard fighting, scurvy, suicide, or just plain accidental drowning, death occurred to at least a few members of every crew, on every long voyage. To make matters worse, *Endeavour* would be alone, without a companion ship to rescue James and the crew in case something went wrong. Speaking of these dangers would have rendered James and Elizabeth's last night together maudlin, detracting from the romance of a man and woman hours away from a three-year separation.

For all the anxiety, however, the coming morning held incredible promise. James Cook would not only begin an epic voyage, he would make history. His unorthodox decision to leave a promising career in merchant sailing thirteen years earlier, then start all over again at the bottom of the Royal Navy's enlisted ranks, would finally be vali-

dated. He had already become the first man in Royal Navy history to
rise from the bottom of those ranks to an officer's commission and
command. Now, rewriting the rules for career advancement, he was
joining the very short list of men given command of voyages around
the world.

Preparation had consumed Cook all summer. Each morning he
had ferried across the river, leaving Britain's great symbols—the Admiralty building, Westminster Abbey, the Tower of London—behind
him on the Thames's north bank. On the south shore, Cook had
turned left and entered the East End waterfront tenement and ware-
house slums Charles Dickens would someday make famous in *Oliver
Twist*. Walking the narrow cobblestone path, Cook could smell the
rot of trash piled in alleys, the stench of urine pooled at the base of
walls outside taverns, and almost taste the thick, black grease of
cooking oil and smoke. Some days there were riots, too, brought on
by the heat and the overcrowded slums. *Endeavour* and Cook weren't
so much setting sail from the chaos as fleeing.

The goals set forth for Cook's journey were lofty and came at a
crucial moment for both Britain and the world. The year 1768
was in the middle of what writers were calling the Age of Enlightenment, with mankind shaking off centuries of darkness to embrace
learning and reason once again. Science was sexy, peace reigned, and
a growing belief in personal liberty was blurring the lines between
the upper and lower classes.

Enlightenment or no, however, a handful of nations were behaving as nations had since the beginning of time, jockeying for global
dominance. And no nation was pushing more frantically than Great
Britain. The tiny island nation (England, Scotland, Wales, Ireland)
controlled the seas from India to the Americas. She had recently
vanquished archfoe France in the Seven Years' War—taking full possession of North America, temporarily ending the French military
threat they had endured since the Norman Conquest, and even gain-

ing concessions from the argumentative Spanish (who had belatedly joined the war on the side of France), thus rendering the Iberian Peninsula's residents little more than a respected nuisance.

The focus of world exploration in February 1768 was the Southern Hemisphere. Most everything of note that could be discovered above the equator—save the legendary Northwest Passage—had been. The Portuguese and the Spanish, then the mercantile Dutch, had seen to that. But below the equator lay vast swaths of mystery. The bumbling but ambitious king of England, George III, devised a plan to send a single vessel of discovery around the globe. The voyage would be hailed as a scientific expedition (and science would truly be a vital aspect of its mission). The greater aim, however, was the discovery and conquest of the legendary Southern Continent—Antarctica. Since Ptolemy in the second century, the idea of the Southern Continent had bewitched powerful men, burgeoning from the theoretical—its existence at the bottom of the world was necessary to counterbalance the arctic land mass—into a mythic opiate promising wealth beyond wildest imaginings. "The scraps from this table," theorist Alexander Dalrymple had written, sure that the Great Southern Continent was bigger than all Asia, "would be sufficient to maintain the power, dominion, and sovereignty of Britain by employing all its manufacturers and ships."

Kings of many nations, and the men they sent to explore for this lost continent, believed so much in this Southern Hemisphere promised land that they somehow disregarded the obvious: a continent so far south was likely to be just as snow-blasted and awful as its arctic counterpart to the north.

Britain was eager to find and colonize Antarctica because she was in danger of losing her lucrative American colonies. Colonial resources were the lifeblood of Britain, providing raw materials to British manufacturers, who then exported finished goods to other nations and back to the colonies. Without this colonial flow, England's great thinkers believed, Britain's international influence

would shrivel. As Horace Walpole wrote candidly, "We shall be reduced to a miserable little island, and from a mighty empire sink to
as insignificant a country as Denmark or Sardinia. Then France will
dictate to us more imperiously than we ever did to Ireland."

America was the crown jewel of Britain's possessions, a bountiful
land blessed with dense pine forests for fashioning ship's masts, rich,
dark soil for growing tobacco, and thousands of miles of coastal fishing grounds. But that same coastline was the bane of Britain's attempts to collect colonial revenue, laced with the sort of coves and
hidden inlets that concealed cargo ships long enough for their haul
to be off-loaded and for customs duties to go unpaid. Between 1763
and 1768, the British began cracking down. Militant colonists
fought back, beginning efforts to drive the British from America altogether. King George III—pudgy, with eyes that bulged comically
from his head, of limited education but with dreams of a grand
legacy—vowed that scenario would never occur. He said he would
rather level the colonies than see them independent.

Prudently, George III began searching for other resources. In
1764 and 1766 he sent major probes into the South Pacific. Each expedition consisted of two vessels traveling together. Neither ventured far enough south to discover any evidence of Antarctica.

As the situation in the colonies worsened, George III placed
greater expectations on the next voyage of circumnavigation. Instead
of two ships, a lone vessel would make the journey to find Antarctica.
The captain of this circumnavigation would have to be bold and
eager, given to following orders to the letter, and uncaring that the expedition was, because of the extremely stormy and unknown southern latitudes through which he would sail, likely a suicide mission.

So it came to pass that James Cook, the brilliant, upright, and
middle-aged career sailor—a man of "genius and capacity" in the
words of one admiral—woke on the morning of August 6, bid good-
bye to his pregnant wife and three small children, and boarded a
coach for Deal wearing his dazzling new blue uniform. He had been

plucked from obscurity, granted a commission, and offered command of the expedition. The pain of leaving was tempered by the
thrill that Endeavour was all he'd waited for, dreamed of, counted on.
Cook had always lived by a self-determined set of rules, and it was finally paying off.

As for preserving the legacy of King George III and ensuring the
power of Great Britain, Cook was unaware he'd been so entrusted.
His aims were modest—to fulfill his orders to the letter and return to
Elizabeth. He was focused and prepared for the challenges to come,
The instant the coach pulled away from Mile End Road, however, his
life, and his entire motivation for being, would be forever changed.

CHAPTER 2

Adam Raised Cain

Had George III known who was entrusted with preserving his legacy, he might have looked elsewhere. For Cook had a rebel past. His father, also James, had fought to topple George's grandfather from the crown during the first Jacobite Rebellion in 1715. That the son of this rebel, fifty-three years later, would sail off to claim new lands in the name of George III was an ironic oversight.

The basis of the Jacobite cause was restoration of a Catholic monarch in Protestant-run England. But its failure made *Catholic* and *pariah* synonymous, so Cook the elder kept his faith to himself after crossing the border from Scotland into England. When he found a job slopping hogs in the northeastern England region of Yorkshire, he considered himself lucky and set to making a career of it.

Over the next ten years the immigrant earned a reputation for intellect and hard work, endearing him not just to his employer but also to a farm girl eight years younger, Grace Pace. Their flirtations brought out a minor impulsive streak in the thirty-one-year-old immigrant. The pair married out of necessity, and a child was born just four months later, in January 1726. They named him John, after the immigrant's father.

Two years later, on October 27, 1728, their second of eight children was born. Another boy. Circumstances being more upright, the child was given his father's name.

Lying in a fertile valley just north of the vast Cleveland Moors, young James Cook's hometown of Marton-in-Cleveland was scant miles from the North Sea ports of Staithes and Whitby, but light-years away from London's sophistication and worldliness. England was still an agricultural society when Cook was born in 1728, and young men were trained to follow in their fathers' footsteps. With Cook's father risen to foreman of the largest farm in the region, Airyholme, just outside the village of Great Ayton, young James seemed destined for the same future.

Not that the foreman's job was a meager position. In fact, because British landowners were required by law to leave their property regularly to serve as justices of the peace, regulate local inns and pubs, and even ensure development of roads and bridges, the foreman had total control of the farm in the owner's absence. The landowner, then, was like a king commanding his subjects. The foreman was his instrument of power.

Because Airyholme was the largest local farm, the foreman's role carried even more heft, and James Cook senior enjoyed a rank and status shared by few in Great Ayton. Every Airyholme employee reported to him. Everyone as far as the eye could see respected him. James Cook senior didn't share in the profits but worked with the proprietary zeal of an owner.

It was a work ethic young James never forgot. And though father and son were different on the surface, that's because young James was battling hard to be contrary. In fact, the two were very much the same. Between birth and the age of seven, young James displayed rebelliousness, a tendency toward being a loner, and competitiveness—

all traits of his father's. And while older brother John was responsible, a carbon copy of their mother, James rejected familial structure, often wandering off to explore Airyholme's vast acreage. James was especially fond of examining the structure of birds' nests. In the confined world of the farm, where his family was subservient to the landowners, James sought a world limitless and free. It was to become his life's common theme.

At the same time Cook distanced himself from his family, he began seeking approval from a series of surrogate fathers, adopting their manners and morals as indicators of how he should act upon arriving at every new station in life. Cook intuitively trusted these men, honored and looked up to them; saw infallibility and strength. Their copied traits were Cook's pathway to greatness, filling him with deep notions of honor, duty, and country. And because Cook's real father had suppressed his Catholicism after fleeing Scotland, young James even looked to the surrogates for views of God and morality, truth and light.

The first was Thomas Skottowe, owner of Airyholme. The year was 1735 and young James was seven. Skottowe made note of Cook's intelligence and paid for him to attend elementary school in Great Ayton, a great honor in a largely illiterate society. In school, Cook was a charismatic loner, known for having "a steady adherence to his own schemes," an instructor noted, adding with puzzlement, "but there was something in his manners and deportment which attracted the reverence and respect of his companions."

In 1745, Cook ceased his formal schooling and left the farm for good. There was a curious symmetry between his flight from home and his father's flight from Scotland thirty years previously. For a second Jacobite Rebellion was then raging across the border in Scotland, and even spreading into England. Cook—father and son—ignored the rebellion. But the ongoing Jacobite struggle neatly bookended the individual struggles of father and son for personal independence and self-actualization.

Along the dirt donkey paths of North Yorkshire, seventeen-year-old James walked east to the cobbled streets of Staithes, a small fishing village with a reputation as a smuggler's haven. Apprenticing informally as a shop boy to Thomas Skottowe's brother-in-law, the brooding William Sanderson, Cook spent his days stocking shelves, slicing slabs of cheese and bacon, and weighing herring. The shop was gloomy and damp, blasted by winter gales. A North Sea chill and the taste of salt air swirled about. The shop was also right on the ocean, so close, in fact, that Sanderson would surrender the shop to the sea in late 1745 and build another only slightly back off the water. That proximity to the ocean slowly eroded Cook's yearning to become a grocer and increased his desire to chase adventure. Slowly, the sea claimed the impressionable young man.

In the afternoons Cook listened to herring fishermen as they leaned on the shop's counter, describing their day at sea. Hands gnarled, backs broad, faces leathery from wind and sun, the coarse men spun yarns about North Sea gales, the rocky English coastline, and the mysteries of life beyond sight of land. Enigmatically, they also sprinkled their conversation with complex references to the workings of sun and stars and currents.

At night Cook slept beneath that same counter. He pored over books on mathematics, geography, and astronomy by candlelight, trying to learn between those pages what Staithes's fishermen had learned through life experience. Cook studied with focus, ignoring anything unrelated to the sea, including grammar, literature, and spelling.

And so it went for a seemingly wasted but hugely formative year. Cook lived in the store's vacuum, studying by night and stealing flirtatious glances at the ocean by day. Without his noticing, two symbolic connections between the outside world and his own life passed in that time. The first was the death, on October 19, 1745, of the man who had redefined *adventure, Gulliver's Travels'* Jonathan Swift. Cook would not only come to exemplify the word, but live a series of adventures that made Gulliver's pale.

The second incident was the death in April 1746 of the Jacobite cause that had brought about Cook's English birth. After a series of brilliant attacks, Bonnie Prince Charlie and his forces of the second Jacobite uprising were defeated a hundred miles short of London and their goal of putting a Catholic back on the British throne. King George II, a German who had been placed on the throne of England to maintain Protestant dominance, and who spoke fractured English with a guttural German accent, remained in charge. Call it historical irony, call it coincidence, but shortly thereafter Cook fled Sanderson's shop. It was September 1746. The time had come for Cook to begin his life of adventure.

Throwing his few belongings over his shoulder, Cook began hiking south along the cliff-studded coastline to Whitby and the office of John Walker, a prominent Quaker who owned a fleet of cargo ships and a man who would become Cook's next surrogate father. Cook planned to ask Walker for a job. Sanderson had arranged the interview as a parting gift.

Walking from Staithes to Whitby, Cook was burdened only by a few items of clothing but must have been bursting with relief that he would never spend another day working in Sanderson's dank little store. By leaving the shop he was admitting failure as a grocer. Hard on the heels of his perceived failure as a farmer, the few people who knew him well might have been worried about Cook as he wandered farther from his roots, hoping to begin a life at sea. He was displaying all the traits of a lost soul, traveling from town to town in search of a niche, perhaps never destined to find his place in the world.

Cook, however, clearly believed himself capable of great things. This was a teenager who had had the audacity to teach himself mathematics and astronomy. Though there would always be detractors in Cook's life—those who were outraged that a man would dare rise above his preordained rank in Britain's strict class society—Cook never lost sight of his lofty goals.

* * *

The path Cook followed to Whitby is now part of England's nationwide network of hiking trails, and easily one of the most stunning. A dozen miles in length, the trek skirts rugged coastline. Sweeping views, full exposure to the very raw elements—it's the sort of walk that fills a man with a sense of infinite possibility.

Cook arrived in Whitby flushed and tired, but rather than rest, he raced to the waterfront. Whereas Staithes was small and quiet, Whitby was a shipbuilding and cargo transportation center for the entire North Sea and Baltic. Perched on the banks of the river Esk, hemmed from behind by a steep hillside, Whitby had a population of over ten thousand in 1746. The ruined Abbey of Saint Hilda perched on the bluff overlooking town.

Cook gaped at the international armada of cargo ships. The squat behemoths were stately, with masts reaching up to tickle the heavens and yards spreading wide like the arms of God. For the first time, Cook heard the sounds of foreign languages being spoken, as sailors from Baltic ports in Finland, Sweden, Russia, and Germany strolled the docks. From farm boy to shop boy to sailor—Cook had finally wandered to where he belonged. Or at least he hoped so.

Cook entered the spartan office on the first floor of John Walker's home and requested employment. The middle-aged shipowner leaned back in his cane chair and appraised Cook. Walker saw a lad uncoordinated and handsome, with an angular nose that seemed to own his face and bushy, brown eyebrows that stretched his forehead taut when he was deep in thought. Cook, like his father, was sturdy, standing over six feet tall, with shoulders broad and posture ramrod. He made eye contact. His every mannerism betrayed his eagerness to learn and please.

However, Cook was also seventeen, old for a beginning apprentice. Those eighteen months working indoors had made him pale and a little soft. And there was a rebellious, cocksure side to the youth that bordered on arrogance. Would he be able to take orders?

Walker also had reservations about Cook's compatibility with the sailors populating his ships. The sailing life was profane and hard, and Cook seemed something of an innocent. "Those who would go to sea for pleasure would go to hell for pastime" was a popular waterfront saying. Sailors were transient, poor, foulmouthed, and disease-prone, but surprisingly literate, with almost all able seamen possessing the ability to read and write. Most of the sailors would die at sea, so they drank as if there were no tomorrow. Because of risk and mortality, 60 percent of all sailors were under the age of thirty, with the average age being twenty-seven (only 2 percent were older than fifty). The average ship's officer was in his early thirties. Earnings were often squandered gambling or getting drunk in seaside bars. Fights were common because of the heavy drinking and the close living quarters. The fights tended to be bloody and fatal, as sailors were in the habit of arming themselves with a sharp knife at all times.

At sea they faced not just storms, but lightning, freezing temperatures, fire (the seaman's greatest fear on board wooden ships), and sudden death from a crashing mast or amputation from a snapped rope. Sodomy—"buggery"—was officially outlawed, but sharing hammocks often passed for fellowship in the dingy, rat-infested, foulsmelling holds, even by men who preferred heterosexuality onshore. Personal space was nonexistent. Sailors slept in hammocks six feet long, strung just fourteen inches apart. That fourteen-by-six was a sailor's sole refuge.

To join the sailing life was to voluntarily step outside society, changing even facial appearance and manner of dress. Wind and sun prematurely creased and coppered faces, "like they'd been hammered into uncouth shape upon Vulcan's Anvil," one writer noted. Sailors on land walked with an irregular gait, feet shoulder width, torso rolling side to side as if standing on a pitching deck. This waddle, much like a mallard duck's, was comical but functional, learned as a bracing maneuver on the high seas.

Sailors dressed distinctively, wearing baggy breeches coated with tar to keep out the wet and cold. The sailor's shirt was often of a checked pattern, made of whatever thick material he could afford on his annual salary of just one pound sterling. His jacket was the heavy, blue wool fearnought. Head cover in good weather and bad was a floppy watchman's stocking cap. Beneath, sailors often kept pigtails in place by applying a thin layer of tar to their locks. All this gooey, black pitch coating clothes and hair was how sailors of the era earned the nickname Jack Tar.

For men whose fates were at the whims of the elements' raw fury, sailors were surprisingly apathetic about God. They put more faith in omens and apparitions, so much so that ministers of the day singled out sailors for their irreligiosity. "Great is the defect among seafaring men in regard to virtue and piety," one religious writer noted, not understanding that the sailor's world was one of rage and chaos, in tune with the elements but out of sync with land-bound behavior. More intuitive clergy taking passage on merchant vessels learned to prefer the sailor's rampant profanity over any tendency toward prayer, because the only time a sailor began praying was when his ship was in danger of sinking.

For the sailor's whole world was the sea, and it shaped every aspect of his thoughts. Their labor was performed under temperamental conditions, in four-hour shifts known as watches, on ships that spent months away from land. In addition to changing their notion of religious worship, this led to a strong collective identity and a language apart from any other. Sailing jargon and commands—rope names, sail names, portions of the ship, types of weather and waves—constituted a language of technical necessity noteworthy for its clarity and brevity. Syllables saved, however, were spewed through swearing. Sailors were considered incapable of uttering a sentence without an expletive. In addition to being descriptive, the swearing served as a form of protest, an "us versus them" volley of oaths differentiating transient sailors from the middle and upper classes with their polite manners.

The anger stemmed from awareness that men of the sea fit in nowhere else. On land they were out of place, outcasts from polite society and likely to get drunk and wake up in prison. On ship they were subject to random punishment meted out by the captain and his officers. On the other side of the ship's rail lay the tempestuous sea, that physical embodiment of peril. Some sailors could swim but most could not, and a man overboard was likely to drown in the time it took a square-rigged sailing ship to turn around and sail back to his rescue. In the North Sea and Baltic, where the men of Whitby sailed, going overboard meant a painful death through hypothermia and drowning. Swimming only prolonged the agony.

If sailors acted like the whole world was against them, that's because it was. They couldn't even die in peace.

But James Cook wanted to be a part of it. At seventeen, he'd been out of step with society as long as he could remember anyway, and he was sure the sea was his long-sought niche. Walker decided to give the boy a chance. A jubilant Cook was told to find the *Freelove* in Whitby harbor and report for duty.

When Cook located the functional *Freelove*, he nervously clambered up the gangplank, stepping carefully to avoid toppling into the cold, green water. Cook stepped on board, his hard-soled shoes clacking against the wooden deck. As he digested the sights and smells and sounds of his new world—masts and rigging, paint and varnish, seagulls and creaking timber—Cook's body swayed uneasily as a deck rolled beneath his feet for the first time. His new life had begun.

Cook was ordered to sign the muster book. He was issued a hammock and blanket, told where to hang them, then put to work. For a seemingly simple profession, there was much to do and much to learn. Like all new apprentices, Cook quickly set to "learning the ropes"—literally, the knots and names of lines, and the million and one ways to employ the Gordian jumble in good weather and worse—and how best to clamber up the tar-covered ratlines in a gale, then balance on a spindly, bucking yard to unfurl a sail.

Less swashbuckling tasks for the ordinary seaman included latrine duty. The ship's toilets—"seats of ease"—were planks, one extended over either side of the bow. A hole was cut, and the edges sanded. A man did his business precariously, backside dangling over open ocean. When the weather was perfectly calm, there was no problem. Everything splashed into the sea. But when North Sea winds and waves reared up, foiling gravity, it was an ordinary seaman's task to be lowered over the side and polish splatter from the hull before the ship nosed into port.

Once comfortable aboard ship, Cook's next step would be competing for advancement. With Britain shifting from an agrarian to an industrial nation, farmwork was scarce. Scores of teenaged boys who might formerly have worked the fields with their fathers were found employed as apprentices and ordinary seamen on Whitby's colliers. The competition for promotion and employment was fierce.

James Cook, however, was the competitive type. He excelled as a sailor. Beginning in 1746 he made a dozen voyages per year. His first trip aboard *Freelove* was to haul coal along the British coast. Then, as the years passed and he grew more capable, Cook was transferred to a variety of Walker's other vessels, such as the *Three Brothers*, and began open-ocean passages across the North Sea. Between voyages, Cook slept in the attic of Walker's red-brick house on Grape Lane alongside his fellow apprentices. He continued his practice of studying mathematics and astronomy by candlelight. Instead of the floor, as in Sanderson's shop, however, Walker provided him with a table in the corner.

Sailing had become Cook's passion, and he soaked in every nuance, every nugget of information that would make him the consummate seaman. When his three-year apprenticeship ended, Walker continued Cook's employment, promoting him up the ranks. Cook's responsibility was increased. He became adept at the logistics of loading a cargo ship, of how best to balance weight in the hold. He learned to order supplies, and how to oversee a hull and mast's refurbishment between voyages. He learned what sort of sail combination worked best in what sort of wind. He learned how to drop a weighted rope—a "lead line"—over the side of a ship to measure the ocean's depth, especially close to the tricky English coast, where rocks and swirling currents made passage delicate. He learned to record speed and distance with something known as a log line. This piece of wood was attached to a rope, then thrown overboard. A sandglass was used to time how quickly the rope unspooled.

Most important, Cook began learning the fundamentals of navigation. He became adept at determining latitude with a sextant. By accurately measuring the sun's height over the horizon, then consulting latitudinal charts, north-south position could be determined.

Longitude, however, was far more difficult to measure (Sir Isaac Newton, the greatest mind of the early eighteenth century, called longitude "the only problem that ever made my head ache"). It was still an inexact science. Instead of the sun, the moon and the exact time were the keys. By figuring the height of the moon from wherever the ship might be, then figuring the distance between the moon and certain prominent stars, then comparing those figures with the moon's height as computed at Greenwich's Royal Observatory, *then* comparing the time at the ship's location (using the sun to tell time) as compared with Greenwich mean time, *then* calculating the time difference converted to degrees, with one hour equaling fifteen minutes . . . it was possible to calculate longitude exactly.

In all that calculation, the two imperatives were a complete book of lunar tables showing exact distances between moon and stars at Greenwich, then a clock to tell time at the ship's location. Neither, unfortunately, had been invented when Cook was learning his navigation basics. A complete set of lunar tables would not be published until 1755. And a clock had not yet been invented that could withstand the humidity, pitching, temperature changes, and gravity changes inherent in shipboard life. As a result, even the world's most experienced navigators were rarely exact when estimating longitude.

Instead, navigators often fell back into the primitive art of dead reckoning, combining compass, log line, and observation of wind and currents to guess approximate location. In learning dead reckoning, Cook also learned to keep a sharp eye on the wind and the sea's activities, and their influence on the ship. Around the Whitby docks he became known for his intelligence and gentle—if distant—bearing.

By 1752, Cook had worked his way up from apprentice to seaman to first mate. In the merchant world, that made him second-in-command to the captain. Whitby was proving to be a quiet and unglamorous, yet ideal, training ground for the budding mariner. As he moved from his teens into his midtwenties, Cook was a solitary and single man, without the wife and family that might have detracted from his growing obsession with career. When not at sea he studied and planned for the next voyage. Like any sailor, Cook enjoyed nights in the taverns fronting the harbor, but he was careful with his money and wasn't the sort to get falling-down drunk. Quaker Walker noticed these attributes and began taking a greater interest in Cook's career development. The young farm boy was turning out to be perfectly fitted for life at sea, unafraid of physical labor nor cowed by hard weather, but deeply fond of those cerebral pursuits necessary to guide a ship through troubled waters.

Walker began sending Cook on journeys to glamorous London. Cook was smitten with the big city, fixating on the bright lights and bustle of Thames-side ports rather than on the seedier aspects—the poverty, overcrowding, open sewers, illness. London was where Cook laid eyes on officers of the Royal Navy for the first time, with their powdered white wigs, polished shoes, and bright blue uniforms piped in gold. Their ships were sleek, muscular, and overpopulated. Cannon seemed to poke from every orifice.

By comparison, Cook's Whitby cats looked stubby and slow. Cook was not a man prone to envy, but he had a weakness for status and wealth. The Royal Navy officers in London seemed to have both. In

Cook's mind, they were true men of the sea. He found himself wondering what it would be like to be one of them.

For all Cook's idealism, life in the Royal Navy was hellish. Life in the Whitby merchant fleet was a pleasure cruise by comparison. Unlike the motivated career seamen in Whitby, sailors in the Royal Navy were the dregs of society. Many were lost men and derelicts, physically abducted by press gangs and thrown aboard against their will. They knew nothing of life on ship and were prone to seasickness. While merchant sailors could expect regular payment for their work, navy sailors might not get paid for years at a time. The longer duration of navy voyages—to America, Africa, India—meant ships were deliberately overstaffed at the start of a voyage to compensate for the coming multitude of deaths. Hundreds of men died of typhus on every voyage.

The single greatest killer, however, was scurvy. The disease is caused by an absence of vitamin C in the body, the result of spending months at sea without the fresh fruits and vegetables providing this vital substance. Vitamin C is responsible for producing the fibrous tissues that provide strong capillaries, bone, dentin, and cartilage. Without it, the body begins slowly breaking down. Listlessness sets in, teeth fall out, and victims become anemic before dying. In Cook's time, there was no known cure.

Many, of course, suspected food had something to do with the problem. The standard weekly ration included bread, beer (one gallon per day), beef or pork (four days out of the week), peas, and oatmeal. Storage was a problem, however, and shipboard food was atrocious once it began rotting, especially later in a journey when rats had broken into rations, eaten some, then soaked the rest with urine. Maggots also infested food, with the remedy for killing maggots (placing a piece of dead fish atop the infested food, drawing the maggots from the food into the fish) almost as foul as the maggots themselves.

On top of all their other hardships, sailors in the Royal Navy were subjected to severe punishment should they misbehave. Discipline was harsh and random, and so pervasive that it left an indelible mark on the English language.

Lesser crimes were punished with "cobbing." That is, a gruff group of sailors would take the offender to the gun room and beat him senseless. A more public punishment was "gauntleting," when the entire ship's company formed two lines and the miscreant was whipped using knotted ropes. The term *running the gauntlet* originated there. The more serious the crime, however, the slower the man was compelled to move through the gauntlet, right down to wheeling him down the line lashed over a barrel, hence, "had him over a barrel."

The next level of punishment was meted out by having the offender tied to the mainmast and lashed with the cat-o'-nine-tails. This many-tentacled whip was made of leather and was used by many nations, some of whom tipped the end with metal or bone. Even the Royal Navy found this too draconian and forbade such appendage. However, the cats in the antipodean prison colonies were often tipped or turned into a "thieves' cat" by knotting the strands down their length. These were often wielded by marines or sailors assigned duty as prison guards.

The cat was kept in a red baize bag to conceal the blood covering its tendrils—which brought forth the term *the cat's out of the bag.* In bad weather, punishment on board ships had to be done belowdecks. This posed a problem, however, for few spaces had room for the attendant victim, observers, and the master administering the captain's "award." If a space was too small, it was said to be "too small to swing a cat." If the captain felt that the master administering the punishment wasn't trying hard enough, he, too, would receive "six of the best."

For truly bad indiscretions, a sailor could be "flogged around the fleet" (six of the best on each of His Majesty's ships in the port at the time). Keelhauling was one step above that (tied to a rope and dragged along the ship's bottom from one side of the hull to another underwater, scraping the body against barnacles, often killing the victim by drowning or from bleeding). The ultimate punishment was hanging, done from a mainmast yard.

About the only thing navy life had going for it was the generous daily ration of 94-proof rum mixed with water, a concoction known as grog. The ration was a pint a day, split between a morning and an afternoon serving. And on long voyages, sometimes even the grog ran out.

In East End bars such as the Mayflower and the Angel (with its bar paneled to resemble a ship's hull, whose rear windows looked out onto the Thames), Cook rubbed elbows with seamen from His Majesty's fleet. He chose to ignore stories of brutality and focused on the glory. His Majesty's sailors spoke rapturously of the spice trade or the Americas or failed expeditions in search of unseen places such as the Great South Land and the Northwest Passage. Of Calcutta, Saint Helena, Capetown, New York. Of entire fleets lost in a single ferocious gale or of days without movement in the equatorial doldrums. Of the horrors of working the slave trade, sailing's most unpopular detail. Of battling ferocious currents off Africa and Tierra del Fuego. Of the legendary Spanish ghost ship that was last seen along the North American coast under full sail, despite the death of her entire crew from malaria, yellow fever, and scurvy. Of sailing from the cold gales of England to latitudes where the air was warm and soft like a lover's kiss, the sea a soothing turquoise instead of gunmetal gray, and where the women weren't encumbered by clothing.

The old salts also whispered of hostile natives in those faraway lands who practiced cannibalism. The shock wasn't that these tropical savages ingested human flesh—cannibalism was alive and well in Europe—but that they had a taste for *live* people. European cannibalism was confined to cadavers and men dangling from the gallows, whose blood was drained as a cure for epilepsy and as a tonic for healthier living. Local citizenry would line up after a hanging, cups in hand, to let the free samples of life flow into them. Also, "the spirit of life" was routinely consumed by European soldiers of the seventeenth and eighteenth centuries. This was obtained by slicing off and eating the genitals of men killed in battle. Phalluses of the newly dead were alleged to contain concentrated life forces.

But the tropical savages hunted and killed men expressly to roast them on a spit or boil them alive. The only organ unfit for consumption was the gallbladder, for it was considered too bitter.

In such fantastic tales Cook's world grew larger, his vision for his future grander. Whitby—blustery, storybook Whitby, with the river Esk flowing through the center of town and sheer, gray cliffs flanking the harbor like titans—was no longer big enough to contain Cook's dreams. "Someday," Cook confided to a crestfallen Walker after returning from one trip to London, "I want to be in the Royal Navy."

In 1755, at age twenty-six, Cook was an old salt, given de facto control of every ship on which he sailed. Cook's leadership style was at once casual and demanding, and men took orders well from him. Years plying coastal waterways and the stormy North Sea had made Cook a true navigator, an expert on currents and depths and wind patterns and rocky shoals that needed to be approached carefully at night or in fog, for the English coast had no lighthouses.

Walker, meanwhile, decided it was time to formally discuss promoting Cook to ship's captain. Financially, Cook would be set for life. As for power, he would be a true commander, with all the authority the position entailed. And the ship wouldn't be a second-rate vessel like the old and slow *Freelove*, but the dashing new *Friendship*, the finest and newest addition to Walker's fleet.

In the spring of 1755, Walker summoned Cook to his office. The pubescent teenager who'd tramped hopefully from Staithes so long ago was now a man. He was confident and knowledgeable, an excellent choice for command. Walker was lucky to have him and he knew it.

Cook stood before Walker's desk, knowing what he was about to hear.

Walker offered Cook command of the *Friendship*. He reminded Cook that *Friendship* was his best vessel. He reminded Cook that staying in Whitby was the smartest thing he could do, for his immense talents would be wasted in the Royal Navy. Wasted, Walker reinforced. Cook would never be granted command. That honor only went to officers, and officers were always born of the upper class, entering the navy at a young age and guided by influential connections up through the officer corps. The best Cook could hope for (and this was the main point of persuasion, because Walker knew Cook seriously believed he was destined for greater things) was to be a master, always laboring in the shadow of a captain. He might do great things, but another man would always get credit.

Cook was a deliberate man, practical in almost every way, but that adventurous streak ran through him hard. Because of it, Cook not only chased danger and adventure throughout his lifetime, but made three highly unusual and impulsive choices. One got Cook into the Royal Navy, another got him married, and the third got him killed. In retrospect, two out of three were brilliant decisions.

As politely as he knew how, Cook spurned Walker. He announced his plans to sail for London, where he would throw away nine years' seniority and advancement by enlisting in the Royal Navy. At twenty-six, James Cook would be an able-bodied seaman, starting all over again. In parting, Cook told Walker of the Royal Navy, "I want to make my future fortune there."

On June 17, 1755, seduced by grandeur and guided by his dream, Cook enlisted in the Royal Navy.

CHAPTER 3

In the Navy

ook was assigned to *Eagle*, a sixty-gun ship moored on the English Channel at Spithead. Despite his dreams, Cook had few misconceptions about life in His Majesty's navy. Being just another faceless crew member was akin to being an inmate. The captain had total authority, a fact of life guaranteed by Admiralty law. Any action or word counter to his will was punishable as mutiny. "They could make life," it was written of captains, "as tolerable or un-bearable as they wished." This powerlessness imbued hopelessness into the fabric of crew life and crushed the will of independent thinkers like James Cook.

That was the life he chose, but descending into the belly of *Eagle* for the first time, Cook couldn't help but be dumbfounded. She may have been spit-and-polish above decks, but as Cook backed down the companionway, he was assaulted by the noise of a hundred conversa-tions and the smells of mildew, urine, and body odor. He stooped—thick beams meant the space between decks was sometimes just five feet—under the orlop deck to hang his hammock and stow his sea chest. It took a moment for Cook's eyes to adjust to the darkness.

Body shapes materialized. Men were playing cards, drinking, nap-ping; marking time between birth and death, oblivious to their squalor, holding out little hope of a better world. To Cook's amaze-ment, almost four hundred men called the dank belly home. On a Whitby collier the crew was a couple dozen men—small enough to feel like a family.

The crew casually appraised the new man. Cook's clothing, walk, and facial appearance told them he was a real sailor. That was an odd-ity itself. Real sailors didn't inhabit their netherworld. Real sailors were up top, barking commands, or making a good living on mer-chant ships.

The new man was tall, very strong. His hands were large and cal-lused. He descended the companionway and snaked through the hold with surefooted nonchalance. He was quiet but not impolite. No one bothered him as he found a beam for his hammock and a small parcel of deck for his sea chest. And though the more forth-right members of the crew would eventually get around to asking Cook what the hell a man like him was doing there, the crew's inter-est in Cook ceased once he found a spot to bunk. He was obviously not a man to be trifled with.

Over the next few weeks, *Eagle*'s officers noticed his appearance, too. After probing his knowledge with questions about wind and drift and the function of different ropes, Cook was told to move above decks. After just a month as an able-bodied seaman, Cook was promoted to master's mate.

Cook's next surrogate father entered his life when Captain Hugh Palliser took command of *Eagle* three months later. Palliser was just five years older than Cook but had been in the navy twenty years longer. He was handsome and polished in a way Cook admired, with myriad political connections. Palliser was from the Scottish border territory, just like Cook. Palliser was acutely self-conscious of his humble beginnings. This was also Cook's Achilles' heel. And both men knew it was impossible to ignore that breeding was a far greater determinant of success than job performance in eighteenth-century London.

With that in mind, Palliser did everything in his power to help Cook. The push began in October 1755, when *Eagle* sailed for the unknown wilderness of Canada to fight against France in the Seven Years' War. Britain, which saw America as a land of endless resources, aching to be exploited, wanted the French out.

Once in Canada, Palliser arranged for Cook to be trained as a surveyor and cartographer, then promoted to warrant officer. Cook was moving upward quickly. From lowest to highest, the Royal Navy's enlisted ranks went able seaman, master's mate, warrant officer, then, after a written examination, ship's master. Only the rarefied air of commissioned officers (in order: third lieutenant, second lieutenant, first lieutenant, captain, post captain, admiral) lay beyond ship's master. Cook, however, lacked the breeding to be an officer. Master was as far as men like Cook were allowed to go.

On May 30, 1757, Cook and Palliser enjoyed the first of what would become many moments of shared glory. *Eagle* had come back from Canada and fought a ferocious battle off Ushant with the French fifty-gun *Duc D'Acquitaine*. Though three of *Eagle's* crew were killed and eighty wounded, *Eagle* won out. The captured French vessel was led back into Plymouth. For his action, Palliser was promoted to another command. Cook, after passing a written examination at the Trinity House in Deptford, became a full-fledged ship's master on June 29, 1757. He had risen from the lowest rank in the Royal Navy to the highest available to a noncommissioned officer in just two years and twelve days.

The next morning, Cook was transferred from *Eagle* to the twenty-four-gun frigate *Solebay*. Her home base was in Scotland, at Leith on the Firth of Forth, near Edinburgh. Cook traveled overland from London to his new base, passing through Whitby and Great Ayton on his way north. He greeted Walker warmly and spent a

week regaling the Quaker with all that had happened in the previous two years.

Cook's visit with his father was more tentative. The purpose wasn't
a homecoming, but a search for approval. The new ship's master desperately wanted to show his family that he'd done well since leaving
the farm.

Unlike a decade previous, when Cook had left for Staithes on foot,
Cook returned home by carriage. His sixty-three-year-old father had
built a cottage in Ayton by then, moving off Airyholme into retirement.

Cook never wrote of that day, so what happened can only be
guessed. But after two weeks with his parents before moving on to
Leith, Cook was galvanized. His journal entries were suddenly filled
with swooping letters and bold pronouncements. No longer the dis-
appointing youth who'd spurned the farm, James Cook had measured up to his father's expectations. The realization emboldened
him to push himself even harder toward greatness. He became more
sure of his intelligence, still a humble man, but less afraid to engage
in intellectual debate, even with superiors or university-trained men.

As if the assignment had been preordained with the express purpose of allowing Cook to return home in triumph, Cook served only
two months on *Solebay*. On October 18 he was transferred to a larger
ship, the *Pembroke*, and was again sent to fight the French in Canada.

As 1758 moved into 1759, the British had penetrated deep into
Canada, just outside the pivotal city of Quebec. At Quebec, the
Saint Lawrence River narrowed from several miles wide to just several hundred yards. No ship could sail farther into Canada without
coming under fire from the French guns perched on the cliffs
overlooking the river. As long as the French held Quebec, they
held Canada.

The British needed to maneuver their ships closer to the city in
order to attack, but were afraid of running them aground in the tur-
bulent, rocky waters. They were reluctant to use captured French
river maps, for fear they were fakes designed to ruin the British fleet.

Cook was ordered to survey the Saint Lawrence and prepare an original set of maps for the attack.

Alone in a small rowboat, in that no-man's-land between the British front lines and the French outpost above him on the Plains of Abraham, Cook charted the Saint Lawrence. He gauged currents and calculated depths, located sandbars and rocky shoals, noted where the banks were conducive to assault boats unloading troops.

On July 31, 1759, using Cook's information, red-haired British general James Wolfe landed a force of nine thousand troops and marched into position to attempt a frontal attack by land. Wolfe was repulsed.

Clearly, a more daring strategy was required. Wolfe decided that in his next attack his troops would scale the steep cliffs from the river up onto the Plains of Abraham, where he would attack the French from behind. The sticking point was getting ships upriver to drop troops at the base of those cliffs. Not only was the shore lined with unseen rocks and of varying depths, but the current was highly unpredictable. Wolfe had been impressed with Cook's earlier maps. He asked Cook to find a path through the rocks and currents for the landing craft to put the soldiers ashore. The reconnaissance was perilously close to French forces.

Cook, eager to prove himself and just as eager to display heroism, enthusiastically swore that he would find such a path. Working under cover of darkness, Cook covertly sounded depths and gauged currents, then briefed Wolfe on an appropriate landing spot. Displaying his growing self-confidence, Cook also offered strategy tips.

The next day Wolfe led five thousand men up the steep cliffs to the Plains of Abraham. The thirty-two-year-old general died while routing the French, but the Battle of Quebec ultimately assured Britain's victory in the Seven Years' War. It also made Cook's name. Buzz around the navy referred to him as "master surveyor and master of the fleet." In essence, James Cook was the best of the second-best. That lantern of hope allowing him to make brash decisions was shining brighter than ever. Cook's improbable career move from Whitby was paying off.

When the war ended, however, Cook's meteoric career encountered its first bump in the road. *Pembroke* returned to England in the fall of 1762, and a stunned Cook was laid off. He was paid the considerable sum of three hundred pounds (about $70,000 today) as thanks from His Majesty. Cook wandered London with full pockets for the first time in his life, confused about his next career move but carefree in his small wealth.

With characteristic intensity, Cook turned his attention to a new type of adventure: love. He began courting Elizabeth Batts, the twenty-one-year-old daughter of a Shadwell merchant. Cook never wrote of the details of their initial meeting, but her family had close ties with the London Quaker community, with whom John Walker did a great deal of business. Regardless, James was so smitten he considered giving up the sea for the lass.

James's adventurous life, however, was part of his allure to Elizabeth. He couldn't very well sweep her off her feet with tales of heroic cartography, then adopt a Milquetoast lifestyle. Cook's swashbuckling job was the type she'd always imagined her husband would have. He was not counting change or measuring hemlines or weighing slabs of meat, but living a life of action. She saw Cook as a man of substance and intellect and reason. A man's man. He spoke of the future in a way that puzzled her eighteenth-century mind, not allowing himself to be indentured to his birthright, but always seeking the status without which he would not be content.

Elizabeth Batts, conversely, was James Cook's dream woman. He meant to keep her intrigued for a lifetime. What dazzled him most was that she had picked him. They were opposites in every way. She was wealthy, a merchant's daughter from the upper 5 percent of British wage earners. Cook was, despite his recent payoff, lower-middle class, earning less than fifty pounds a year. She was just twenty-one. He was thirty-four. She was lighthearted and romantic. He was aloof and scientific. Elizabeth enjoyed being the center of attention and entertaining. He liked to be alone, watching others from a distance when he noticed them at all.

As they walked side by side through the green fields along Mile End Road, Elizabeth did most of the talking, but Cook would have contributed his share—usually a dissertation on some pet theory as on celestial navigation he wanted her to understand. But often it would be a confidence. Elizabeth, as different as the two were, was his soul mate. She was the first person Cook ever told about his dream. Like him, she believed it would come true. Even as he outlined his mission in life, Cook was amazed that such a woman was in love with *him*. The foreman's boy. She worshiped him, brought out the best in him. Elizabeth was a woman who would make going away hard, but coming home would be ecstasy.

On December 22, only two weeks after their first meeting, James Cook and Elizabeth Batts said their vows in the Parish Church of Little Barking. His war payoff went into buying a three-story brick row house with a basement and two rooms to the floor. It was located on the main thoroughfare leading eastward from London to the coast, Mile End Road. A pub was across the street and a gin mill next door. The Thames was a brisk mile's walk distant.

Her friends (he was too much a loner to promote anything but acquaintances and had no friends of his own save the surrogate fathers) rolled their eyes at the brief courtship, predicting doom. But the bond between Elizabeth and James would become one of history's great unsung romances. Cook would never be unfaithful, even when the ocean took him away for three and four years at a time. Even his most disgruntled crew members would never dream of leveling the charge of infidelity. And while she survived him by six decades, Elizabeth never remarried. He had written dozens of letters to her during his years at sea, mailing them when he came to major ports. In her later years she burned those letters so the world would never know their private sentiments.

Cook's furlough made a fine honeymoon, but in the spring of

1763 the navy recalled him. The Treaty of Paris, signed on February 10, 1763, officially ended the Seven Years' War and gave Britain control of Canada. A cartographer was needed to chart the new acquisitions. Career doubts dispelled, restless after his longest stint ashore (four months) in fifteen years, he eagerly accepted a Palliser-arranged assignment charting the waterways of Newfoundland. The island lay at the easternmost end of the Canadian land mass, with the North Atlantic to one side and the Gulf of Saint Lawrence to the other. A jagged triangle of inlets, harbors, coves, peninsulas, and just plain rock, Newfoundland measured roughly 325 miles long and 300 miles wide. The fertile Grand Banks fishing grounds along the island's southern coast was its greatest resource.

Done with the precision and thoroughness on which Cook had built his reputation, a proper survey could last a decade or more.

To his great surprise, Cook was given a small schooner, the *Grenville*, along with a crew, and allowed to work without supervision. He still remained a master. His pay was not increased. But the appeasing title "the King's Surveyor" was tacked on to his name. A proud Elizabeth saw him off in April 1763.

Nine months after their wedding day, with Cook back charting Newfoundland, Elizabeth gave birth to a son, who would be the first of six children. Cook had already selected a most appropriate name: James. The next year, Nathaniel was born.

On August 6, 1764, as Cook finished his second summer in Newfoundland, disaster struck. A powder charge exploded aboard the *Grenville* and Cook's right hand was almost torn off. His thumb dangled by a tendon. Blood drenched his uniform, and his face was pale as Cook went in and out of shock. *Grenville's* crew wrapped the injury tightly and rushed Cook to Neddy Harbor, on the island's northwest side. There, a doctor aboard a French fishing boat began the difficult task of attempting to save the hand.

Once again fortune was smiling on James Cook. In London the surgery would have been as devastating as the powder blast. Disease

and filth were so rife in London hospitals that almost any surgery re-
sulted in gangrene or pyemia. He would have lost the entire arm.
But Newfoundland was a pristine environment, and the surgeon was
masterful. Back surveying within a month, Cook's only reminder of
the explosion was the deep purple line circling his thumb. It would
slowly fade to red, then dull pink, but would never disappear altogether. The terrible irony about this episode was that the half-moon
welt on Cook's hand would one day be used to identify his body.

Spending spring and summer in Newfoundland, with winters
back in England, Cook was typically thorough in his survey. As
he advanced into his middle and then late thirties, the survey
loomed as the high point of Cook's Royal Navy career—and likely the
end. In peacetime, unemployed naval personnel were laid off until
the next war. Many were forced to earn a living between wars sailing
on civilian merchant vessels. Cook faced a similar fate once he finished surveying Newfoundland, so he was in no hurry to conclude.

It helped that Palliser had been named governor of Newfoundland in 1764. Continuing his personal pledge to support men with
North Yorkshire backgrounds like his own, Palliser did everything
in his power to assist Cook. By bestowing attention on Cook, Palliser
gave the survey great prominence. This—and the glorious memory of
the strategy lecture to Wolfe—empowered Cook to begin writing letters to nobility, telling of the survey's progress. He also wrote to the
Royal Society, describing in great detail a solar eclipse he'd witnessed
on August 5, 1766. James No Middle Initial Cook was the King's Surveyor, after all, and he felt obligated to write relevant letters, even if it
seemed presumptuous.

Scarred and getting older, Cook and his survey wore on. He spent
his summers charting Newfoundland, and winters perfecting his
charts for publication. The quality of Cook's work was so great that
his charts would still be used in the twentieth century.

Cook was far senior to any of the *Grenville*'s crew, and even older than most commissioned officers in the Royal Navy. Yet no matter how sure he was that great things lay ahead, he only shared that thought with Elizabeth. For all the romance and career growth and bravery displayed by Cook, he was still a provincial outsider to the London blue bloods—an almost-forty outsider with pipe dreams. He lacked the bearing and polish of a Royal Navy officer. With his lumbering gait, scarred hand, fractured grammar, and low North Riding burr almost incomprehensible to Londoners, he was no man's idea of an officer. Yet even when others his age were moving into retirement or to posts away from the sea, Cook continued to believe.

When *Grenville* returned to England for the winter of 1767–68, Cook went about the business of fine-tuning his charts and discovered within weeks of his arrival that Elizabeth was pregnant again. Unbeknownst to him, however, that winter would be anything but usual. Mere miles from his small home, yet aristocratic worlds away, two men on a private fishing trip along the Thames were preparing an unlikely gambit. Their sights were set on an expedition that would change the shape of the world forever.

The mission would be that of the *Endeavour*.

CHAPTER 4

Politics

Mile End Road, London

I have a difficult time finding the site of Cook's home. At a cozy Piccadilly shop smelling of secondhand books and old leather chairs, I find a guidebook telling me the house is not numbered 7 Assembly Row anymore, but 88 Mile End Road. That broad boulevard, however, has lengthened substantially since Cook's day. He and Elizabeth lived on the outer fringes of town, a short walk from lush meadows. When I step from the London underground at the Mile End stop and find 88, what used to be Cook's house turns out to be an abandoned building next to a men's clothing store. I look for some sort of historical marker, but there is none.

This is odd. In London, homes owned or lived in by famous people often bear a ceramic plaque denoting that individual. Frédéric Chopin, for instance, is honored by a sign showing where he spent the night of his last concert—and Chopin wasn't even British. Throughout the city, prior residences of authors, writers, and explorers are honored. It's almost a pastime, walking through London's varied districts, spotting the plaque that notes a Brontë or a Chichester once called the house home.

This is not the case at 88 Mile End Road. The owner of the men's clothing store next door is standing on his stoop, watching me. He is Pakistani and polite and has never heard of a Captain Cook. I explain that in London, of all places, there should be some sort of memorial to Cook. "One of those plaques," I say, sounding very American.

It's cold and the sunlight is paling at four in the afternoon. A hard wind is charging up Mile End, past the press of shops, pedestrians, and the bustle of cars, reminding me that winter is much closer than summer. In trying to retrace Cook's path to the Deptford Yards, I've walked from Deptford, through the East End, had a pint at the Angel, trekked across the Thames on the Tower Bridge, which wasn't built until a century after Cook, then got lazy and traveled by underground because I was running out of daylight. Now, finally finding Cook's house, I find myself staring at a plaque denoting that Jack the Ripper once killed someone in the alley next door, but there is nothing to tell me who once lived at 88 Mile End Road.

"Maybe you are thinking of Captain Hook," the clothier suggests. "There is a statue in Hyde Park for Peter Pan. It is that way."

"I've seen it. But I'm looking for Captain Cook." I crunch on the last name so there's no misunderstanding.

He mistakes the emphasis for aggression and suddenly wishes I would leave. I can see it in the way his hands move up from his hips to intertwine across his chest, and how his milky eyes stop trying to make contact with mine.

I head back toward the Thames. I walk and walk, because I have nowhere to go. Maybe in the morning I'll hit the National Gallery and see the Joshua Reynolds portraits of Cook and Banks, but for now all I want to do is earn a large hot meal by walking hard across London as the sun sets.

My pace down Mile End increases until it is brisk, but the road is flat and straight and looks as if it will never end, so I feel like I'm walking on a treadmill. But after a while, a curious thing happens: the street numbers, which had gone down, rise again. Mile End Road, it turns out, is divided into east and west sections. I have been too far east, but now, with each step, I am coming closer to a second number 88.

The houses get narrower, their brickwork more pronounced. Most have a shop downstairs and a residence up top. As in Newport, these homes have survived the centuries. These are the same buildings Cook knew.

I enjoy the irony of an old tavern along the way, and its proximity to Cook's house. For the name—The '45—refers to 1745, when Jacobite rebel Bonnie Prince Charlie tried to overthrow the king of England during the second Jacobite uprising.

Then it is before me. From an old map, I know I am walking along the block that was once Assembly Row. In Cook's time an entryway to the gin mill was alongside his house, and a cobbled courtyard behind. They still exist. I stop at the entryway, which now leads into a paved parking lot filled with cars and trash. What's left of Cook's home stands next to a unisex fashion store, whose block-lettered, red-and-white neon sign stands in stark contrast to the polished marble plaque adorning the single remaining brick wall of Cook's home, approximately where the front door once stood. Quite a few complimentary things about the man and his accomplishments are carefully etched. "On this site," the plaque begins with a nicely written bit of British understatement, "stood a house occupied for some years by Captain James Cook . . ."

It goes on to list Cook's accomplishments, and the day he died. I pull out a notebook and write down the words. Then I look hard at the facade when I'm done, imagining what it once was—a honeymoon home, then noisy with children, and the tranquillity of the small garden in the small backyard. Homecomings took place where I stand, as did the beginnings of epic adventures.

Winter 1768

To assess the astounding (even *miraculous*) career metamorphosis James Cook underwent in the winter of 1768, one must focus on a most fascinating political scenario that draws an unsuspecting Cook to its center. Four men—Lord Sandwich, Joseph Banks, Hugh Palliser, and King George III—were connected to Cook's highy unusual ascendance. These were the men who stood to gain most from Cook's command.

Existing history books would have us believe the preposterous—

that a middle-aged noncommissioned officer with modest political connections was given command of the most desirable assignment available in peacetime England circa 1768. This came at a time when the Royal Navy had a glut of commissioned officers, many even serving at half pay just to remain employed.

There is also an undeniable set of facts: Never in the history of the Royal Navy had a sailor risen through the ranks and been awarded a commission. Never had a ship's master been selected for command. Never had an English circumnavigation been led by an officer below the rank of post captain (one step above captain).

Cook was extremely talented, and equally qualified, but he was not merely plucked from the noncommissioned ranks and selected to command *Endeavour* based on merit. The Royal Navy was far too political a monster, and circumnavigation was the brass ring of peacetime naval leadership. No, Cook had help.

Though planning for *Endeavour*'s voyage had been under way for two years, it was likely a short time after Valentine's Day, 1768, that John Montagu, the fourth Earl of Sandwich (simply, Sandwich), was invited by Joseph Banks to spend an afternoon fishing on the wind-blasted Thames. History records neither the invitation nor the secret meeting that ensued, but Banks and Sandwich were regular fishing companions. Sandwich had worked his political magic for Banks previously, and both enjoyed a flurry of life-changing actions shortly after this time.

Sandwich was an old forty-nine. Tall and pear-shaped, with a long face that looked horsey until it grew round after his thirtieth year, the two-time First Lord of the Admiralty (the Royal Navy was run by a nine-member panel known as the Navy Board; the First Lord was head of the board) had once been a rising political star. Before the age of thirty, the born politician had leveraged his abundant relationships with Britain's 200 ruling families and 174 peerages to rise to his initial term as First Lord of the Admiralty.

As the man in charge of the Royal Navy, world travel—more

specifically, world conquest—became a Sandwich forte. A detailed map of the world was stowed inside his head. He didn't view it as an assemblage of continents and oceans, but of scattered landmasses rightfully belonging to England—even those not yet discovered. Land equaled resources, resources equaled trade, trade equaled money. If England didn't get to her landmasses first, why, another country would acquire that money and power. Discovery of Antarctica was Sandwich's personal grail.

In 1749, during his first reign as Lord of the Admiralty, Sandwich directed that two vessels, *Porcupine* and *Raven*, be sent to explore the strategically located Falkland Islands, then to push even farther south until they slammed hard against Antarctica.

By doing so, Sandwich was openly defying the papal bulls signed by Pope Alexander VI in 1493 and the 1494 Treaty of Tordesillas, both of which divided the world and all its spoils between Spain and Portugal. A mythical line had been drawn north and south, 370 leagues west of the Azores. Everything to the west belonged to Spain, with everything to the east belonging to Portugal. That is why, for instance, Brazil became a Portuguese nation and the rest of South America became Spanish.

Sandwich was saying, in effect, that no such line existed. Sandwich believed France to be Britain's permanent and most dangerous enemy, with Spain a close second. In a rapidly shrinking world, where a nation's might was judged by its power in both the Atlantic and the Pacific, Sandwich was sending *Porcupine* and *Raven* to establish military strongholds in the South Atlantic—at the Falklands, three hundred miles off South America's east coast—and in the South Pacific—on the Juan Fernández Islands, five hundred miles off South America's west coast.

From the Falklands and Juan Fernández, Britain would be able to resupply ships on long voyages, both before and after they sailed into the Pacific. Ships would be able to stay away from England longer. More new lands would be discovered, more colonization would ensue, and more trade routes would open. Sandwich's beloved England would rule the world like no other power in history.

When the Spanish got wind of Sandwich's scheme, they filed a formal diplomatic protest. Citing the papal bulls, the Treaty of Tordesillas, and the 1713 Treaty of Utrecht as evidence of Spanish land rights, the ambassador demanded Britain recall *Porcupine* and *Raven*.

The British replied warmly, shrugging their shoulders and telling the Spanish that Britain had no interest in stealing Spanish colonies or depriving the Spanish of trade routes. *Porcupine* and *Raven* were merely vessels of discovery, "exploring for the advancement of knowledge."

The Spanish weren't amused. Another protest was filed.

And though Britain had the greater naval might, the Admiralty wasn't in the mood to go to war over cold, gray islands in the Southern Hemisphere. England backed down. *Porcupine* and *Raven's* orders were rescinded. "This plan for the discovery of new countries and islands in the American seas," Sandwich curtly promised the Spanish ambassador, "will be continued at some later time."

That later time was two decades later, once Sandwich had risen to a new level of power by being named Britain's secretary of state. In 1764 he sent HMS *Dolphin* and *Tamar* to explore for Antarctica and to find the Northwest Passage. They found neither. Sandwich was out of politics by the time *Dolphin* and *Tamar* returned from their circumnavigation in May 1766. The only incident of note was Commodore John "Foulweather Jack" Byron's record-setting global sprint of just twenty-two months. He had been spooked by "giants" in Patagonia and had lost interest in further discovery.

Another voyage was arranged immediately. This time it was King George III taking up the torch for exploration. *Dolphin* was ordered to sea again, with HMS *Swallow* as her escort. Captain Samuel Wallis was in command. *Dolphin* and *Swallow* sailed from Plymouth in August 1766. The ships hadn't yet returned when Banks and Sandwich scheduled their winter meeting in 1768.

Sandwich had fallen on hard times even before Wallis sailed. In

1765 he had been forced from politics after a very public defense of King George III was seen as opposing personal liberty. Between 1765 and 1768 he had indulged in his affection for orgiastic sex and playing drums alongside a men's chorus performing Handel's oratorios. Sandwich ached to return to power, but his vilification had been so complete—London newspapers called him "the most hated man in England"—that it would take a political miracle for him to find a way back.

Oddly enough, Banks, a twenty-five-year-old playboy and fellow member of the Royal Society, a group dedicated to the advancement of the sciences, had an idea that might change Sandwich's fortunes.

Born the day after Valentine's Day, 1743, Banks was no man's image of a botanist. A social gadfly, he had unruly dark brown hair, chestnut eyes, and a nose with a tip round like a tulip bulb. The playboy's paunch that would define him in old age was a mere pooch. He networked shamelessly. His list of friends was long and influential. Banks was a whimsical man with a carefree air, waltzing through life, making up the rules as he went along. Banks's personality was winning, though. And what might have appeared as blatantly selfish behavior in other men was written off as Banks just being Banks.

His father had died when Banks was just nineteen, leaving a sizable fortune and several estates to his maverick son. As Banks charmed his way through his formal education, he found himself obsessed with, of all things, botany. The attraction began at fourteen, while he was attending rough-and-tumble Eton. Until then, Banks was famous among his friends for disdaining studies, and many thought Banks's new passion was an elaborate joke. But Banks was so taken with plants that he was soon corralling classmates into helping him catalog local flora. In college, he possessed a greater knowledge of botany than his professors and had to hire a private tutor to sate his thirst. Young Joseph swaggered away from Oxford without a degree and purchased a home in London, near Piccadilly. The year was 1764.

Soon after, Banks became a Fellow of the Royal Society. For a man like Banks, who knew the London social calendar by heart, membership in the Royal Society was a wonderful way to validate his existence. This body of 360 British members and 160 foreign members gave Banks the chance for inspirational osmosis from rubbing against great minds such as Voltaire, Linnaeus, and Joshua Reynolds.

By 1766, Banks ached to be the equal of his Royal Society peers. However, he had never published nor advanced the course of his young field, two vital methods of achieving scientific renown. Banks decided to make a journey to the vast new frontier of Canada, where he would catalog as many new plants, animals, and birds as possible. He turned to fellow Royal Society member and fishing companion Sandwich for help in arranging passage on a Royal Navy vessel.

Sandwich secured a berth to Newfoundland for Banks on board the thirty-two-gun frigate HMS *Niger*. The voyage would last ten months. Banks was thrilled to be embarking on such a grand adventure, but soon found himself seasick, homesick, and unsexed.

Adventure, however, is a bewitching seductress. That time on *Niger*, for all its hardship, saw adventure insinuate itself into Banks's persona. Instead of staying up late and sleeping even later, he slept when the sun set and woke when it rose. He discovered a well of ambition within himself and became tireless in his collection of samples, even seeming to gain strength through long hours of work in a country where swarms of mosquitoes and blackflies made life tedious.

In the midst of his metamorphosis, Banks had a chance encounter with a man he would soon come to know quite well. Cook paid the *Niger* a visit on October 27, 1766, though neither he nor Banks mentioned their meeting in their journals. However, one of the specimens Banks obtained in Newfoundland was an Indian canoe. There being no space on *Niger*, Cook ferried it back to England aboard *Grenville*, only to see it washed overboard by a Channel storm.

Niger docked in Portsmouth in January 1767. Immediately, Banks complained that the terror and seasickness of being on board ship in fierce weather "almost ruined me," but he was already making plans for a next voyage. He would be the commander, and the destination would be either Lapland or Iceland.

Those destinations were forgotten once Banks heard about a far greater voyage being planned by the Royal Society. On June 3, 1769, Venus would pass across the face of the sun. This "Transit of Venus" would not occur again for almost a century. By observing the Transit from different points on the earth it would be possible to precisely measure earth's distance from the sun. Once this "astronomical unit" had been established, stellar parallax could be used to determine distance from every star in the heavens.

Astronomer Royal Dr. Nevil Maskelyne's plan was to place observers at three widely spaced points on the globe to ensure the most accurate recording possible: Hudson Bay, northern Scandinavia, and an unspecified tropical island in the Pacific. For the first two locations, the Royal Society could arrange passage for a Fellow on one of the many ships shuttling regularly about the Atlantic and North Sea. The South Pacific was a different matter, however, and would require the purchase of a specialized vessel, which a scientist would command.

The Royal Society turned to King George III for funding, requesting four thousand pounds to purchase a substantial ship and hire a crew. The thirty-year-old ruler (whose mother was known to admonish him when he acted out as a child, "George, be a king!") approved the money, quietly recognizing that once the scientific aspects of the voyage had been completed, the ship could search for Antarctica.

Most importantly, King George decreed, the voyage would take place under the auspices of the Royal Navy, with a Royal Navy officer in command. The Fellows would be ferried, as passengers known as supernumeraries, to the Transit. George was unpopular with the navy, and the gesture was a political bone. But there was also precedent: in 1698 the navy had experimented with allowing a scientist to command a voyage, when Edmond Halley (discoverer of Halley's Comet and Venus's Transit) had skippered the HMS *Paramour*. For all Halley's genius with astronomy, his indecisiveness and ignorance of the sea had alienated the ship's officers. Their mutiny was upheld by the Admiralty.

Nevertheless, Banks began scheming for a way to gain command. He couldn't envision a two- or three-year journey at sea, on board something as claustrophobic and regimented as a vessel of His Majesty's Royal Navy, being condescended to by some lowly captain whose personal wealth and societal status were greatly inferior to his own.

At the same time, another member of the Royal Society publicly demanded that *he* be given command. Hydrographer Alexander Dalrymple based his claim on extensive knowledge of the South Pacific. In fact, he was the world's premier authority on the Southern Hemisphere, specifically the unknown lands between the bottom of South America and the bottom of Africa. Dalrymple, a vain, self-educated bureaucrat of Scottish origin, had written books, drawn maps, and argued passionately for the existence of a hidden Southern Continent. No man, Dalrymple argued to the Admiralty, was better suited to lead the Transit. Not even an officer in the Royal Navy.

The Admiralty publicly mocked Dalrymple's request. It was, the navy sneered, "entirely repugnant." First Lord of the Admiralty Sir Edward Hawke swore he would "rather his right hand be cut off than see a civilian command a naval vessel." Dalrymple was welcome to travel as an observer, nothing more. He refused angrily and, in time, would become the Transit voyage's most impassioned critic.

Even before Dalrymple's rejection, Banks had realized that assuming command meant finding a way to circumvent the Admiralty's authority. Banks devised a plan predicated on the Admiralty selecting the commander. However, once the ship sailed, Banks would take over. For his plan to work, Banks needed the Admiralty to select a man awed by authority and wealth and intellect. And the lower in rank, the better.

The rub was that command of circumnavigatory vessels was not given to mere captains. That honor was bestowed upon officers of advanced rank, either a post captain or an admiral. Royal Navy commanders leading successful circumnavigations banked great political clout. Their deeds made London newspaper headlines. Used judiciously, lasting power ensued. The Admiralty knew this and carefully husbanded the right to play power broker.

Banks turned to the one man who could solve his problem—a man with political clout and insider knowledge of the Admiralty: Sandwich.

When Banks came calling, he found a political junkie in deep withdrawal. The two men rowed out onto the Thames on the winter afternoon. Sandwich would have listened between the lines, getting to the kernel of Banks's meandering dialogue. It would have been obvious Banks didn't care about the Transit of Venus. Nor, truth be told, science. That was good. Their mutual ground was hunger for power, a motivation Sandwich understood completely.

Sandwich realized the Transit voyage represented the opportunity for a definitive circumnavigation. Sailing under the pretense of science, the Royal Society's vessel would prowl the Pacific without raising French and Spanish suspicion. They would locate Antarctica, once and for all—or not. Any islands discovered along the way would be charted, vetted for potential settlement, and claimed in the name of England. If men perished, it would be in the name of England's glory.

Once Sandwich and Banks finished their cold day on the water, His Lordship went to work. He hatched a scheme that involved giving command of the Transit vessel to the most high-ranking non-commissioned officer on a ship, the master. The master was in charge of all navigation and sailing. While the master did not actually have authority over the vessel, only the captain knew the ship as well or had more control over day-to-day operations. Ship's masters were competent, thorough—and malleable. What made the plan audacious was that no master had ever commanded a Royal Naval vessel—especially not for a circumnavigation.

Sandwich huddled with an acquaintance who'd recently returned from a posting in Newfoundland and been placed on the Navy Board: Hugh Palliser. Sandwich found him most helpful.

The master Palliser recommended was thirty-nine, a rather advanced age for a man whose profession carried a fantastic death rate. Tall, confident, and handsome in a square-jawed way, the newcomer to Sandwich and Banks's contrivance spoke infrequently, but when he did, it was with a North Riding accent so low and thick it sounded like a Scots burr. He walked with that splayfooted, almost bowlegged manner of the professional sailor, as if anticipating a sudden roll of the deck. His character was beyond reproach. He loved his wife. The master carried himself with the air of a man caught between two worlds: more dignified than the typical bawdy, drunken sailor but lacking the polish of a blue-blooded officer. He had few friends. In short, he was perfect for the job.

So it was that Sandwich and Palliser had Cook named commander of the Transit of Venus circumnavigation in April of 1768. For a month there was debate within the Admiralty as to an appropriate rank to lead a scientific voyage, with opinion leaning toward Cook's remaining a master. However, Sandwich was fearful that the precedent would offend the Royal Navy's officer corps and arranged for Cook to be commissioned a first lieutenant on May 25, 1768.

Coincidentally, Wallis had returned from his *Dolphin* circumnavigation just five days earlier. He brought incredible news: he had discovered the most wondrous island paradise imaginable, a lush and mountainous oasis. It was a sailor's dream, loaded with fresh water and endless quantities of animals and vegetables for reprovisioning. And the natives not only didn't eat people, but the men were friendly and the women much, much more so. Wallis officially named the discovery King George the Third Island. The locals, however, called their paradise Tahiti.

Serendipitously, the Royal Society considered Tahiti an ideal place for observing the Transit. In fact, Neville Maskelyne (or "Dr. Masculine," as the *Dolphin's* purser called the Astronomer Royal) had wished for an island in Tahiti's exact location.

Of more interest to Sandwich was that Wallis and his men reported seeing distant mountains as they sailed from Tahiti and were reasonably certain they rose from Antarctica. If Wallis was right about those mountains, controlling Tahiti was tantamount to controlling the gateway to Antarctica and its vast resources.

Making matters more urgent were rumors of a French expedition to the South Pacific already under way. The voyage was being led by Antoine de Bougainville, France's top explorer. The race to find Antarctica was heating up. World dominance was at stake. As the days to its departure counted down, the Transit of Venus expedition became more and more vital to British national interests.

James Cook, meanwhile, cared little about world dominance and had only a passing interest in de Bougainville. After twenty-two years believing privately that he, a commoner and farm boy, was destined to rise above his preordained station in life, Cook had just been asked to command a vital British mission to the South Pacific. The dream was being realized.

PART TWO

Endeavour: Living on the Edge of the World

CHAPTER 5

The Great *Endeavour*

The fiery summer of 1768 was a hectic time for Cook. Between May, when he was commissioned and took command, and August, when he planned to sail, Cook had a near impossible list of tasks to accomplish. He needed sailors, warrant officers, and officers. He needed supplies and provisions. He needed a small amount of armament. And he needed to know where he was going.

The only item Cook didn't need was a ship. Back in April, immediately after being informed of his new command (but well before his commission gave him the right to be so blunt), Cook strongly recommended to Palliser and the Navy Board that the ideal discovery vessel would be a Whitby collier, or "cat." This was in direct conflict with the Board's recommendation for either a fourteen-gun sloop or a twenty-four-gun frigate. Cook wasn't cowed. If he was going to spend three years roaming the earth on a ship's deck, it had to be a ship in which he had confidence.

A Whitby cat was the Mack truck of its day, blunt-nosed and relatively slow, but reliable and built to take abuse. The wooden hull (oak for frames, planks, deck beams, stem, and stern; pine for decks

and masts) was of a heavy construction to support cargo in the hold
and the ship's weight when she was beached for cleaning. No glue or
screws were used in construction. Instead, dowels known as trun-
nels were hammered through the timber, then secured in place with
a wedge of wood. Cats had a top speed of ten knots, though they av-
eraged just four. In effect, if a cat was selected for the Transit voyage,
Cook would travel over twenty-five thousand miles around the
world at the pace of a brisk walk.

He made his arguments: The cat's shallow draft made it less susceptible to running aground in shallow waters; ample cargo space made
cats perfect for a long trip; and if the oak and pine constitution could
absorb punishment from the tempestuous North Sea, it could stand
up to anything. Finally, Cook noted that the Whitby cat *Earl of Pembroke* just happened to be lying in the Thames. He would be grateful
if the Admiralty could find the funds to purchase this vessel.

The demand was typical of Cook's confident professionalism. A
lesser man would have assumed command timidly. Contradicting
the Admiralty to suggest a bold voyage of discovery, underwritten by
King George III, be undertaken on a slow, ugly coal ship would be
unheard of. But that wasn't the way Cook worked. He was low-key,
which caused men like Banks and Sandwich to underestimate him.
However, when Cook wanted something, he found a way to get it.

The *Earl of Pembroke*'s purchase was approved. Refitting began immediately at the Deptford Yard, one of the Royal Navy's six major
yards. Also known as His Majesty's Docks, in reference to their first
being built by Henry VIII two hundred years before, the Deptford
Yard was just around a Thames bend from the Tower of London.
Cook's favorite pub, the Angel, was near the yard. His home on Mile
End Road was a brisk walk distant. He couldn't have asked for a better location to oversee the refitting.

It was vital that Cook physically view the work being done. The
British fleet had almost doubled in size during the Seven Years' War.
And though the dockyards were the largest commercial enterprises

in London (each at least ten times bigger than any private business), lack of space made expansion impossible. As work backed up, ships had to wait longer and longer for simple repairs, and many rotted before it was their turn.

Corruption was rife. In some cases work went unperformed but the Admiralty was still billed for it. The victim would be the captain unlucky enough to take command of the unfixed vessel. Because a ship's massive wooden hull easily concealed decay below the waterline, the captain would only discover the problems once he was at sea, when his vessel sprung leaks and deteriorated from rot and aquatic worms burrowing holes into the wood. Saving the lives of himself and his men would be a matter of finding a major port as soon as possible, then putting in for an overhaul.

Cook virtually took up residence at Deptford to ensure this wouldn't happen to him. Soon after the purchase, the Admiralty changed *Earl of Pembroke's* name to *Endeavour*. She was almost four years old, with a square stern, single-thickness bottom, and no decorative bowsprit. She was only 106 feet long and 29 feet wide and weighed 379 tons. Her bottom was painted white, the waterline black, and a natural wood finish eight plank-widths tall rose from waterline to deck. The deck accoutrements were painted red, save for the natural finish of the masts, which were also wrapped in tar-covered rope at critical junctures.

Overall, *Endeavour* was low and squat, wholly ungraceful. To justify giving such a swashbuckling name to the roly-poly vessel without ornamentation—and avoid confusion with an HMS *Endeavour* gunship already in commission—the Admiralty referred to her as a puny bark instead of a ship. So HM Bark *Endeavour* was born.

On June 9, the Royal Society wrote the Admiralty suggesting the newly discovered King George's Island be *Endeavour's* destination. In addition to the esteemed Charles Green, the Royal Society was assigning another pair of astronomers to make the trip and ensure perfect measurement of the Transit.

At the end of the letter, almost as an afterthought, the Society noted that Joseph Banks and his suite of "seven persons or more" would be joining Cook. Banks had paid ten thousand pounds for the privilege, a figure totaling several million dollars in modern money and almost three times King George III's patronage.

Clearly, Banks was leaving no stone unturned in his desire to take command. Royal Society gossips already had Banks leading the glorious crusade. "They are to proceed," historian John Ellis wrote botanist Carl Linnaeus in the summer of 1768, "under the direction of Mr. Banks, by order of Lords of the Admiralty, on further discoveries of Antarctica. And from thence proceed to England by the Cape of Good Hope"—around Africa.

That would have been news to the Admiralty, who hadn't yet given Cook specifics of the voyage. And while Cook must have shrugged off such scientific gossip as nonsensical, he must have suspected a struggle for control was imminent when hearing the size of both Banks's financial investment and entourage. The perception was likely heightened when Banks began making occasional journeys across the river to Deptford, to watch *Endeavour's* overhaul. Cook ignored the young man, not introducing himself as he continued working long hours during June and July preparing for the voyage. He was simply glad to be on the Thames, where (flow of raw sewage aside) an ocean breeze took the edge off London's miserable summer weather.

On July 22, Cook was officially ordered to receive the contingent of Royal Society scientists and their servants as supernumeraries. Space was already tight aboard *Endeavour*, but Banks sent word that his personal suite included two artists, a secretary, four servants, and two greyhounds. Cook ordered the ship's carpenters to begin construction of new cabins.

On July 30 the pilot came aboard to maneuver *Endeavour* down the Thames to the English Channel and the open ocean, where Cook would then join the ship and take command.

On that same day, the Admiralty issued Cook's orders. They were labeled "secret" and came in two parts. The first section told Cook to guide *Endeavour* to Tahiti in time for the Transit. The second section would remain unopened until the Transit was completed and Cook sailed from Tahiti.

Finally, it was time for Cook to say good-bye. He left Elizabeth and the children and began the seventy-mile journey to Deal by coach. There was an overnight stop, so he didn't arrive until noon on August 7. Stretching his long legs, feeling his hamstrings uncoil and his back straighten after too many hours of rough road pounding his spine, he reveled in the completion of one journey and the start of quite another. The cool salt air of the Channel was a refreshing difference after London's torpor. And the sight of the ocean, even the roiling gray waters of the English Channel, was calming. And deep in the back of his mind, Cook must have felt a sense of independence. In London he was a ship's master made good, a commoner who didn't know his place in a class society, whose coming assignment would prove either utter folly or an arena for genius to shine.

But standing on the edge of the ocean—his playing field, his home away from home—Cook was about to become a man beyond question. A little nervous, a little unaware of international diplomatic protocol, a little less poetic than the scientists he was about to share his ship with, James Cook staring into the gray void of the English Channel was a man staring upon the squeaky-clean canvas of destiny, about to scrawl his name.

Cook quickly differentiated *Endeavour* from the gaggle of hulls sharing the harbor. The fresh white paint of the base of the hull disappeared into the waters below with all the unknown depth of an iceberg. Varnish up the oak sides of her hull made the planking shine as if polished. Unpretentious and functional and strong like a bull, she was quite the same as the man who would command her. Without fanfare, but with the excitement of the grand voyage coursing through him, Cook was piped aboard by boatswain John Galthrey. One of these men would survive the circumnavigation. One would not.

Cook proudly reviewed his ship. The decks were clean and or-
ganized, with her new sails furled loosely along those horizontal
yards stretching out from the three masts like the arms of Christ's
cross. Perched above the deck, six small boats for shore exploration—a pinnace, longboat, yawl, barge, and two rowboats—were
mounted upside down, atop a raised platform. Directly below
their bows was the entrance—*companionway* in sailor-speak—into
the cramped area belowdecks where the crew lived. The upper
deck was pocked by companionways, forested by masts, shaded
by sail, cluttered with boats and capstans and coiled rope, all
squeezed into an area as long and wide as the aisle of a modern su-
permarket. It offered no more escape from claustrophobia than
belowdecks.

Cook enjoyed a smidgen more personal space. His quarters were
partitioned from the crew's and raised slightly, in an area known as
the "after fall" deck. This deck was accessed down a separate companionway amidships, directly behind the mainmast. Cook would have
two rooms to his name. The smaller cabin, his sleeping area, would
measure a few feet square. It would be the equivalent of sleeping in a
bedroom closet.

The great cabin, however, with its rear-facing, paned windows as
tall as a man, would be his truest sanctuary. In the shipboard world
of condensation, with space at a premium and the crew breathing air
through hull slits the size of a brick, those great windows were an
idiosyncratic, oversized touch of home.

With the windows as a claustrophobia-reducing mural, a confer-
ence table atop a green baize rug would allow Cook ample room to
spread maps and logs and journals, or even to retire for contemplation. He would be able to sink deeply into the comfortable padding
of a favorite chair while sipping a glass of port, bewitched by the
ocean *Endeavour* had just traveled through. A guard at the door
would insure his privacy.

Unless bent on mutiny, a sailor would never dare intrude into the great cabin. The only visitors into Cook's inner sanctum would be his ship's officers. Cook had crossed the Atlantic ten times, and his open-ocean experience was unquestionable, but the Pacific was a different beast, vast and argumentative. The Admiralty was sending along a complement of officers to point out its unique weather and wind patterns. The men could also brief Cook about the Southern Ocean, that tempest in the Southern Hemisphere's high latitudes. Each of the officers and warrant officers was previously unknown to Cook. His second-in-command would be Lieutenant John Gore, a redheaded American just one year younger than Cook. Barely two months earlier, Gore had returned from Tahiti, where he'd sailed aboard the *Dolphin*.

Under Gore, and third in command, was the modest and tubercular Second Lieutenant Zachary Hicks.

Endeavour's master was Robert Molyneaux, twenty-two, highly capable but with a fondness for drink. Because a ship's captain needed to rely on the master at all times, Molyneaux's drinking would become a source of contention. Cook didn't dislike Molyneaux, but he would never fully trust him, either.

The master's mate was Charles Clerke. He was a farmer's son, like Cook. But unlike the intense thirty-nine-year-old skipper who'd come to the sea late, twenty-five-year-old Clerke was a bawdy young man with a crackling wit who had escaped to the ocean at twelve. Like Gore, Clerke had also been on *Dolphin*.

The crew were sailors, carpenters, sail makers, a one-armed cook, cabin boys barely out of childhood. Elizabeth Cook's cousin sixteen-year-old Isaac Smith was on board as an able-bodied seaman. There was a goat (for officers' milk and for luck—it had also sailed on the *Dolphin*), hens in coops, sailors' pets such as cats and monkeys, and two greyhounds. Banks's dogs, he said, were for hunting game on Antarctica.

Unlike her days as a coal-carrying Whitby cat, *Endeavour* crammed seventy men between her decks. Over twenty more would soon be added, including Banks, who would join the voyage in Plymouth.

But those on board in Deal were the lucky ones, for they saw history made the afternoon of August 7, 1768. Cook discharged the Thames pilot and took the helm of *Endeavour* for the first time. Master Molyneaux barked commands. The sound of wind snapping slack canvas taut filled the air, as one sail after another found the wind. And *Endeavour* was on the way, sailing out of Deal and past the white cliffs of Dover for a five-day shakedown cruise to Plymouth.

Belowdecks, once the frenzy of getting under way had passed, the crew adjusted to the shipboard routine of watch duty—four hours on, eight hours off, around the clock. Cook referred to them as "the People." They hailed from England, Scotland, Wales, Ireland, and even Italy. Their assortment of accents sang through the air. They exchanged small talk, fought for additional living space, formed cliques by trade and nationality, and tried to hide animosity.

The People's greatest motivation for signing on for *Endeavour*'s long, long voyage, other than escaping dreary London, was sex. The crew of *Dolphin*, the British vessel that had discovered Tahiti, had wasted no time touring dockside bars, telling fantastic stories of tropical women exposing their breasts and offering rapturous nights on the beach or quickie forays into the jungle.

Those brazen, tanned, voluptuous, ready, acrobatic, half-dressed-if-they-dressed-at-all women didn't even wait for a ship to drop anchor. They were so eager to express their love for the rotten-toothed dregs of London society they actually swam out to the ship—through the surreal blue Tahitian lagoons, where the bottom could be seen from fifty feet up—and climbed on board. Climbed on board! They were mermaids, only better. To a sailor opposed to shivering through a London winter, no fantasy could be a more compelling motivation to sign on for extended duty.

The best part of it all was the price for sex: one slim metal nail. A nail was worth a fortune in Tahiti. The men of *Dolphin* had pried so many nails from her hull that *Dolphin's* captain had feared she would be disassembled before leaving Tahiti. Thus, even though some crew deserted in Plymouth, scared off by the long voyage, Cook had no shortage of replacements. Only the youngest member of the crew, twelve-year-old cook's servant Isaac Manley, seemed oblivious to island charms.

Upon arriving in Plymouth, Cook increased the number of crew by enlisting local hands, prepared to receive the scientists, and added a complement of twelve Royal Marines, who came aboard *Endeavour* to prevent mutiny. Cold and brutish, with a deep fondness for their knuckles and their firearms, the marines were hooligans in uniform, more likely to provoke a fight than prevent one. Sailors sarcastically called them "bootnecks" for the marines' habit of sewing old leather boot tongues into the necks of their uniforms to protect their throats from sailors' knives.

On August 14 ship's carpenters finished the new cabins. Cook summoned botanist Banks and the other supernumeraries from London and prepared to set sail.

Banks arrived August 16, hungover. He and Cook had never been formally introduced. The moment was cordial but tense. Banks shook hands with Cook without making eye contact, then descended to his room from the quarterdeck.

When Cook showed Banks his apartment, the young botanist pretended grave unhappiness. He stepped inside, promptly bumped his head on the ceiling, and then proclaimed that he could not stand up straight in his apartment. Furthermore, lack of a window rendered the room claustrophobic. To alleviate the problem, Banks genially announced, he would use the apartment to store clothing and personal effects.

For sleeping, however, the twenty-five-year-old Banks intoned that he and his companion, the plump, unkempt naturalist Daniel Carl Solander, would require the great cabin. Cook, two inches taller than Banks and unable to stand up straight in his cabin either, shrugged and agreed, just so long as Banks realized that the great cabin was also to be used for spreading charts and preparing journals. Banks found that acceptable and added that he had a few items—professional in nature, of course—that would also litter the great cabin. Then he and Solander were rowed back into Plymouth to wait at their hotel for the northwest wind that would carry *Endeavour* from port.

The wait for the wind lasted ten long days. With the exception of Banks and Solander, *Endeavour*'s crew and passengers were confined to the ship. Finally, Cook felt the northwest breeze. The date was August 25, 1768. Immediately a pendant was hoisted signaling Banks and Solander to hurry on board. What started as a cloudy day soon cleared, and men were sent up the ratlines to unfurl mainsails and topsails and topgallants. Sensing that Cook would—*must*—wait for them, but not wanting to take chances, even Banks and Solander made haste to *Endeavour*.

Finally, anchor was weighed. The grunts of men straining to turn the capstan could be heard above the screech of low-flying gulls. Cook stood on the quarterdeck, just behind the wheel, calmly giving orders to ship's master Molyneaux, who then sang them loudly to the crew. Banks, not possessing sea legs, slowly made his way to the back of the ship as *Endeavour* swung around to catch the wind. The red ensign hanging from her stern snapped smartly. He silently stood beside Cook as Plymouth Hoe, then Drake Island, and then England herself faded to memory. Banks's unspoken plan—once his seasickness, which would last seven days, went away—was to quietly assume command of *Endeavour*. The action would be necessary to further his botanical dreams and self-motivated march to glory.

Cook focused on the voyage. As England slipped away, his body hummed with anticipation of all that lay ahead—the challenge of command, the danger of the unknown, the loneliness of years away from home. It was the moment he'd planned for, trained for, dreamed about, a surreal validation of years of hard work.

Cook savored the moment. It was not his nature to be overwhelmed easily, or to indulge in giddy displays of enthusiasm. He merely watched his new vessel plow through the seas, a thin smile on his lips, likely wishing Elizabeth could be there to share the moment. Then, shipboard routine settling in, he gave Molyneaux a last order before going below. *Endeavour* would set course for Madeira, Cape Verde, Rio de Janeiro, Tierra del Fuego, King George the Third Island, and whatever lay beyond. "I want to go," Cook would write in his journal, "as far as I think it possible for man to go."

Cook was unaware that on August 26, the day after *Endeavour* finally sailed, Elizabeth gave birth to a third son, Joseph. He was baptized on September 5. On September 13, as his father was mooring off the Portuguese island of Madeira to take on wine, Joseph Cook died in the cramped brick row house next to the gin mill at 7 Assembly Row, on Mile End Road. He was nineteen days old.

CHAPTER 6

Rio

In 1971, the Apollo 15 spacecraft *Endeavour* would travel to the moon on a twelve-day mission that would see her three-man crew establish Hadley Base, history's first lunar outpost. In 1992, the Space Shuttle *Endeavour* blasted off from Cape Canaveral as a replacement for the exploded *Challenger*. Before returning she would make 141 laps of Earth, crossing the Pacific in roughly the same amount of time it took a Whitby cat to weigh anchor.

In terms of bravery and scope, their namesake's voyage was no less bold. When Cook sailed from Madeira at midnight on September 18, 1768, by the light of a full moon, his hold full of wine, onions, fresh and salted beef, and even a bull for later slaughter, he was effectively leaving the civilized world behind and embarking on a voyage into the outer limits. As exciting and bold as space travel would be two centuries later, so, too, was Cook's voyage. There would be no Mission Control to guide his actions or counsel him in times of peril. No global weather satellite would forecast the heavens. For most of her journey *Endeavour* would sail through waters unplied in the history of mankind.

The closest similarities between the three *Endeavours* were the name, the impossibility of rescue, and the simple awareness inside the head of each crewman that once the voyage began, safely stepping beyond the confines of the vessel was not an option.

Cook's entire crew quarters were so small they could easily fit inside the Space Shuttle's cargo hold, yet he carried more than a dozen times as much personnel. His food stores were not carefully premeasured, guaranteed to last the entire voyage, but a combination of condensed soups and salted meat designed to last mere months. Cook would have to forage for replenishments, praying that whichever new island he stumbled upon—*if* he stumbled upon a new island in the great unknown—would be the equivalent of nature's cupboard, containing edible wildlife for salting and storage, and nonpoisonous plants. And while the value of a human life is never a relative commodity, Cook's complement of ninety-four (officers, supernumeraries, and crew) greatly outnumbered Apollo commander David Randolph Scott's crew of three and the Space Shuttle's Dan Brandenstein's seven and gave Cook a greater responsibility.

Endeavour pushed south hard from Madeira, racing past Africa before veering south-southwest toward South America, Tierra del Fuego, then the Pacific. Along the way, Cook planned to stop in Rio de Janeiro to resupply. Though his holds were full, Cook didn't want to take any chances of running low, for Rio would be the last port of call before the long push to Tahiti.

Cook appeased the demanding Mr. Banks with confidence and skill. As *Endeavour* sailed across the Atlantic toward South America, the two men wordlessly sparred for control of the ship. Cook's strategy was to appear oblivious. Cook knew that over a three-year journey a pecking order would establish itself. Better to let that happen on its own than force a confrontation. Cook had been around vainglorious men his whole life. He saw Banks's weaknesses, foolishness, and bent toward dissipation. Cook wasn't worried about his opponent.

Banks's strategy was the bold pronouncement: the need for more space, the need for more time to collect specimens, the need for men to climb up the ratlines and extricate tangled birds for his collection, and the outrageous (to sailors) need to use the ship's precious rum stores to preserve his fish specimens. And always, the need for *Endeavour* to sail faster. Banks's only prior sailing experience had been aboard the thirty-two-gun frigate *Niger*, a much larger, quicker ship. He complained constantly that *Endeavour* was too slow. His cause was undermined, however, by recurring episodes of seasickness. Vomiting and green around the gills, Banks gamely struggled to adjust to shipboard life.

Meanwhile, *Endeavour's* thirty sails (maneuvered by almost twenty miles of rope) pushed her along at one hundred miles per day, depending upon the weather. The crew settled into a routine of working, sleeping, playing cards and dice, whittling, and drinking, as Cook grappled with the odd sensation of command. Aboard ship, even the lowliest of seamen considered themselves a judge of a captain's abilities. The collective safety of the crew depended upon each man performing his job to the best of his abilities—especially the captain. As *Endeavour* voyaged through these early months, Cook knew he was being closely studied and his actions compared for better or worse with other captains the People had sailed under.

Being captain wasn't easy. The People could collapse into their hammocks after four hours of watch, but Cook was constantly on call for one important decision or another, never allowed the luxury of total relaxation. His cabin was small, containing a swinging cot, a small desk and chair for writing private notes to Elizabeth (ship's journals were written in the great cabin), hanging lantern, small shelf above the cot, and chamber pot. Recreation consisted of studying past voyages of exploration and reading from Sandwich's thoughtful going-away present, a book on gentleman's etiquette.

A flattered Cook correctly understood that Sandwich was opening the door for future alliance and social prominence, but it was a deal with the devil. Cook's character had always been above reproach. He must have known in his gut that aligning with Sandwich would inevitably lead to ethical compromise and moral decay. Sandwich was too infamous as a symbol of debauchery for Cook not to have such naggings. Already the seeds of compromise had come to fruition (or had, perhaps, been planted in childhood and were finally germinating). By taking command of *Endeavour*, Cook had severed himself emotionally from his wife, abrogating responsibility for his children's upbringing, and inextricably linked himself with a man infamous throughout Britain for betrayal. It can be said that those deeds were done to fulfill a dream, and that Sandwich could hardly be blamed for Cook's eagerness to command *Endeavour*. But what would come next? To which moral precipice would Sandwich's friendship lead Cook?

An immediate litmus test would be Cook's handling of power. As captain of a Royal Navy vessel on an ocean thousands of miles wide, Cook could say anything he wanted, do anything he wanted, go anywhere he wanted. He could flog men on a whim and cheat on his wife with abandon. He could spend his days getting drunk and his nights howling at the moon. Or he could simply surrender to cowardice and abandon his mission when the sea unleashed her terrors. Explorers had done it for centuries.

The erosion of great character doesn't happen overnight though, and it was unlikely Cook would abuse power on *Endeavour*. He was bound by a dystonic belief system superseding his infatuation with Sandwich. It centered on achievement, advancement, and pleasing authority figures. Not only would perfect execution of his orders and a successful circumnavigation make for exponential career growth, it would result in personal fulfillment as well. Ironically, though the search for his land of hopes and dreams drove Cook, he was so hungry for praise that its discovery was secondary to pleasing his superiors. Cook sometimes even viewed Banks in this light, due to social position. And while Cook often foisted himself into a social circle above his station—reporting the eclipse to the Royal Society in 1766, developing friendships with Palliser and Sandwich—he was still a second-class citizen. To be a true commander of men he would eventually need to court more than authority, he would have to confront it and realize he was any man's equal.

On November 20, 1768, Cook got his chance. A month after crossing the equator for the first time in his life, Cook engaged in his first act of international diplomacy, battling toe-to-toe with a pompous Portuguese viceroy—and lost.

His Excellency Don Antonio Rolim de Moura was sixty-one and had enjoyed a long career in the Portuguese diplomatic service—long enough to know that England and Portugal were very good friends. But while Britain was an ascending superpower, the viceroy knew that Portugal had effectively peaked as a world power in 1500, shortly after the Treaty of Tordesillas. If Portugal was to remain a player on the world stage—however minor—she had to maintain control of her last great colonial outpost, Brazil.

She had been there since January 1, 1502. *Rio de Janeiro* means "river of January" in Portuguese. This refers to both its location near the entrance to Guanabara Bay—which early-sixteenth-century explorers mistook for a river estuary—and to the date it was discovered, January 1, 1502. Though Portuguese explorers arrived first, French colonists didn't hesitate to establish a rival Calvinist settlement in 1555. Both parties warred with the local Tupi Indians.

Then as in Cook's time, the Portuguese were desperate to hold on to Brazil. They subjugated the Tupi, then expelled the French in 1567. Over the next century the stunning harbor with its white, sandy beaches, heavily forested mountains, and rocky sentinels guarding the entrance remained a small colony. Settlers scraped by through farming and fishing, as well as the export of brazilwood and sugarcane.

Then gold and diamonds were discovered in Brazil's interior. By 1704 a road had been built from Rio to the gold mines of Minas Gerais. Overnight Rio became a major center of transportation, commerce, and wealth. Her harbor filled with ships of many nations. When the Dutch and the French became too keen about exploiting the Brazilian marketplace, the Portuguese feared there would be another conflict. They turned to the British for protection and commercial assistance. Savvy British merchants were only too happy to move in. They soon dominated trade, engendering a quiet Portuguese animosity.

In 1710 the French returned and took control of the city. With little military might of their own, the Portuguese were forced to cite the Treaty of Tordesillas to wrangle Rio back from the French—that, and paying a substantial ransom. In 1763, Rio became Brazil's capital. His Excellency Don Antonio Rolim de Moura was eager to ensure that it remained Portuguese, and when French explorer de Bougainville had sailed into Rio's harbor in 1766, the viceroy had treated him so poorly that de Bougainville later filed a formal diplomatic protest. The Portuguese ignored it.

But de Bougainville had a history of colonial aggression, setting up a French garrison on the Falklands in 1764. The viceroy couldn't be faulted for being wary of de Bougainville.

Cook, however, was British, an explorer, carrying a shipload of scientists and very light armament. All Cook wanted was to resupply his vessel and take advantage of Rio's port facilities to recaulk *Endeavour's* bottom. There was no reason Cook should have expected anything but regal treatment.

However, from the moment *Endeavour* sailed into Rio's majestic harbor, the People lining the rail to take in the stunning landscape, the viceroy treated Cook as a military intruder. The viceroy was sure

Endeavour was a spy ship, for the notion of a voyage founded on science was preposterous. Her crew were not allowed to go ashore. Cook, alone, would be allowed to purchase provisions, but only through an agent extracting a 5 percent commission. When Cook drafted a rebuttal to the viceroy, then had Hicks row it ashore with a small crew, the viceroy not only refused to read Cook's document, but imprisoned Hicks's crew and returned the second lieutenant to *Endeavour* under guard.

When Cook put on his best dress uniform, complete with powdered white wig, blue topcoat (only the Royals, or "jollies," as they were known, wore red in the British Navy), and plumed hat, then went ashore and personally protested to the viceroy that his vessel was being treated unfairly, that Portugal and England had been allies for fifty years, and that at least forty other vessels in the harbor weren't being treated in the same shabby manner, the viceroy simply shrugged and said he was under orders from the king of Portugal—the same king of Portugal, Cook quickly noted, who ruled Madeira, which had treated Cook and *Endeavour* wonderfully. The viceroy was unmoved. "He had an answer," Cook wrote in disgust, "for everything I had to say."

"He certainly did not believe a word about our being bound to the southwest to observe the Transit of Venus," Cook wrote. "But looked upon it only as an invented story to cover some other design we must be upon, for he could form no other idea of that phenomenon (after I had explained it to him) than the North Star passing through the South Pole (these were his own words)." So not only was Cook being outfoxed by a petty tyrant, the man was dim-witted, to boot. Cook didn't know how to act. Even simple diplomacy was to no avail.

Acutely aware that rankling the Portuguese was not a good way to kick off a world cruise (and sure to be reported to his Admiralty masters during his absence), Cook tried not to provoke the viceroy. Cook did, however, taunt him twice a day by firing the ship's cannon with the customary Royal Navy morning and evening salutes.

Cook ordered *Endeavour*'s crew to stay on board—including Banks. Cook was losing enough face through the viceroy's actions. He didn't need a headstrong botanist making matters worse.

Banks would hear none of it. The Brazilian coastline was choked with uncataloged plants and animals. During *Endeavour*'s week in tiny Madeira he'd collected and pressed over seven hundred plants. Brazil, by comparison, was a botanist's dream come true. It had been frustrating enough bypassing the African coast on the journey south. He had no plans to sit in the sweltering great cabin, within sight of a botanical bounty, and admire the plants from afar like an unrequited lover. He was going ashore, and that's all there was to it. The scientific community had been most impressed that Banks would command this vessel of discovery. Now that Brazil's wonders lay before him, Banks could hardly sail on without cataloging this immense new world. Bucking Cook's authority, Banks and Solander climbed out the great cabin's large stern windows and snuck ashore by rowboat. Much to Cook's amusement, the viceroy refused to allow the pair to land.

By the time *Endeavour* prepared to leave Rio, a frustrated Banks had only managed to slip ashore at nights, under cover of darkness.

The final insult came as Cook was finally leaving Rio after three weeks in port. Sails up, slowly making his way into the Atlantic, Rio's shore batteries suddenly opened fire, launching two shots across Cook's bow. The action would have been unusual, but explainable, if *Endeavour* were sailing *into* Rio—perhaps mistaken for an attacker.

But for a ship to be attacked on her way out? The move was a pure power play by the viceroy, a show of force by a frustrated man whose once powerful country was being globally usurped.

Cook couldn't fire back. *Endeavour* would be blown out of the water. Her arsenal of twelve small swivel guns (usually fired only to repel boarders) and six small cannon was no match for garrison cannon. A frustrated Cook sent his cutter ashore with a small crew to clear the problem. After several hours of debate with the garrison commander, word came from the viceroy that *Endeavour* might safely pass.

It was a humiliated and angry Cook who finally led *Endeavour* back into the Atlantic. He'd learned a valuable lesson in international one-upmanship. Rio would be the last time Cook ever let a foreign official get the best of him.

Christmas raised Cook's spirits. He hove to (drifted with the sails furled) and let the men drink to excess, dance on deck, and engage in fistfights for entertainment. New Year's, 1769, was passed more quietly as Cook pushed *Endeavour* down the length of South America. Instead of remaining near shore—"coasting"—Cook sailed into the high seas, several hundred miles offshore. Wind conditions were more favorable there, and Cook was unlikely to run into any Portuguese military vessel bearing the viceroy's odd notions of diplomacy (or even sent by the Viceroy to sink *Endeavour*), but Banks grew more and more frustrated that little time was allocated him for research.

Cook considered himself a scientist of sorts, with his abiding interest in astronomy and surveying. He didn't see the relationship between science and botany, however, and was privately amused by Banks's aching to go ashore just to pick flowers. The indefatigable Banks, used to men making light of his profession, didn't care what Cook thought of him. For the five weeks it took Cook to maneuver toward the southern tip of the continent, Banks hounded Cook to sail closer to land. Cook made a few small attempts to mollify Banks, even sailing close enough to the Falklands so that Banks could see his—and Cook's—first penguins. But when Banks asked Cook to put ashore on the remote islands, Cook refused.

He had more pressing issues on his mind. He had been humiliated in Rio; he was about to sail *Endeavour* through the Strait of Le

Maire (the ferocious passage from Atlantic to Pacific discovered in 1616 by Dutch explorers Jakob le Maire and Willem Cornelis Schouten), one of the most treacherous waterways anywhere on earth; and after that, he would face five thousand miles of open ocean before Tahiti. Whereas Wallis merely stumbled onto Tahiti by accident, Cook would need every bit of navigational prowess to locate the small blip of land in all that vast Pacific water.

Last of all, Cook was becoming comfortable in command. The farther he sailed from England, the less he was impressed with Banks's societal position. The young man's constant whining about going ashore was becoming tiresome.

Cook was, however, quietly impressed with one aspect of Banks: his journals. Cook was used to the sailor's traditional terse jottings about weather and wind and liked that Banks wrote in a different style, using a great deal of description and largely disregarding punctuation. Cook began to believe that as a world explorer, the words he chose would someday create a mental image for King George III, Lord Sandwich, the Admiralty masters, and everyone else reading *Endeavour's* journals. Cook vowed to try harder. Slowly, very slowly, he began discovering the adjective.

This seemingly minor departure from protocol was a long time coming. Explorers for centuries had seen magnificence—purple-orange sunsets splashed across the horizon, gales so vicious hardened sailors puked like landlubbers, water a thousand dazzling shades of blue—then recorded those sights in listless, lucid terms. By opening his mind to Banks's artistic sensibilities, Cook began adding an ethereal tinge to discovery. The farther away from home he sailed, the more descriptive his prose. The words were his dreams slowly come to life, vividly etching themselves onto the page.

On the other side of the growing tension was Banks. He'd promised all his scientist friends back home that he would command a great voyage and return with an otherworldly array of previously unknown flora. He'd paid the considerable sum of ten thousand pounds to make the journey, a figure that not only dwarfed the four thousand pounds paid by King George to outfit *Endeavour* but made Cook's salary of 105 pounds per year look puny. And for all that investment and braggadocio, Banks's only return after five months at sea were the seven hundred plants collected at Madeira and a few plucked in the Brazilian night. If things didn't change, Banks was not only fated to spend three boring years on a very slow boat, but would endure scientific humiliation on his arrival back in London.

Cook and Banks's confrontation built to a head as Cook sailed south, preparing to enter the Strait of Le Maire. Just fifteen miles wide and long, it can take a week to transit when the winds are blowing hard. With rugged Tierra del Fuego to his right and left, Cook angled *Endeavour* toward the strait. If the bottom of South America is shaped like a bare foot, Cook was preparing to enter a gap between the big toe and the sole.

Endeavour sailed into a dynamo. The Strait of Le Maire is where currents from both the Atlantic and the Pacific collide. Icebergs spike from the surface during winter. The water is shallow, just a few hundred feet. The waves are taller for being compressed between two specks of land; more unpredictable for being the spearhead of an oceanic collision. And the prevailing winds, born in the Antarctic, blow from the west, so Cook was sailing directly into the wind during the passage. By the time those winds made their way north to the equator, they would heat, expand, and rise thousands of feet into the heavens. But in the Strait of Le Maire, almost sixty degrees south latitude, the air was still cold and dense, displaying its ferocity at sea level.

Almost immediately, *Endeavour* was in trouble. In addition to the wind, the tide was against her, and stormy weather made the bow pitch up and down so violently that the seats of ease were dipping underwater. Cook immediately retreated from the strait to wait for better weather, taking care not to broach as he turned *Endeavour* around in the huge waves. He backtracked up Tierra del Fuego, on what is now the coast of Argentina, and ruminated about the difficult waves and winds he'd just seen. Cook had never sailed through anything that intense. He was anxious about crew and ship safety on the next, inevitable, attempt.

Oblivious to Cook's anguish, Banks wouldn't stop carping about the need to go ashore and pick flowers. Cook finally gave in. Unable to make forward progress until the strait calmed, Cook backtracked up the Argentine coast just offshore, then had Banks and Solander rowed ashore into Thetis Bay. The two returned to the ship happy that night, carrying "plants and flowers, most of them unknown in Europe and in that alone consisted their whole value," Cook noted sarcastically in his journal.

No sooner had he arrived back on board than Banks was badgering Cook to let him go ashore again. Cook said no. The weather had become too unruly to launch a small boat, let alone risk the lives of the crew members needed to row Banks and Solander ashore.

And still Banks persisted. Cook said no once again, reminding Banks that the safety of the vessel was more important than botany. Banks would not be discouraged, though, and he turned on the charm. Cook, about to make his second attempt at entering the strait, refused again.

When the wind had calmed and the tidal race shifted into *Endeavour*'s favor, Cook sped down the coast and successfully squeezed his ship into the violent passage.

Banks seized the moment. He strolled to Cook's side and casually asked if he might be allowed to go ashore to explore the stunning array of flora and fauna no doubt existing on these unexplored shores. Cook, worn down by Banks's insistence and the ordeal of safely sailing into the strait, was too tired to say no. Halfway through the strait, Cook put Banks ashore in a half-moon cove known as Bay of Good Success. The date was January 15, 1769.

Thinking ahead to the long open-ocean passage to Tahiti, Cook decided to replenish *Endeavour's* stores. He sent the People ashore to forage for food, encouraging them to take long walks as a form of exercise. Going ashore himself, Cook was surprised to find plenty of freshwater, firewood, wild celery, and berries.

The local people, a primitive tribe who wore sealskins, streaked their copper skin with paint, and lived off shellfish and seals, amused him. This was Cook's first encounter with indigenous people other than the Native Americans of Newfoundland. As if they were animals in a zoo, he watched them, wrote about them, treated them with paternal ownership, then decided "they were the most wretched people on earth" and began to feel sorry for their lot in life.

Much to Cook's surprise and happiness, the natives treated him like a king. James Cook, the foreman's boy! It was a strange, but not wholly unwelcome, sensation. After the humiliating one-upmanship of Rio and the draining tasks of dueling with Banks and the Strait of Le Maire, an embattled Cook didn't discourage their worship.

Meanwhile, Banks and Solander sent word back to Cook that they were heading as far as possible into the countryside to do research, leading a party of eleven, which included ship's astronomer Charles Green, ship's surgeon William Monkhouse, and two sailors whose sole function was to act as porters. This display of independence was Banks's last-ditch attempt to wrest power from the captain. With every additional mile of separation between London and *Endeavour*, Banks's power decreased. He knew it. He was powerless to stop it. This grand voyage was not his after all. Running away for a spell was important to Banks. If nothing else, time away from Cook's authority would salvage some wounded pride. The party was going, Banks messengered to Cook, into the mountains. They would be back for dinner.

Halfway up the large hills above the Bay of Good Success, things began going terribly wrong. Banks's party left a thick forest and entered a waist-high thicket of birch. The ground gave way beneath them, turning from solid earth and rock to a muddy, ankle-deep bog. The day, which had started sunny and warm, turned frigid as they made their way through the small jungle. Their feet were soaked and uncomfortably cold. The birch scratched their hands and faces.

Then Alexander Buchan, one of the artists Banks had brought along to paint pictures of the new botanical discoveries, suffered an epileptic seizure. He dropped into the bog, writhing. Fearing that the seizure would detract from plant-gathering time, Banks ordered one of the sailors and two of the servants to stay with Buchan and make a fire. Meanwhile, Banks would lead Solander, Monkhouse, Green, one sailor, and the other two servants on to the summit. He was sure rare species of alpine plants would be found there.

Snow began falling, lashed by harsh winds off the strait. Then the sun went down. Solander, a fragile man, was exhausted. He lay in the snow and refused to get up. Banks had him dragged to a sheltered spot, where Dorlton, one of the servants, made a fire. Meanwhile, Richmond, the other servant, had gotten lost. Banks ordered Dorlton and one of the People to leave the shelter and find Richmond, giving them a bottle of rum for first aid and insurance against the cold.

When Dorlton and the sailor found Richmond, the three got very drunk—too drunk to remember their location. The sailor struck off alone, wandering around in the darkness until he found Banks and the rest of the party. Dorlton and Richmond, however, passed out in the midst of their stupor. They froze to death in the night. Banks found them the next morning. One of Banks's greyhounds was curled up against the bodies, asleep. Banks ordered the men buried, then shot and cooked a vulture for breakfast.

Under a sunny sky, Banks led the stunned scientists back to *Endeavour*. He was too embarrassed by the deaths to confront Cook.

After assuring his greyhounds were fed a warm meal and placed in a warm bed, he took *Endeavour*'s skiff for a paddle on the bay. Though the servants were Banks's responsibility, in the end they were passengers on Cook's vessel. Banks knew Cook's viewpoint on shipboard loss of life—inexcusable, except in extreme cases—and couldn't bear the prospect of a day aboard ship explaining the deaths. He paddled well into the afternoon, dropping his seine net every now and then for the sake of appearance.

It was over, Banks knew—this quest for command. His recklessness had killed two men. Lesser men, to be sure, mere servants. But men nonetheless, and the crew would never allow Cook's measured leadership to be usurped now. A leader ultimately puts his own safety after that of his crew—Magellan being the perfect example—and Banks had clearly demonstrated that his personal quests came before crew safety. Whatever loyalties Banks had cultivated before then were lost. The crew began treating him as a benign peer.

Cook was stunned and saddened by the deaths. As a former ordinary sailor, he sought to protect his men at all costs. Cook vowed to keep a tighter rein on Banks, especially when it came to overnight botany expeditions in wild countries.

With their rivalry diminished—but never gone—Banks could relax and be himself. That meant slightly foppish, slightly foolish, and prone to seeking sexual pleasure whenever possible. Serious Cook wasn't allowed, and didn't care to have, any of those traits. Cook and Banks began a more open dialogue, and the great cabin—though Banks's sleeping quarters—became a regular meeting place and arena for discussion between Cook, Banks, and the scientists and artists on board. Despite his lack of formal education, Cook held his own in these gatherings and displayed a keen ear for subjects new and interesting to him.

With his brown hair slowly streaking gray and his broad shoulders drawn back in a display of perfect posture, Cook was the antithesis of these casual men with their bohemian airs and young faces. But they were to be together for three years. The scientists were free to be scientists and the captain clearly the captain. Informality followed with this dropping of pretense, and Banks and Cook began developing a deep, yet unusual, lifelong friendship.

CHAPTER 7

The Promised Land

On January 25, 1769, *Endeavour* sailed in Pacific water for the first time. Two hundred and fifty years after the first European had laid eyes on her broad waters, Cook was on the verge of making the Pacific his kingdom.

The one aspect of global discovery that hadn't changed, even as the balance of power had shifted worldwide, was the path explorers took after entering the Pacific. The prevailing winds blew east to west, then rotated counterclockwise up the coast of South America to the equator. Rather than battle prevailing winds, ships allowed the winds to push them north along the coast of Chile. Then, at the equator, where the winds shifted direction and began blowing from the east, ships merely went in the same direction (another sailing addition to modern English, the term *go where the wind blows*).

When Cook sailed past Cape Horn and crossed into the Pacific, he didn't go north with the wind. He didn't even go west, toward Tahiti. Reveling in his command and in the realization that his was the only British ship in the Pacific (and thus had no superior for thousands of miles in any direction), he indulged his craving for adventure by pointing *Endeavour* due south toward the Antarctic. Correctly surmising that he would never find *Endeavour* in such high southern latitudes again, Cook was taking a stab at discovering Antarctica. He wasn't due in Tahiti until April, or maybe June if he wanted to push deadlines. Why not gambol about the Pacific? The world was Cook's oyster. He could go anywhere with impunity. No one could stop him, tell him he was wrong or foolish or headstrong. Even if His Majesty wanted to send someone after this forty-year-old whose wanderlust was finally, totally, blessedly realized, it would take at least a year to mount an expedition, then another to find Lieutenant Cook. It was as if Cook, the brash farm boy made good, was going to dispel seventeen centuries of improper reasoning on his own with one bold gesture.

Banks was suffering even more bad luck in the form of four days of diarrhea after eating bad albatross, so Cook realized he would hear few complaints from his most vocal passenger.

Cook pressed *Endeavour* south. The crew grew anxious, for Cook's exploratory probe was a sharp deviation from the linear nature of exploration. Instead of going straight from Point A to Point B, Cook's whimsical new definition of adventure meant going from Point A to Point Z and then, maybe, to Point B.

The ship's officers were confused, Banks was throwing up down below, and the People were worried they'd be shipwrecked before getting the chance to seduce the mass of naked women treading water off King George Island, eagerly awaiting their arrival. All in all, the only happy man on *Endeavour* was Cook.

The southerly indulgence lasted five days. When Cook reached the sixtieth parallel and had still found nothing resembling a landmass, he had had enough. The weather was cold and raining, the sea was getting larger and more unpredictable, and there was no sign of Antarctica. On January 30, Cook gave the order to turn *Endeavour* north by west, toward Tahiti.

The crew rejoiced. And though Tahiti and its women were still two months distant, the island became the talk of the ship. With the exception of short stints ashore in Madeira and the Strait of Le Maire, the People had been crammed aboard *Endeavour* for six months. Tensions were rising. A certain testosterone ventilation began taking place, brought on by claustrophobia, the crew-wide appearance of scurvy symptoms such as swollen gums, anxiety about reaching paradise, and the nonstop conversations about having sex for the first time in many months. Talk of land and its pleasures became as common as normal shipboard routines such as drinking and gambling or carving wood or bone. Even the officers were drinking and playing backgammon more than usual.

That ventilation turned into a subdued, crew-wide belligerence as day after day passed without sight of land. Instead of ceasing when the weather got warmer and the seas smoother, the tension rose. Cook's distance recordings and latitude calculations showed that land was getting close. As long as food and water and liquor remained in supply, violence wouldn't become a problem.

Cook was a visible daily presence on deck, scanning the horizon with the same eager eye of the People. His daily uniform was informal and light, befitting the increasingly hotter tropical climate: comfortable black leather shoes with a single buckle, white breeches, and a billowing white shirt unbuttoned at the collar and often rolled to the elbow. His long brown hair was pulled back in a pigtail. The formal dress uniform—Number One Dress Rig—with its heavy blue topcoat, powdered wig, and hat was stowed, being saved for formal appearances such as the occasional Sunday service or a burial at sea—neither of which happened much on Cook's vessel. However, stepping ashore to greet foreign dignitaries or to claim a new land "in the name of King George III, and all His Heirs and Successors" was another instance calling for the Number One. Cook, despite its stifling weight, ached to don the rig and do just that.

On the morning of March 25, exactly two months after sailing into the Pacific, Cook sighted seaweed—a sign of land. He breathed a sigh of relief and passed word of the sighting, hoping the coming landfall would calm the men.

But land would come too late for one member of Endeavour's crew. The victim was William Greenslade, a shy marine.

Like all sailors, Cook disdained the marines' presence, but fully understood the Admiralty's rationale for sending them. Guiding almost a hundred men for three years was incredibly difficult. The strain of constant decision-making—day in, day out; around the clock from the time Endeavour sailed from England until the day she returned—about men and navigation and stores and an endless list of other pressing needs, could make a man lose his confidence, lose his moral compass. Lose his life.

Hence, the marines' quarters on Endeavour were situated between Cook's and the crew's as a barrier. In their white gaiters and shocking-red tunics, with bayonets and muskets in hand, the marines seemed intent on intimidating by appearance alone. Their leader was Sergeant John Edgcumbe, a no-nonsense man with a nose for other men's weakness.

On March 25, the morning Cook spied seaweed, Greenslade had been given a dual responsibility: first, to guard the door of the great cabin while Cook and Banks conferred inside; second, to keep a length of sealskin in his possession for some fellow marines. It was a rude joke, foisted upon him by Edgcumbe. When men must do without creature comforts for long periods, odd things take on value. And so it was with sealskin. Waterproof and malleable, sealskin had first come aboard Endeavour after hunting expeditions off Tierra del Fuego. It was the perfect material for sewing tobacco pouches and had quickly become a valuable commodity.

The marines had a small square of sealskin they were dividing among themselves—except Greenslade. The introverted young man had become an outcast within the bawdy, garrulous marine detachment. Edgcumbe was the senior NCO and felt it his job to maintain cohesiveness among his men. Instead of trying to draw Greenslade in, Edgcumbe had encouraged the others to bully and harass the shy young man. Day by day since leaving Plymouth, Greenslade's despair had grown. He had not a friend on the ship and home was years away.

Despite—or, perhaps, because of—the ostracism, Greenslade wanted a piece of sealskin for himself. Knowing the act of rebellion might prove his undoing, Greenslade cut a small square with his bayonet. He stuffed the rough, thin, waterproof gold in his pocket. Then he resumed his time on watch, spending the next two hours thinking about that thing in his pocket, tortured as to whether he should put it back or proclaim his manhood. He would get caught. That much was obvious. So why risk it? Why not just admit the moment of weakness and reunite the cut section with the original?

Edgcumbe returned. The sergeant put his face right in front of Greenslade's as the scared young man stood at attention and demanded his sealskin. Suddenly Greenslade regretted his stupidity, then felt his strength and confidence slip away. Edgcumbe's face was so close he could feel the older man's spittle and taste his hot, rancid breath, as Edgcumbe vowed he would take the matter to Lieutenant Cook. "People should not suffer scandal because of the ill behavior of one," the sergeant grunted. He would recommend to Cook that a lashing of the most severe nature was the only proper punishment for insubordination. Edgcumbe, swatch of sealskin in hand, turned and walked crisply down the corridor to the marines.

Greenslade was still on duty and couldn't leave his post. He stood at attention, ruminating, until his watch was done. Then Greenslade fled to the sanctuary of his hammock. Even there he was not safe, though, as his cohorts taunted him for the theft. Greenslade tried to close his eyes and ignore them, but that provided no comfort. He felt homesick and alone. He felt tortured by the day-in, day-out mental harassment. But he saw no immediate way out. The obvious solution was desertion at King George Island, but that would only bring on more problems when he was inevitably caught—a lashing, at the very least. And even if he succeeded, home was still half a world away. Even in paradise, desertion was no guarantee of happiness.

Greenslade knew what he must do. The tortured young man left his hammock and walked up on deck. Pretending to use the bathroom, Greenslade went to the bow and jumped over the side. Alone in the Pacific, he could only watch as *Endeavour* sailed away.

Sadly, the tragedy was preventable. Banks had witnessed the growing tension among the marines, saw them cull Greenslade from their herd. "Before night," he told Cook later, "they drove the young fellow almost mad." But Banks never anticipated the suicide, nor did he inquire into the depths of young Greenslade's torment. Only when the end finally came and Greenslade had leapt was Cook finally told of the sealskin incident.

Cook listened to the news incredulously. Edgcumbe clearly didn't care that Greenslade was dead, having carefully delayed his report on the incident until thirty minutes after watching Greenslade leap. "They painted it in such colors," a disgusted Cook noted of the collective marine vilification of Greenslade, "and stood up for the honor of the core so highly, that before night they drove the young fellow almost mad. He was seen to go upon the forecastle, and from that time on he was seen no more."

Cook, who knew the pain of being on the fringe of society, mourned the young man's passing. "I was neither made acquainted with the theft or the circumstance attending it," he lamented, "until the man was gone."

More than ever, Cook hoped the seaweed blossom was a true portender of land. Time ashore was critical. *Endeavour* was becoming a powder keg. The men needed to refresh themselves mentally and physically, or *Endeavour's* objectives would never be met. Mutiny would happen instead, and the People would easily—and happily—overwhelm the marines.

Cook was navigating by an advanced technique known as "running down the latitude." Unlike skippers who depended upon dead reckoning's educated guess to determine position, Cook used lunar tables for longitude and sun sights to determine latitude (the north-south orientation on the globe). However, because exact longitude was still hard to determine, Cook sailed *Endeavour* north to Tahiti's exact latitude, then turned sharply west. Though he was still several hundred miles from the islands, the logic of running down the latitude held that if Cook could hold course, he would eventually sail right into Tahiti's azure lagoons. Two ship's compasses were set just before the wheel to assist the helmsman in following that course exactly. If contrary winds became a problem, and he had to sail to windward, the helmsman would watch the action of the sails and air to keep the ship as close as possible to the proper course.

While Cook was an accomplished navigator with a cartographer's notion of geography and had thirty-three-year-old astronomer Charles Green (like Cook, raised a Yorkshire farm boy) to guide him through the more complex celestial-navigation computations, there was a great deal of luck involved in finding Tahiti. The breadth of the Pacific and the small size of the South Pacific islands (though these twenty-five thousand islands are scattered across millions of square miles of ocean, their combined mass is only roughly the size of America's west coast) demanded precision navigation, good weather, and benevolent winds. Finding Tahiti in that watery mass was a literal search for a needle in a haystack. At just thirty-three miles long and sixteen miles wide, Tahiti was the sort of landmass a ship could easily bypass in the night.

As the days turned into weeks, then months, since *Endeavour* had last seen land at Cape Horn, Cook must have felt a lot like Christopher Columbus—another unproven captain who had known landfall was imminent, but wasn't sure when or where. Cook grew increasingly isolated from every other man on board as the days passed without a sighting. He was beginning to worry.

On March 28, Cook and Green spent the morning along the rail with sextants, shooting the sun and moon, then using their known distance from Earth to compute *Endeavour's* location. To Cook's dismay he was sixty miles off course, still three degrees south of Tahiti's seventeen-degree south latitude. At that great distance, Tahiti would be hidden by the earth's curvature when *Endeavour* finally sailed into the proper longitude.

Cook blamed himself, recording that the fair weather and benevolent winds wouldn't push him this far off course. On March 29 and March 30 he noted "errors too great to be accounted for," hinting that he had made gross navigational mistakes earlier in the voyage.

Deciding to double-check their computations before making a sudden course change, Cook and Green spent between 10 and 11 A.M. the morning of March 29 getting to the root of the problem. They were determined to fix *Endeavour's* exact position by the sun and the moon. After the hour of shooting, then several more hours of mathematics in the great cabin with Green, Cook discovered that *Endeavour* was truly off course. He gave the order to sail north and west, into the proper latitude. The crewman sighting land first would be rewarded with a bottle of rum. Cook anxiously waited for the fevered cry of "Land ho!"

Finally, on April 4, Banks's servant, Peter Briscoe, sighted an island. The land wasn't Tahiti, but one of the atolls (a coral island consisting of a reef surrounding a lagoon) of the Tuamotus, an 870-mile-long chain of eighty atolls five hundred miles east of Tahiti. The crew cheered the sight of land, but was disappointed to see tall, dark, naked men carrying twelve-foot spears gathering on the beach, instead of women. "Only their privys were covered," a relieved Cook wrote. "And they were copper colored people."

The Tuamotu atoll of Vahitahi is little remembered by history, but it was the first of Cook's many discoveries (other Tuamotu atolls had been discovered by Portuguese navigator de Queirós in 1606). Cook's desire to race for shore and step on the unknown islands was strong, but he sensed that the warlike locals could only become a problem. Cook sailed close to the reef, however, and would write in his journal of tall trees, something inland resembling a lake, a lack of anchorage, and then women in white skirts emerging from the jungle as *Endeavour* sailed away.

Endeavour passed quickly through the scattered Tuamotus. Another island was discovered the next day. Cook's self-doubt earlier was forgotten. The enormous stress of being so low-ranking but commanding such a high-profile voyage—stress that he had shouldered for almost exactly a year since given the *Endeavour* command—slipped from his shoulders. He had endured the Portuguese viceroy. He had quieted Banks. Through an innovative diet of antiscorbutics—sauerkraut, malt, and wort that provided a constant supply of vitamins—he had lost no man to scurvy. He had sailed over twelve thousand miles since leaving England. He had found land and knew that Tahiti was just a few hundred miles over the horizon. Life was all good for James Cook. For the first time that entire voyage, Cook truly allowed himself to relax and enjoy the wondrous new lands he'd dreamed of visiting since childhood.

When a third island hove into view at dusk on April 6, Cook shed the stress entirely. His stoic facade dropped. Reverting to his days as an able seaman, Cook greatly amused the crew by climbing the mainmast's tar-covered ratlines all the way to the very top. From this bucking, swaying vantage point (the mainmast's upper reaches experienced more lateral motion than any other part of the vessel), Cook surveyed his new tropical kingdom.

He studied Bow Island as a soft tropical breeze caressed his face. The People lined the decks and hung on lower reaches of the rigging, peering out onto paradise. Coconut palms were visible. White sand beaches. Outrigger canoes. Dark-skinned locals hiding in clumps of trees. For the men who'd never circumnavigated before—especially Cook—the enchanting sights and smells of the South Pacific were like a landing on another planet.

The stunning blue water entranced Cook, as did the tropical sunset with its otherworldly oranges and purples that brought forth a sense of inner calm, and even the shape of the island. He stayed atop the mast long after the sun had set, when his image of the island was just a profile illuminated by the moon and stars. "I was admiring," he wrote of the island, "its extraordinary structure: In shape it appeared like a longbow." The island today is called Bow Island.

Earlier in the voyage, when Cook was unproven to the crew or after he'd been humiliated in Rio de Janeiro, it might have been disconcerting to the People to watch their leader getting pie-eyed over land and dirtying his white shirt on the ratlines. They would have compared Cook with more traditional Royal Navy officers they'd sailed under and found him a tad unorthodox. But Cook had earned the People's respect with his expertise and benevolence (though there had been scattered examples of disciplinary flogging, Cook's reluctance to use the lash had been an important surprise to the People), and the unorthodox sight of a ship's captain scampering up the rigging was endearing. Until his gymnastics, Cook had been impossible to read and enigmatic to know, appearing aloof and outwardly stern despite his lack of harsh discipline. But now the People understood him. They knew passion shimmered beneath that hard surface. And though he'd said nothing, given no command, nor done anything more than daydream atop the mast, the foundation for total authority Cook had laid in Tierra del Fuego led to a higher realm of leadership in the Tuamotus. His People felt the sort of kinship only the best leaders enjoy, the kind that says their men will go anywhere, do anything, because their trust runs so deep. Many men standing on deck that evening would voluntarily sail with Cook until his death.

No one had dared to follow Cook's climb, not even the officers. So Cook stayed aloft, alone.

When Cook finally climbed down, it was with great care, for *Endeavour*'s bow was heaving up and down as she bashed across the Pacific under full sail. The equatorial latitudes were near, and the prevailing winds blew from behind *Endeavour*, shoving her those final five hundred miles to Tahiti at a blistering pace.

A week later, towering, green volcanic mountains poked through a squall to announce themselves. James Cook, the farm boy from Airyholme, had found Tahiti.

CHAPTER 8

Rendezvous

For all the beauty of Bow Island and the Tuamotus, they were underfed geographic waifs compared with the voluptuous sprawl Cook and the People ogled sailing along the Tahitian coast. Tropical birds wreathed the masts. It was a world of vivid greens and blues; of mountains and valleys; and clear lagoons with sandy, white bottoms and beaches of volcanic black. The air smelled of ripe flowers and silky humidity. Tahiti's pointed, mile-high peaks thrust boldly into the sky like giants without shoulders.

But the most amazing sight of all was the population. These weren't the shy natives of the Tuamotus, hiding their women and discouraging visitation. Thousands of native outriggers filled with bare-chested men and women were paddling to greet *Endeavour* as she maneuvered into Matavai Bay, a stunning natural harbor on the northwest shoulder of Tahiti and site of present-day Papeete.

Cook gathered the People. They ached to go ashore, calling out to Cook, begging for him to give the order that would allow them to plunge into the pleasures of paradise. First, however, Cook had a few things to say. He was extending his authority over his men from merely shipboard life to deportment ashore. Having won their trust and affection, Cook wanted to control the People's hearts and minds. They were *his* People. He wanted them to forget that they were the dregs of London society and see the potential for great good within themselves. He realized that lust coursed through their veins, but he wanted them to set that aside and be moral and upright and honest. That was like asking a famished man not to eat, but Cook was sure he could pull it off.

Boldly, Cook laid down a series of laws designed to protect the Tahitians. The men listened carefully. Their biggest fear—an irrational fear, they knew, but vibrant nonetheless—was that Cook would confine them to the ship. Contact with women would be impossible. The People stood at loose attention, jammed shoulder to shoulder on the tightly packed deck. Cook was atop the quarterdeck wearing his Number One Dress Rig, looking down and holding a sheet of parchment in one hand. Warm air drifted past the men, who stood stone-still, afraid even to speak for fear it would anger their commander and lead to confinement aboard ship.

Cook cleared his throat and began reading: "The local citizenry are to be treated with civility, and friendships are to be cultivated."

A bawdy titter tiptoed across the deck. Cook smiled, waited for it to pass him by, then continued.

"There will be no trading with the ship's stores. Any man found doing so will suffer punishment and loss of pay. The only persons trading with the natives, in fact, are to be individuals I will designate specifically for the task." He had in mind Banks and Solander.

"Next, any man losing a firearm or tool will be punished." That might mean lashing or hard duty or merely confinement to quarters, but such losses were not permissible under any circumstances.

Finally, "no sort of iron, or anything that was made of iron, or any sort of cloth or other useful or necessary articles" was to be given in exchange for anything but provisions. In other words, no nails for sex.

The men groaned. Cook continued, "The People are to be on their best behavior."

And that was all. The crew cheered in relief, though they were puzzled about which new rate of exchange would replace nails. Romance and kind words never crossed their minds, and those men given shore leave quickly fled to enjoy island charms.

To the men's chagrin, during the first few days ashore island sex turned out to be more complex than London barroom legend implied. More exactly, sex wasn't a matter of unlimited congress, but took on four distinct guises. How a woman responded to a sexual overture depended on her view of sex. This was confusing to the People because they never knew which woman practiced which form.

The islanders enjoyed ritual sex for religion, orgiastic sex for religion, and marital sex; and a group known as the *ariori*, who trolled the beaches, engaged in sex for commerce and mere fun. How to differentiate when and with whom sex should be engaged? And, secretly, would it be possible to meet a nice island girl and establish a relationship, then maybe get married—with the implicit knowledge that marital loyalty would mean the temptation to desert, and a severe lashing if discovered. For the lonely sailors, establishing this knowledge became top priority. They trolled the beach in search of the answer.

Meanwhile, Cook was preparing for the June 3 Transit. His top priority was establishing relations with the local king. Following that, he meant to find the perfect spot to build the Transit observatory. The two actions were linked, for trees and rocks were considered the personal property of various leaders. Cook needed to knock down more than a few trees to build his Transit observatory and the fort that would protect it. Cook's immersion in Tahitian culture, then, began as a study of local hierarchy in order to accomplish *Endeavour's* mission. Once he knew the men in charge, Cook could not only discuss toppling trees, but also establishing a permanent garrison on Tahiti. He envisioned the island as a strategic base for His Majesty. Not a colony, just a base. Though not a sentimental man,

Cook bridled at the thought of colonization. He had an instant fondness for the Tahitian people born of a growing sense of his own omnipotence. This was his world. These people were a part of it. Cook was not the first European to stumble into their waters, but in spring of 1769 he was the most powerful man within several thousand miles. He had the cannon and muskets to back up any decree. There was immense satisfaction in that, a certain freedom to make the rules and bend the rules and assert his dominance. If anyone was going to bend the Tahitians' will, subjugate them, settle them, it would be Cook—not some Admiralty lackey. And colonization would likely mean a repeat of the Europeanization of Africa, where the locals were first seen as noble savages, then beaten down as enemies, devalued as less than human beings, and enslaved. Cook was more interested in forging alliances with the Tahitians than stripping them of their dignity.

In fact, Cook was so eager to make friends with the local warlords that he immediately set to learning their language and customs. Cook found that the Tahitians were a class society, bestowing monarchy and poverty; banishing the oppressed or rebellious. They had religion, taboos (known as *tapu*), forbidden foods, and sacred land. The Tahitians didn't merely have one king, but many, with varying levels of power. This was most confusing to Cook.

There was, for instance, the *ari'i*. This was a chief. He was obviously a special person, for his commands had heft and were immediately obeyed. His body and clothing were not to be touched by others and were protected by *tapu*. His land was protected, as were his symbols of power such as his rod and spear. His holy place of worship was a coral structure that looked like a fort and was called a *marae*. About the island were scattered dozens of *ari'i*.

But even more powerful than the *ari'i* were a group known as *ari'i rahi*. Three such men wandered the island, feet never touching the ground because a group of subjects carried the *ari'i rahi* everywhere on royal litters. All worshiped them. Logically, these men were the most powerful men on the island.

Cook's problem was that the three *ari'i rahi* held no sway over the *ari'i*. So essentially, no one was in charge. Out of desperation and expedience, Cook decided he would be king. It was of utmost importance that he get the Transit observatory built, and there was little time to waste. Cook wasn't trying to assume command to play the part of colonial master, but to carry out his Admiralty orders. His motives were pure. So while James Cook was in Tahiti, he would be the supreme power and would broach no loss of face to a lesser local man. And as he stepped into the perceived power vacuum, they were all lesser in Cook's eyes.

Within two weeks of arriving, Cook found his perfect spot for the Transit observatory, naming the beachfront property Point Venus. Without obtaining permission from the locals, he ordered a work crew to begin knocking down trees. A wooden fence with pointed uprights and berms of black volcanic sand would surround the fort. Tents inside would have room for forty-five men, a cook's oven, and an armorer's forge. An observatory in the center would house telescopic equipment and the special Transit timekeeping apparatus packed in storage the year before in Greenwich, then stowed so carefully aboard *Endeavour*.

Marine sentries were posted around the fort's perimeter to protect the work crews and prevent theft.

All went well between the Tahitians and *Endeavour's* crew until the marines began creating problems. When a local attempted to steal a marine's musket from Fort Venus (the Tahitians were proving themselves a light-fingered bunch), the marine simply grabbed another musket and shot the thief dead. The Greenslade incident was still fresh on Cook's mind, and he had no problem taking the local's side, especially if supporting the marines jeopardized the Transit mission. Cook detained the marine sentry, then found the family of the dead local and apologized. Just in case, however, the Tahitians thought this gave them license to steal, Cook had *Endeavour* moved closer to shore. In addition to the swivel guns and cannon inside Fort Venus, cannon from *Endeavour* were trained on the coast.

Shortly thereafter, Alexander Buchan, the epileptic artist who had suffered so greatly during Banks's snowy night in the Strait of Le Maire, was hit by another seizure and died. Not sure about local custom in such a situation, afraid of offending the Tahitians or provoking them unnecessarily, Cook sailed *Endeavour* out to sea for the burial.

While all this was going on, Banks, who was displaying a remarkable affection for the local women, became something of a sidekick to Cook. Banks's naturally haughty nature had been replaced by gregariousness, and the Tahitians liked him very much, which allowed him to get close to them. On the other hand, the studious Cook treated the island as a case study, observing the people without getting too close. Between the two of them came forth an alliance that led to greater understanding of the Tahitians. They shared journal pages, with Banks's subjective eye for observation supplementing Cook's analytical bent. Both men had a great many questions about Tahitian culture and spent hours in conversation about exactly what the more obscure rituals, such as infanticide, implied. And while the crew were confined to Matavai Bay, forbidden to travel farther than a bare slope known as One Tree Hill, Banks was given permission to range far and wide. He cut a splendid figure strolling the beach in his waistcoat, bending down with fanatic zeal to caress and pluck new botanical discoveries. He often spent the night far in the woods, away from the beach, sleeping without any sort of weapon or military protection. "I found them to be a people so free from deceit that I trusted myself among them almost as freely as in my own country," Banks wrote. He added: "Love is the chief occupation. The favorite, nay, the soul luxury of the inhabitants; both the bodies and souls of the women are molded into the utmost perfection for that soft science idleness. Love reigns here."

What Cook and Banks could not see was that the European presence was bewildering the Tahitians, damaging their moral fiber ir-reparably. And it was all because of metal. The Tahitians' boats were made of wood, their art form was primarily wood carving, and even weapons such as war clubs and hatchets were primarily made from wood. Sharks' teeth were their carving tools, but they were difficult to procure and dulled rapidly. With the European introduction of metallurgy, however, a whole other caliber of chisels and awls came into being. The metal tools dulled slower, were more effective, and lasted a lifetime, which meant that killing a shark was no longer a prerequisite for pursuing a woodworking hobby.

The less benign use for steel was as a killing tool. But no matter what it was used for, metal was a life-changing commodity to the Tahitians. Its accumulation became an island obsession. Women ex-changing sex for a single nail may have seemed a ridiculous price to the sailors, even cavalier. But nails could be melted down and formed into tools or bartered for valuable other commodities. Nail by nail these women were accumulating a Tahitian fortune. It was ironic that the sailors thought they were taking advantage of the women, for the women saw themselves doing the same to the sailors.

A more subtle change was expressed through the thievery. This bent owed more to curiosity and the human desire to covet others' possessions than to a societal bad streak. When the Tahitians looked at the massive European vessels sailing into their waters—Cook was the third explorer to guide a ship this way, after Wallis and the Frenchman de Bougainville—they saw a treasure chest. There were obviously more riches on board than any society could use in a lifetime. Stealing from such an ample supply was hardly theft. More like leveling the playing field, redistributing the wealth. The British were outraged and grew furious that more and more possessions—many seemingly worthless—disappeared into Tahitian hands. This simple clash of two cultures meant that nei-ther acted appropriately in times of friction. With each theft, tensions escalated, and it was only a matter of time before some sort of minor warfare began.

The situation came to a head in early May—just four weeks before the Transit. A local man snuck into Fort Venus and stole that very special, very precious astronomical quadrant. If it was not returned, *Endeavour's*—and Cook's—raison d'être was done. Cook could explore for Antarctica all he wanted, but if he returned to England minus Transit of Venus information, blaming it on a local's theft, he would have been the laughingstock of the Royal Navy. An Admiralty inquest into the voyage's failure would be held, and the most embarrassing tidbit of the theft would come to light: the quadrant had been stolen from Cook's tent.

Cook flew into a rage. He abducted a local chief, Tuteha, and held him ransom for the quadrant. He also seized every canoe in the bay and placed them under marine guard. Banks and Green discovered from another chief, Tepau, who the thief was. With glee, Banks slipped two small pistols into his pockets and bade Tepau lead them to the man. It was a hot, sluggish day. Tepau walked with Banks from house to house (the Tahitians did not cluster their homes in communal villages, but spread out across acres of woods) calling out the name of the guilty man. The thief's neighbors, afraid Cook would fire *Endeavour's* cannon into their homes, hastily pointed where the man had gone with the quadrant's pieces.

"Pieces?" Banks asked.

The precision instrument had been taken apart. The different pieces had been divvied up between the thief and a few friends. They were preparing to use them to make ornamental necklaces and bracelets, as well as household decorations.

Banks and Green scavenged the island on that sweltering day. Somehow they located every piece of the quadrant. At one point a crowd of a hundred Tahitians surrounded the pair, and a nervous Banks was forced to produce his weapons to scare them away. On their way home, a triumphant, sweaty Banks and Solander met Cook and a party of marines coming from the shore. Banks informed Cook of Tuteha's innocence, and Cook had the chief freed immediately upon their return to Fort Venus.

Tuteha took personal responsibility for the quadrant's kidnapping and had two hogs sent to Cook. However, there was the matter of appearances, and Tuteha—an *ari'i*, a man whose very body was *tapu*—had lost a great deal of face when the English had manhandled him without apology. After sleeping on it a night, Tuteha sent word back that Cook must atone for his violating *tapu*. An ax and a shirt were the price of forgiveness. Until these were delivered, all the fresh food and water Cook's men had come to depend upon after months eating stale, tasteless meals at sea would no longer be available.

Cook was surprised to find that the Tahitians rallied behind Tuteha, giving him overwhelming authority to enforce his mandates. Other *ari'i* and *ari'i rahi* participated in the embargo. When master Molyneaux and Green sailed *Endeavour's* pinnace twenty miles east to circumvent the blockade, villagers refused to sell them hogs or fowl. Tuteha had forbade it. With that, Cook threw in the towel. He went with Banks and Solander to present not only the ax and a shirt, but also a poncho. Tuteha accepted the gifts before a throng of villagers, then celebrated his personal victory by treating the Englishmen to a display of wrestling by local men. The supply of fresh food and water resumed, but English and Tahitian relations had clearly passed the honeymoon stage. Each culture was wary and respectful of the other, not always happy with the other's behavior but making allowances in the name of peace.

The thieving, however, continued. At one point Cook even had a pair of stockings stolen from under his head while he lay awake on the beach. English displays of force continued as well. Cook began seizing canoes instead of chiefs to assert himself; it was as if neither side in the symbiotic partnership could help itself.

When June 3, 1769, the day of the Transit, finally arrived, Green had restored the quadrant to working condition. "The astronomical clock," wrote Cook in his most scientific manner, "made by Shelton and furnished with a gridiron pendulum, was set up in the middle of one end of a large tent, a frame of wood made for that purpose in Greenwich, fixed firm and as low in the ground as the door above the clock case would admit, and to prevent it being disturbed by any accident, another framing of wood was made around this, at the distance of one foot from it. The telescope made use of in the observations were: Two reflecting ones of two feet focus each, made by the late Mr. James Short, one of which was furnished with a glass micrometer."

Cook divided the observation into three teams, with Green and himself at Fort Venus, Clerke and a team on the other side of the island, and a team led by Gore rowing ten miles across a channel to Tahiti's sister island of Moorea. Banks showed his feelings about the Transit by traveling with the Moorean contingent. He would spend the day of the Transit specimen-collecting, then share his tent with three local girls that night.

Cook's major fear had been a cloudy day, but June 3 dawned bright and clear. From nine in the morning until three in the afternoon, Cook and Green watched the tiny shape of Venus crawl across the sun. The entire Transit lasted six hours, from approximately twenty-one minutes, fifty seconds past 9 A.M. until 3 P.M. The midday temperature rose to 119 degrees. The telescope's metal was scorching to the touch, and the most minor instrumental adjustment became a premeditated act.

In the end, though, viewing conditions were ideal. "This day proved as favorable to our purpose as we could wish," Cook wrote. "Not a cloud was to be seen the whole day and the air was perfectly clear, so that we had every advantage we could desire in observing the whole of the passage of the planet Venus over the sun's disk. We very distinctly saw an atmosphere or dusky shade round the body of the planet."

Because of that dusky shade, however, the perfectionist in Cook was deflated by the results. When Sir Edmond Halley had surmised a century earlier that the Transit could determine distance from the sun, he had noted that observers would have to record the precise time Venus began and ended its trek across the sun. But Halley didn't possess a telescope as strong as the one used by Cook and Green and couldn't know that an atmosphere blurring Venus's out-line surrounded the planet. This "dusky shade" meant that Venus didn't just leap onto the sun's face as a distinct disk, but slowly insin-uated itself as a hazy shape.

Because of that blurred edge, Cook and Green couldn't agree on the exact time the disk had entered and exited the sun's face. The *Endeav-our* mission's calculations weren't conclusive. The Transit results would have to wait for Royal Society analysis. Through no fault of his own, Cook, the consummate overachiever, fretted he may have failed.

He spent five more weeks resting and replenishing in Matavai Bay, then spent a month exploring the neighboring islands. On Au-gust 9, Cook sailed *Endeavour* from Tahiti. His relations with the Tahitians were left tenuous. He had become a powerful figure to them in his short time ashore, a rival to their own *ari'i* and *ari'i rahi*. His swift action to combat theft had not deterred its taking place but had commanded the respect of locals. Cook was, they could see, a compassionate man, more likely to punish his crew with the lash for their indiscretions than to punish a Tahitian. But he'd also made it clear, through taking possession of their canoes, pigs, and fish catch, that he was a man of bold decision and backbone. Their one and only king.

Sailing away, Cook finally opened the top-secret orders from the Admiralty. *Endeavour* ceased to be a scientific mission and became military. Cook's orders were to search for the Southern Continent, chart New Zealand, and discover any other lands he could find. The only limit would be his personal courage. For in the history of the South Seas, men had again and again come close to making great discoveries, then turned back when the Pacific's storms and vastness overwhelmed them and their ships. Cook had read of these men and knew the routes they had sailed. He would sail the ocean hard and not be deterred by adversity, personal doubt, or even, if it came to that, a mutinous crew.

Cook knew the remainder of the journey would have to be bold or the entire voyage would be seen as a waste of the king's money and the Royal Society's time. He hadn't discovered Antarctica for Sandwich, nor had he conclusively fulfilled *Endeavour's* prime mission by gathering exact data for the Royal Society. In reality, all he'd accomplished was to find Tahiti, discipline the Tahitians, and earn a measure of respect from the People and Banks. Cook would have to do better than all that.

Cook aimed *Endeavour* due south once again. He was eager for a new challenge and anxious to explore whatever might lie ahead. Pacing the quarterdeck as Tahiti faded over the horizon behind the stern, Cook was the most powerful man in the Pacific. This made him want to chart it all, see it all, claim it all in the name of His Majesty King George III, then secretly revel that only James Cook was master of these far-flung islands and peoples. He was like his father the foreman, but on a much grander scale.

Belowdecks, as Cook basked in triumph of things to come and the regret of power left behind, the People lined up to see Dr. Monkhouse, the ship's surgeon. They carried a legacy of Tahiti they would remember the rest of their lives. Venereal disease had found its way onto *Endeavour*.

CHAPTER 9

Coasting on the Edge of the World

A s *Endeavour* plowed south on an Admiralty-ordered probe to the fortieth parallel (from whence Cook would run down the latitude to New Zealand), Cook spent the majority of his time in the great cabin poring over maps and books dealing with the Southern Hemisphere. What lay before him was a blank canvas. If South America and the Indian Ocean can be seen as parentheses bracketing the eastern and western borders of the Pacific, the maps of 1769 showed almost nothing but water in between. Starting from South America and working left—toward the west—the parentheses would contain a few dots for small islands: Juan Fernández closest to South America, Easter, the Tuamotus, then Tahiti close to the middle. Then would come a scratch representing New Zealand. Farther west would come another scratch representing the west coast of what is now Australia. Then the parentheses would close on the Indian Ocean.

The scientist in Cook examined the prevailing reasoning supporting Antarctica's existence: because the Northern Hemisphere's great landmasses ended at 70 degrees north latitude, the Southern Hemisphere could only maintain symmetry by hoarding all its land in one solid mass toward the South Pole. Cook found no flaw in the logic. The erratic winds that had driven back previous Southern Hemisphere explorers Novais and Tasman were obvious signs of land.

It was A.D. 140 when the Greek geographer Ptolemy wrote *Geographia*, in which he posited a landmass sprawled across the Southern Hemisphere, contiguous with Africa and South America. He named it Terra Incognita, or "unknown land." In the name of symmetry, Ptolemy said, this unfound land was necessary as a counterbalance to the Northern Hemisphere, preventing the world from wobbling off its axis, then careening into space.

Other major lands in the area, however, were becoming known. Chinese and Malaysian fishermen had been frequenting one prominent landmass for centuries. It was known for its offshore bounty of sea cucumbers. Not until 1616 did the first Europeans set foot on the landmass—and then it was by accident. The Dutch vessel *Eendracht* was en route to Batavia when strong winds blew her far to the east. The crew arrived at what is now Australia's western coast, calling the discovery New Holland.

In 1642, Anton van Diemen, governor-general of the Dutch East Indies, longed to know if New Holland was the Great Southern Continent. He commanded thirty-nine-year-old explorer Abel Tasman to investigate. Tasman's charter was to discover "the remaining unknown parts of the globe." It was a charter Cook would assume a century later.

Tasman's journey lasted ten months and accomplished little in the way of exploration or expansion of trade. Yet Tasman had opened a small window into the unknown world by discovering what would become Tasmania (though he never set foot there) and a small section of New Zealand. When French cartographer Melchedec Thevenot redrew the world in 1663, he included Tasman's findings. A distinction was established between the Great Southern Continent and Terra Australis, for they were obviously not one and the same. Terra Australis was in actuality New Holland and destined to become Australia.

But the Great Southern Continent—Antarctica—had still not been found. It obviously lay far to the south, if it existed at all, separated from Africa, New Holland, and South America by the tempestuous Southern Ocean.

The British began searching for Antarctica in 1698. Using Thevenot's map, William Dampier, commanding the Royal Navy exploration vessel *Roebuck*, landed on New Holland's western coast in 1699. Upon his return to London, Dampier wrote a book of his journeys, *Voyage to New Holland*. It was Dampier's fantastic tome that ignited Sandwich's fire to seek Antarctica.

As Cook studied the wide variety of maps and books about Antarctica on hand in the great cabin, he often fled to the quiet of his small quarters. Banks may have lost control of the vessel, but he owned the great cabin after Tahiti. Not only did Banks sleep there, but also all manner of samples clogged the table and fouled the air. "Dr. Solander sets at the cabin table," Banks wrote in that oddly punctuated style of his on October 30, "myself at my Bureau journalizing, between us hangs a large bunch of sea weed, upon the table lays the wood and barnacles."

Banks was also in the habit of shooting birds as specimens, then leaving their carcasses on the table alongside not just wood and barnacles but jellyfish and other smelly and slimy sea creatures netted as *Endeavour* meandered south. Although cramped, Cook's sleeping quarters were preferable for study.

Contemplation was best handled on the quarterdeck, where the air was fresh, though growing more temperamental. Squalls lashed *Endeavour*. The cold temperature was a far cry from Tahiti's summer climate, and the rain came down in horizontal sheets. Fowl and pigs from Tahiti began to die, from both the cold and their new diet of ship's food instead of island plants. The yams and plantains acquired in Tahiti began to spoil. There was a day of quiet celebration as a distant cloudbank was mistaken for land, then a day of true bacchanal on August 25 to celebrate an entire year since leaving England. Porter flowed and Cheshire cheese was passed around. The party was raucous despite the sea state, with music, singing, and fistfights as entertainment. The People covertly tapped Endeavour's rum casks, drinking more than their share of the high-powered grog.

Unfortunately, the next morning, while the rest of the crew were struggling with hangovers, boatswain's mate John Reading didn't wake up at all. He'd overdone the consumption and died of alcohol poisoning. His body was weighted with ballast and dropped into the frigid Pacific. Cook read the service.

As September wore on, Cook pushed Endeavour to forty degrees latitude without sign of Antarctica. As literal as ever when it came to taking directions, Cook edged not one degree farther south. On a day when Banks reported heavy weather and that "the ship was very troublesome last night and not less so today," Cook turned Endeavour eastward. "I did intend to have stood to the Southward," he wrote for all those who would someday read his journal and might question his bravery for not pushing farther south, "if the winds had been moderate. But we had no prospect of meeting land, and the weather was so very tempestuous I laid aside this design."

Cook sailed in circles in hopes of stumbling across new lands. He first went east, then northwest, actually crossing his own path once. Finding no land, he aimed southwest and again crossed his own path, then set aside his second flirtation with leisurely discovery and resumed running down the latitude for New Zealand. On October 5, two months out of Tahiti, lookout Nicholas Young won the gallon of rum for sighting land. The surgeon's boy had keen eyes, and it was some time before the rest of crew could see clearly that it was a coast on the horizon, not a cloud or fogbank. Through his spyglass, Cook could make out high elevations and a coastline studded with bays. Two days later Endeavour was just offshore, and Cook could make out houses, fires, and canoes. Then, finally, people. He had found New Zealand, though an eastern shore that Tasman never knew existed. The crew was ecstatic, certain they had finally found Antarctica. Cook said nothing, just went ashore with Banks, Solander, and a contingent of marines to begin the section of his Admiralty orders that he "explore as much of the coast as the condition of the bark, the health of her crew and the state of your provisions will admit of."

New Zealand would become one of Cook's favorite places in the entire world. Over the next six months he charted the entire coastline, encountering Maori on several occasions (killing more than once), and naming every harbor and nook and landmark until he ran out of people and places to name things after, at which point he began repeating himself. With few exceptions, the coast was rugged, with cliffs rising from the sea topped by green hills running inland as far as the eye could see. Cook was amazed to find deep fjords in the south. Mountain summits capped with snow could be seen from the sea. Ship's artist Sydney Parkinson wrote in his journal of the land's great romance. "Mountains piled on mountains," wrote Parkinson, "to an amazing height."

Amazingly, the French vessel *Jean Baptiste* was exploring the same land at the exact same time. Often, the two ships were less than fifty miles apart. The *Jean Baptiste* and her captain, Jean François Marie de Surville, would stand as an illustration of Cook's exemplary seamanship and treatment of both his men and locals. De Surville had grave problems with New Zealand's fierce winds and offshore weather, losing anchors, cables, and a dinghy to one gale. Whereas Cook was feeding his men vitamin-laden foods such as onions, grass, and sauerkraut to prevent scurvy—and hadn't suffered a single scurvy death—sixty of de Surville's men had already died from the malady. Cook's encounters with the Maori weren't always pleasant, but they were respectful. De Surville's were disastrous, contentious. While Cook the longtime cartographer enjoyed sailing close to land and charting the coast, de Surville stayed away from land whenever possible. And whereas Cook had sailed from east to west in his circumnavigation, battling severe headwinds in the high latitudes, de

Surville traveled in the opposite direction. After finishing a short re-connaissance of New Zealand, de Surville sailed east with the pre-vailing winds to meet his death. He drowned while trying to go ashore in Peru.

Cook's few shipboard deaths, his respectful, if strained, relations with the Maori, and his navigational ability in severe weather had become the stuff of legend among the People. It would take all those abilities to follow his orders explicitly and chart New Zealand. Where Tasman showed New Zealand as an afterthought—a jag of coastline suspended in the middle of the Pacific—Cook would find its northern and southern limits. He would find for certain that it was an island, and hence not part of Antarctica. Most important, Cook would find that New Zealand was not one continuous island but two. And though he was quiet in doing so, for it was unlike Cook to name something after himself, he would name the gap be-tween New Zealand's North and South Islands the Cook Strait.

Clearly coming into his own, Cook reveled in the expanse of his South Pacific domain. How many men can bestow any name they wish upon countries and landmarks, go where they wish, kill whomever they wish? For all the kings and queens commanding vast armies in Europe and Asia, this entity Cook had become was quietly more pow-erful and controlled an expanse far greater. While he never laid claim to any place for himself—never cultivated a fiefdom nor assembled an army of his own to rule the South Pacific—Cook knew he could not possibly return to England the same eager underdog he had left it.

It seemed at this moment that Cook had achieved all his dreams, and yet there was something missing. Cook had always been search-ing for a corner of the world to call his own. The farm boy in him still prized land, yet his home on Mile End Road had no land, save the patch of walk directly in front and a small garden in back. What Cook longed for was acres of land like the ones he had known as a child, broad and expansive, hemmed by mountains and woodland.

After sailing the coast of northern New Zealand, Cook entered a wide channel shortly after Christmas, 1769. He didn't yet know that New Zealand was two islands and suspected this channel was nothing more than a harbor. He probed deeper. Seeking shelter from the roiling wind and currents of what would be named the Cook Strait, he aimed *Endeavour* into a side inlet. After a narrow entrance between a plethora of islands, Cook was astonished to discover that the inlet extended over the horizon. The topography was astonishing, seemingly designed for the singular purpose of sheltering a sailing vessel. Like horseshoes laid side by side, dozens of perfect natural harbors lined the shoreline on both sides. These coves were deep. There were no waves. The hills were an astonishing green, and forests with trees tall enough for building ship's masts stretched as far as the eye could see, tapering down into the sea gracefully. There were no cliffs at this enclave, but beaches strewn with smooth stones.

Cook named the passage Queen Charlotte's Sound, after King George III's wife, Queen Charlotte Sofia, an obscure German princess King George III had married in 1761, when she was just seventeen. Pushing *Endeavour* into one of the first coves, Cook found that this wonderland was even more magnificent than he'd dreamed. The coves had freshwater, an abundance of wood, fresh fish eager to nibble a hook, and edible wild plants for preventing scurvy. "A very snug cove," Cook wrote happily in his journal after dropping anchor January 15, 1770.

Just over the hill from Endeavor Inlet, as Cook named the refuge, he found something that excited him even more. While the People could resupply *Endeavour*, or intentionally beach her, then lean the vessel on its side to refinish the bottom with tar and caulk; while Banks and Solander could frolic amid the tree ferns, growing as tall as a coconut palm, and the lush rain forest fronting the inlet; Cook could hike to the commanding summit of a long, steep hill through the rain forest. The trail might be slick after a frequent local rain, and the ocher mud would stick and clump to his shoes. But Cook was a persistent man, fond of exploring on land as well as sea. Walking far enough, he would reach a ridgeline. Walking farther still, that same ridgeline would descend into a green, fertile valley. A river coursed through the valley—not wide, but clear and fast and cold.

In those special walks, Cook was drawn back to his childhood. For the countryside was the spitting image of North Yorkshire. Literally halfway around the world, Cook was surveying the one country most like his own in climate and appearance. He was the foreman. This was his farm. He had no castle, no official claim to the land. But Endeavour Inlet belonged to Cook just as surely as Banks's manor estate back in England belonged to the botanist. Banks noted with some astonishment that Cook was unusually lighthearted inside the confines of Queen Charlotte's Sound. He even deigned to drink with Banks and Solander after one of his days of exploration.

The only problem—and it was severe—was the Maori. While they shared the same physical appearance and even the same language as the Tahitians, the Maori were much more warlike. Though the Maori considered the Europeans magicians of some sort (the Maori faced forward while rowing their canoes, while the British faced backward in their rowboats; they theorized the British must be magical or have eyes in the back of their heads), they didn't fear them. In fact, the Maori's fondest method for greeting *Endeavour* was rowing alongside the ship and pelting it with rocks. Spears were often pointed at Cook and the crew.

Far more terrifying, Cook found one day after landing in Endeavour Inlet that the Maori were cannibals. Particular cannibals, to be sure, eating only vanquished enemies—but cannibals nonetheless. Human bones could be seen in local ovens; uneaten limbs were arranged in communal areas like between-meal snacks. And just in case there was any doubt, one Maori picked up a freshly gnawed femur and mimed chomping meat from the bone one day to entertain Cook.

The threat of cannibalism sent a panic through the People, just as it had haunted sailors of discovery for centuries. In fact, men of the sea named the practice. *Cannibal* comes from *Canibal*, the people-eating tribe Christopher Columbus discovered after arriving in the West Indies. Ironically, the practice has existed worldwide since the beginning of recorded time. Herodotus, Marco Polo, and other writers of history described cannibalistic rituals in their work. From India to South America to Europe, cannibalism was practiced either for religious, wartime, spiritual, or medical reasons. Generally, the practice revolved around the belief that a dead body still had power. Eating the body transferred that power to the diner.

The People were petrified of becoming a Maori feast. They focused on the cannibalistic aspect of Maori living to the detriment of all else. It was an understandable, yet unfortunate, reaction, for the Maori were a complex civilization filled with culture and ingenuity.

They had only lived in New Zealand for five hundred years. They had emigrated from Tahiti in A.D. 1200, with most of the Maori settling on the North Island. The soil was fertile there, and the weather less harsh than on the mountainous South Island. Farming was the major source of food, with the principal crop being sweet potato, or *kumara*. For meat, the Maori enjoyed a wide-ranging diet that included birds, rats, and fish. The clusters of Maori living on the South Island tended to live near the sea and to fish instead of farm.

They were a paternal, clan-based society, with several clans bonding to form a single social structure. Kings were chosen by succession, with the firstborn ascending to the throne. The chief was called an *ariki*. As a carryover from their days in Tahiti, touching the chief was *tapu*.

Most enigmatically, these cannibals had an aesthetic bent and placed a high value on the arts. They were poets, as well as sculptors of wood and bone and stone. They also wore jewelry—even the most common people wore carved necklaces, bracelets, and amulets.

But the Maori's special art form was the tattoo. It was not uncommon for men to cover their entire bodies with designs, including their faces. Of all the civilizations that have practiced tattooing since the Egyptians began the practice in 2000 B.C., the Maori were the most advanced. In addition to their full-body designs, they were the first to introduce colored inks.

None of that had any meaning to Endeavour's people. They only knew Maori ate humans. And while most Maori cannibal dinners were composed of warfare victims, Endeavour's People were still nervous about being so close to flesh eaters. Banks didn't help matters when he purchased a severed head from a passing canoe. The flesh was green, but the hair was still in place.

If the Maori had possessed the sunny disposition of their Tahitian relatives, the potential for conflict with Cook and his People would have been minimal. But the Maori's territorial belligerence was a source of conflict with Cook from the moment Endeavour first came in contact with New Zealand. One of Cook's first acts had been to confront a Maori war party. When the war party attacked, Cook, aided by his complement of Royal Marines, gave the order to fire. Three warriors died. A conflicted Cook wrote about the incident that night: "I can by no means justify my conduct for attacking and killing the people."

The issue simmered as Cook explored New Zealand's twenty-four hundred miles of coastline. When he finally pushed away from Endeavour Inlet after a three-week stay, he was perplexed and even a little titillated by the notion of cannibalism. He took the time to write about Maori cannibalism, with the subtext its possible impact on future explorers. "It is hard to account for what we have been told of them eating their enemies killed in battle, but they most certainly do. It is reasonable to assume that men with whom this custom has been found seldom or never give quarter to those men overcome in battle. The people of Queen Charlotte's Sound told us that a few days before we had arrived they had killed and eaten an entire boat's crew. The heads of those unfortunate victims were preserved as trophies."

Sailing from the Sound in February 1770, Cook discovered that the great strait feeding into Queen Charlotte's Sound actually separated

New Zealand into two separate islands. Pleased with himself, for no other explorer had even postulated such a thing, Cook completed his Admiralty orders by making a clockwise lap of South Island. The sight of whales and seals and great mountain ranges stretching from the bottom of the island to the top rendered Cook romantic, made him forget the jarring notion of cannibalism. He wrote of mountain peaks as far as the eye could see "covered with snow that has laid there since creation. No country on earth can appear with a more rugged and barren aspect." This was the side of him only Elizabeth was allowed to see. For him to jot deeply poetic thoughts in his otherwise circumspect journal showed that he was past fearing rebuke by his superiors.

By late March, Cook had completed his exploration of New Zealand and returned to Queen Charlotte's Sound to replenish stores and make minor repairs to *Endeavour*. Cook spent four days in a section of Endeavour Inlet he named Admiralty Bay. While the People resupplied *Endeavour*, Cook sat down to plan the remainder of his voyage.

Endeavour's job was done. The Transit of Venus was charted, though Cook wouldn't know the extent of his success until returning to London. He'd sailed to forty degrees south and found no Southern Continent. He'd charted New Zealand so thoroughly that mariners would trust his charts for generations to come. In a time before reliable clocks or computers or global positioning satellites, Cook's latitudinal and longitudinal recordings were almost dead-on. It was clearly time to go home.

The question now was which way to sail. Backtracking around South America was quickest, and Cook would have a following wind. But where was the adventure in retracing footsteps? More practically, he would touch the wrath of the high latitudes and the Southern Ocean again. Cook had done his utmost to keep *Endeavour* maintained and seaworthy, but she'd been at sea nineteen months. The weather, waves, wind, and extreme temperature fluctuation she'd endured had been horrendous, especially around New Zealand and South America. She was rotting. Wood fatigue was slowly, inexorably weakening her. *Endeavour* was like a boxer in the late rounds of a fight, still standing but just one solid punch away from knock-out. A harsh storm would scuttle her.

This was a fearful notion for two reasons. First, and obviously, she would sink and many men would die, perhaps even Cook. Second, and selfishly, Cook had not encountered another vessel for over a year, and news of his discoveries was still a secret. If *Endeavour* sank, her accomplishments would be for naught. Taking an overall historical view, Cook understood that the second reason for nursing *Endeavour* home safely was as important as the first.

Cook thought long and hard. He thumbed through Dalrymple's book and pondered explorations past. It seemed the world was getting smaller. The oceans had been crossed and recrossed, forming a grid showing that future discoveries in the Pacific were unlikely. Cook had come to doubt the existence of Antarctica and was confident enough to write about it: "As to a Southern Continent, I do not believe any such thing exists, unless in a high latitude, but as the contrary opinion for many years hath prevailed, and may yet prevail, I should say something in support of mine."

Cook continued to ponder, soaking up the intense beauty of Endeavour Inlet. In this nurturing environment, so conducive to reflection, Cook began to see his true potential. In his mind he became more than a cartographer and a ship's captain, he became a singular figure for the ages: a discoverer. He wrote in his journal of "the pleasure which naturally results to a man from being the first discoverer." Being first is a sensation few men throughout history have known, and was a source of pride to Cook. Later opinion that he was not a discoverer, but a "rediscoverer" (because indigenous cultures already lived on the lands), has merit, but misses the point. Discovery is not merely about finding the new land, but exploring the people and their customs and their plants and animals. While indigenous cultures did a small amount of exploration (there's reason to believe Indonesians pollinated the entire South Pacific), none had the scope or ambition of Cook's. His discoveries were sewing together the fabric of the earth, bringing disparate nations together for the first time. For Cook, the world was a puzzle with pieces missing.

The notion suited his curious brain, and this factored into Cook's decision-making. He didn't think much of other discoverers. That any man could turn a ship around while there was so much to be found was a mystery to Cook. For this reason, Cook decided not to retrace his steps toward home but instead to steer west to finish the job Abel Tasman had left undone a century prior. His plan was to maintain forty degrees latitude and find the eastern shore of New Holland. Once he found it, Cook planned to sail north two thousand miles to the Torres Strait, the narrow gap dividing New Guinea and New Holland. From there Cook would push west again, first through the Arafura Sea, then the Timor Sea, on into the Indian Ocean's eastern fringe and the Dutch port of Batavia. After a bit of rest and relaxation, along with a thorough refitting of *Endeavour* in that top-flight port, Cook would sail from Batavia on conventional trade routes southwest across the Indian Ocean. He would stop again at Capetown, at the southern tip of Africa, then sail north for London.

CHAPTER 10

Trapped

On April 1, 1770, Cook bid New Zealand a bittersweet good-bye (he named the last visible spit of land Cape Farewell) and turned his attention to New Holland. (Forty-four years later, in 1814, explorer Matthew Flinders would formally introduce a new name for New Holland—Australia.) Cook began sailing due west across the Tasman Sea, running down the latitude of the eastern Australian coast. It was autumn in the Southern Hemisphere.

Unknowingly, Cook was heading directly into a sailing black hole as fierce as the Cape of Good Hope and Strait of Le Maire. The Tasman Sea marks the convergence of not just the Southern and Pacific Oceans, but their fierce weather patterns as well. Winds blow simultaneously from the west, south, and north in the infamous Roaring Forties latitudinal wind. For a man trying to nurse a broken ship back around the world, those tempestuous waters were the worst possible place for Cook to be.

On April 16, a gale blew *Endeavour* off course, shoving her hard to the north. If it hadn't been for that storm, Cook would have sailed through what is now the Bass Strait on Australia's southern coast. He would likely have kept on sailing along that southern coast until he reached the Indian Ocean, bypassing entirely the eastern shores he had been targeting. The discovery of eastern Australia would have been credited to someone else, likely one of the French explorers who followed in Cook's wake. If not for that gale, modern Australians might trace their ancestry to France instead of Britain, a blasphemous notion for any Commonwealth nation.

On April 19, Cook first set eyes on Australia. The coastline was rugged and rocky. The Tasman Sea's trademark ferocious winds kept pushing him away, preventing him from landing. The winds and the gigantic breakers booming against the coast tempered whatever joy he might have felt.

Cook pushed north, searching for the perfect spot to put ashore. Everywhere he had traveled, Cook had used his immense cartography skills, mapping and naming, so that upon his return he would hand the Admiralty detailed drawings of the world. Australia, however, was proving difficult to map because fierce waves and horrendous weather kept him far from the coast. Cook contented himself by naming landmarks from a distance: Howe Island, Jervis Bay. After the winds had passed, the towering surf still kept Cook from shore, so he continued his northward push.

The warm weather made the time more bearable. Cook's men took note of campfires on shore at night, and white coastal cliffs visible by day. Cook found it all very pleasant, though Banks was unimpressed. "The country, though well enough clothed seemed in places bare; it resembled in my imagination the back of a lean cow, covered in general with long hair, but nevertheless where here scraggy hip bones have stuck out farther than they ought rubs and knocks have entirely bared them of their share of covering," he wrote.

Natives could be seen onshore, naked and black. Their canoes were crude logs, barely more than dugouts, lacking the ornamentation of the Tahitians' or New Zealanders'. The natives made no attempt to paddle through the surf and examine the massive apparition plowing through their waters. No fleet of canoes and warriors and women paddled out to say hello.

On April 27 a suitable bay for landing was finally sighted. After sending in master Molyneaux and the pinnace to sound for depth, Cook sailed *Endeavour* a ways into the bay on the twenty-eighth. Stingrays could be seen in the water all around. Cook impulsively gave it the name Stingray Harbor. Later, when Banks and Solander fell all over themselves cataloging the immense natural wealth to be found onshore, Cook changed the title to Botany Bay. Cape Banks and Point Solander would forever guard the narrow entrance through which *Endeavour* sailed.

Despite the bay's immense size, Cook sailed in just two miles before dropping anchor. Natives could be seen onshore, some ignoring *Endeavour* while fishing, others keeping a wary eye on the newcomers. A few of the natives carried spears or wooden clubs. White stripes covered their torsos. Their hair was stringy and their beards long and bushy.

As the Aborigines watched, Cook had all *Endeavour's* boats lowered. Fully half the crew prepared to go ashore. Elizabeth Cook's cousin Isaac Smith, seventeen, was at Cook's side. Rowing toward a long, sandy beach, Cook paid special attention to the natives. Their indifference was so obvious that Cook had no problem giving Isaac the privilege of making landfall. "Isaac," he spoke softly to the young man, "you shall land first." Smith leapt from the boat, then waded through knee-high water to the beach. The waves were small but the wind was strong. Cook followed his cousin-in-law ashore.

The beach was rocky in spots, sandy in others, punctuated with tidal pools. A thick forest grew straight ahead, beginning where the sand ended. While several natives ran away, two stood their ground. Cook fired a round of shot to scare them. The natives fled. In fact, the entire tribe fled, leaving their children huddled in a small hut to fend for themselves. Cook found this despicable and decided that the Aborigines were a worthless people. If Cook had taken more time, he would have been fascinated with their culture and level of adaptation, just as he had been with the Tahitians. But due to their secretive nature, Cook never interacted with the Aborigines as he had the Tahitians. For this reason, of all the indigenous peoples he would meet on his travels, he held the Aborigines in lowest regard.

This would set a precedent. Subsequent British generations traveling to Australia would see the Aborigines in a similar light. Their culture, with its interweaving of mysticism, oral history, and nature, would be misunderstood for centuries. The Aborigines were a wandering people, having emigrated to Australia from Southeast Asia thousands of years before, walking south along a land bridge connecting the two thousand miles between Vietnam and Australia. Their religion, however, discounted this march in favor of a view of creation that had the Aborigines living in Australia since the dawn of history. In this view, known as the Dream Time, the Wondinna, or spirits of the forefathers, had formed the land, then traveled across Australia sprinkling the spirits of unborn children. The Wondinna remained with the Aborigines forever in spirit form and were called on for help in making laws and influencing natural events.

All Cook saw, however, was a primitive, aimless culture.

He kept *Endeavour* in Botany Bay for a week. Though the surrounding land was low-lying and swampy, choked throughout with mangroves, Cook noted that it would be a fine area for cultivation. He particularly liked the freshwater streams and plentiful fish and shellfish. These notations would eventually be heeded, though not in Cook's lifetime. Seventeen years later, on May 13, 1787, Captain Arthur Phillip would sail from England, with several hundred prisoners. Botany Bay would be his intended destination—a journey that would mark the beginning of Australia's notorious civilization.

From Botany Bay, Cook sailed northward and in just a few miles passed a vast opening between two towering basalt heads. Peering inside, he saw a massive natural harbor, "where a thousand ships could anchor in peace." Itching to travel after the week in Botany

Bay, Cook never sailed into the harbor, preferring to toss out the name Port Jackson as he scurried past. Captain Phillip would some-day rename it Sydney (after a British political figure) and choose to locate his penal colony within its sheltering cliffs rather than on soggy Botany Bay.

As Cook sailed north, he was oblivious that he had entered a vast natural funnel. Beginning two hundred miles out to sea, the Great Barrier Reef rose. Basically a chain of coral reefs in the Coral Sea, as opposed to one continuous reef, the Great Barrier Reef is the world's largest deposit of coral. The reef is over twelve hundred miles long, beginning halfway up Australia's eastern coast and running all the way into the Torres Strait. At its closest point to shore the Great Barrier Reef is only ten miles out. Inside the reef, the water is placid compared with the outer regions. Navigation, however, is difficult due to atolls rising randomly from the ocean floor. Cook knew none of this. All he saw were relatively calm seas and an Australian coast off his port bow.

But this coral formation angled toward the New Holland coast-line like a snare, waiting to close its victims inside. By the time Cook reached the northern, tropical reaches a month later, he was still un-aware of his predicament. For all he knew *Endeavour* was merely sail-ing up the coast of Australia on seas no less treacherous than those off New Zealand.

The greatest issue facing Cook, however, wasn't the sea, but his bored crew's penchant for mischief. The men were already thinking of liberty in Batavia. The Australian coasting couldn't end fast enough for them. As in any society, petty animosities had developed aboard *Endeavour*. Greenslade the marine had been a somewhat un-derstandable example, because the marines were prone to belliger-ence. But it was now the People Cook was worried about. The act that spurred him to disciplinary action took place on May 22, 1770, when Richard Orton, the captain's clerk, passed out after a night of hard drinking. He slept right through the moment when anonymous shipmates cut off his ears. Then, using the same knife, they cut away his clothing, too.

Cook was mortified. He knew discipline was in order, but to whom? There were no witnesses—or at least none who stepped forward—and a dozen suspects. Severing a man's ears fell far outside the norm, and Cook knew of no precedent. He finally punished a midshipman from New York, just to lay the blame on someone. James Magra was forbidden on the quarterdeck and suspended from active duty.

But Magra was just the scapegoat to prevent the ship from descending into anarchy. The maliciousness toward Orton was the symptom of a crew testing the limits of Cook's authority, seeing if discipline would be relaxed now that the journey was toward home. Cook felt powerless to fix the problem. "This is the greatest insult that could be offered to my authority in this ship," he wrote, then added, dipping into rare self-pity: "I have always been ready to hear and redress every complaint that have been made against any Person in the ship."

Cook had always taken a quiet pride in being in touch with his crew's emotions. Their worries and fears became his, for in his heart he was still one of them. The king of the South Pacific felt like a poseur, knowing that his prestige would be stripped the moment he returned to London. He would be little better than his men in society's eyes. For this reason, he didn't forsake them when he had been given command. They were all one in their love of the sea.

Originally, that love had bred a passion in the People for the great discoveries to come. But exploration was no longer unifying the People, and home was still too far off to think about. The limbo would cause trouble until Cook found a goal behind which the People could rally.

On June 11 that new mission presented itself in most brutal fashion.

Endeavour was several miles off the northeast coast of Australia. Botany Bay was a distant memory and Cook was only five hundred miles from the left turn at the Torres Strait leading to Batavia.

The ocean was calm. As night fell, Cook noticed a scattering of low-lying islands. Unaware he had sailed precariously close to the undiscovered Great Barrier Reef, he ordered regular soundings (a weighted line dropped overboard) to ascertain accurate depth. Sometime after eleven o'clock, content *Endeavour* was safe in seventeen fathoms of water, Cook issued his final orders for the night, then retired to his small quarters. He changed out of his uniform, doused the beeswax candle inside his hanging lantern, and stretched out on his swinging cot. He fell right to sleep.

Almost immediately, *Endeavour* slammed hard into a coral reef and ground to a violent halt. Men on deck were knocked to the ground. Men below were thrown from their hammocks. In the great cabin, Banks and Solander's precious supply of uncataloged Botany Bay specimens flew from the tables. Specimen jars crashed, broke. Chamber pots tipped. A mighty surf pounded the beleaguered *Endeavour*, wedging her wooden hull tightly onto the reef. Cook later journalized calmly that "the ship struck and stuck fast," then mentioned that boats were immediately lowered to assess the damage. They "found that we had got upon the southeast edge of a reef of coral rocks." Cook's tone made it sound as if shipwreck were a regular occurrence.

Banks was a little more forthcoming. "Scarce were we warm in our beds," Banks wrote, "when we were called up with the alarming news of the ship being fast ashore on a rock, which she in a few moments convinced us by beating very violently against the rocks. Our situation now became greatly alarming . . . we were little less than certain that we were upon sunken coral rocks, the most dreadful of all others on account of their sharp points and grinding quality, which cut through a ship's bottom almost immediately."

All hands were immediately summoned on deck by a mate's frantic cry of "Up every soul nimbly, for God's sake, or we all perish." Stumbling from their hammocks, a frantic line of crew clambered up the companionway into the warm tropical night just as Cook bounded up his own companionway two steps at a time to survey the damage. Still dressed in his underwear, Cook began issuing commands immediately.

The People would later marvel at the cool efficiency of Cook. He'd never known shipwreck, but he dispatched commands to begin pumping water from the hold like a man experienced, running down a mighty mental checklist. The sails were quickly taken in. Following Royal Navy protocol, boats were launched to sound depths around the vessel. The cable and anchor were put into the longboat, which then pushed away from *Endeavour*. In effect, they meant to pull her off.

The ship, however, would not budge.

What would become known as Endeavour Reef was ten miles offshore. If *Endeavour* sank, the task of ferrying her People ashore would be treacherous. And even if all hands survived, the realization that *Endeavour* was the first vessel to lay eyes on the eastern coast weighed heavily. No ship was coming along in the immediate future to rescue them.

Cook journalized that he would build a vessel from the remains of *Endeavour* and attempt passage to the East Indies, but that was almost impossible. A life onshore—the life of shipwreck victims since man began sailing the seas—would have to begin. Shelter would be built, food and water gathered, amenities forever done without. The survivors would never again share the company of a woman. Communal infighting would begin, with Cook's command eventually usurped by a more primal order. Men would be cast out. Others would be killed, eaten by marauding cannibals, struck down by disease, or driven mad by the hopelessness. In the end, only one or two might live long enough to be rescued.

But as bad as *Endeavour*'s People imagined such a prospect, in reality it was worse. Unbeknownst to them, the northeast coast of Australia was the living, breathing embodiment of a shipwrecked sailor's worst nightmare. Away from shore, the terrain was jungle instead of farmland. The climate was humid, dank. Insects bit nonstop. Several of the world's most poisonous snakes called the jungle home. Others, such as the reticulated python, weren't poisonous but instilled terror by their great length and girth. The pythons only ate once a month, but when hungry, they coiled in the trees above game trails, then dropped upon their prey. Their immense weight—sometimes three hundred pounds—knocked the victim unconscious, giving the python time to slowly coil around the torso and squeeze life from the prey. The body was then swallowed whole. A large python was capable of eating a man.

Even if a sailor avoided jungles swimming and bathing would be obstacles themselves. Rivers and oceans were the domain of salt- and freshwater crocodiles—fat, greedy, insatiable eaters with pea brains that made absolutely no distinction between a small deer or a large man as prey. The more vicious saltwater crocodile, which was also comfortable in freshwater, grew to twenty feet long. Its method of killing—the *Endeavour* People were better off not knowing as the bailing continued for two, then six, then twelve hours—was horrendous: a sneak attack that wrested a man underwater, spun him around and around to disorient him, and drowned him. The crocodile then stowed the body underwater in a cave or beneath a log to be eaten later, like some waterlogged midnight snack that had once held the ability to reason.

And if a man wanted to venture farther on to the sea, for solace or to fish the abundant waters off the reef, great white sharks with their bullet snouts and uneven rows of white teeth stood ready to fulfill a seaman's darkest terror—being eaten alive. Several times during *Endeavour*'s two years at sea when Banks had accidentally seined a shark, *Endeavour*'s crew had refused to eat the thick shark steaks. Even when Banks noted the inoffensive taste, the People preferred dried stores to this predator. Sharks ate sailors, was their rationale. Returning the favor was like eating the flesh of a fellow sailor. When a ship sank, the first on-scene arrival was sharks. And sailors already dead, buried at sea, became nothing more than ballast-weighted chum. Many sailor's myths revolved around this great evil beast. Had they known that a shark of nightmares—an eating machine dwarfing the feared creatures of the Atlantic and the South Pacific—inhabited the very waters in which *Endeavour* was now stuck, the People might have found it possible to bail even harder.

Yet the crew took their cue from Cook and remained calm throughout, pumping the hold in fifteen-minute shifts. Officers, supernumeraries, and enlisted men all worked—Cook was among them. Midshipman Magra's suspension was ended so he might pitch in. It was a rare moment of equality and togetherness on a Royal Navy vessel. All hands worked to exhaustion.

Like their leader, they pretended not to be worried when two of the four pumps turned out to be broken, and when the water level in the hold rose to three feet. They ignored the knowledge that coral, the worst possible material for a wooden ship to collide with, had embedded itself in the hull in several places. One large chunk had driven all the way through. The jagged edges bit into the wood, pushing deeper and deeper with every push from following waves.

In desperation, Cook ordered everything expendable of great heft heaved overboard. Six of the twelve cannon were dumped, with buoys attached to their barrels in the hope of a later salvage attempt. Twenty-five tons of fresh water. Tons of rock and shell ballast. "Casks, Hoops, staves, oil jars, decayed stores," wrote Cook of other items surrendered to the Pacific. Amazingly, *Endeavour* was lightened by fifty tons—one-seventh her entire weight.

And still she stuck fast. The tide fell. *Endeavour* perched atop that pile of coral like a statue on a pedestal, leaning to one side. Time was running out. Unless Cook could maneuver her off, the combination of coral and waves would shatter the already weathered hull. "We now had no hope, but from the high tide at midnight. It encouraged us to prepare for the event."

Cook and the People nervously watched as night fell and the tide rose. The 11 A.M. high tide that morning had failed to float her free, but Cook had a gut instinct the evening tide would be higher—just high enough to gain *Endeavour's* freedom.

The minutes to midnight ticked past slowly. The rising tide flooded more water into the hold. Cook was becoming fearful about their chances, realizing that even if the ship could be floated off the coral, the vast amount of water in the hold would still cause her to sink. "At 9 o'clock the ship righted itself and the leak gained upon the pumps considerably," he wrote. This was an alarming and terrible circumstance. "However, I was resolved to risk all and heave her off."

Cook's gut instinct about the tide was correct. "At 20 minutes past ten we hove her off into deep water," Cook wrote.

Six years later, in a letter to a friend, Cook admitted that, despite his cool demeanor, he had been afraid of being stuck forever on Endeavour Reef. "[Floating off the reef] exceeded," Cook wrote, "our most sanguine expectations."

But *Endeavour's* problems were far from over. There was still almost four feet of water in the hold. The overworked pumps weren't able to keep up with the water rushing in. When two men sent below to measure the water level reported that it had risen another eighteen inches, even Cook had to fight off an emotional tailspin. "For the first time," Cook wrote, "fear operated on every man on the ship." *Endeavour* was sinking. Men began mental inventory of personal items. Not all their belongings would fit in *Endeavour's* small boats, and the issue was which items would be vital to life on the new land and which items could be left behind to sink.

Cook sent the men below for a remeasurement. To his great relief, they reported back that they'd been mistaken—the water level in the hold had not risen at all. With that single correction, crew morale rose exponentially. "This mistake was no sooner cleared up than that it acted on every man like a charm," a relieved Cook wrote. "They redoubled their vigor in so much that before 8 o'clock in the morning they had gained significantly on the leak."

Then Midshipman Jonathan Monkhouse (not to be confused

with ship's surgeon William Monkhouse) approached Cook with a rather novel idea. Monkhouse had once been aboard a vessel that had sprung a leak mid-Atlantic. The captain had used a technique known as fothering to patch the leak until the ship could find land. Simply, fothering meant coating an old sail in sheep dung and un-raveled old rope (known as oakum), then using lines to wrap the sail around the hull's exterior. The leak was effectively plugged by water pressure's forcing the sail inward, with additional sheep dung spread inside as a cheap caulk.

Cook knew of fothering, but had never seen it done. He asked Monkhouse to take charge of the operation. The midshipman read-ily accepted.

Sail maker John Ravenhill quickly selected a tattered sail from his weathered quiver. Tied carefully with lengths of rope, which were wrapped under and around the hull by a small group of sailors with the ability to swim, the sail was pulled taut over the hole. *Endeavour* had been too long without livestock to have sheep dung, making the fothering less smelly, but also depriving it of the sealant that made it so effective. Monkhouse instead ordered the ropes around the hull yanked tighter, and for water-soaked globs of oakum to be pressed into the porous breech between hull and sail. Meanwhile, the two operational lift pumps (situated on the top deck next to the main-mast, these pipelike fixtures extended down into the hold; pumping was done by operating long handles, much like pumping water from a well) were manned by a crew grasping at the opportunity to get the situation under control.

Monkhouse's plan worked.

Soon *Endeavour* was out of danger and heading for land. Cook's journal entry on Monkhouse's action was, as usual, measured: "He executed it very much to my satisfaction."

Endeavour Reef was almost ten miles offshore, and like hidden land mines, a slough of similar reefs waited to detonate a new hole in *Endeavour* as Cook snaked her to land. Slowly, surely, he wove through the madness, the crew leaning against the rails with eyes peeled for the hint of coral. As the ship drew closer to land, Cook ordered *Endeavour* to be aimed toward a low beach alongside a river, then intentionally run aground.

The hold was emptied of her ballast and stores. Cook and the People removed their personal belongings from the ship and prepared a camp onshore. *Endeavour* was leaned onto her side and ship's carpenters set to repairing the troubles. The keel was damaged, as was the sheathing protecting the bow from shipworm. Most important, Cook was startled to find that a large chunk of coral had pierced the hull, but had held fast without pressing all the way through. If that had happened, the ship would most surely have sunk.

For almost two months the crew got a taste of what life would have been like marooned in this hostile land. They seined fish, ate kangaroo and sea turtle, marveled at flying fox. They fought the local Aborigines, who set fire to the brush surrounding *Endeavour's* campsite in one memorable skirmish. Cook himself shot an Aborigine for trying to steal sea turtle meat from the camp. Banks and Solander spent their usual hours onshore, collecting species of plant and animal. Cook surveyed, explored. It was a time for recuperation of men and vessel, of recapturing strength for the long trip home.

Before *Endeavour* sailed again, Cook took steps to heal old wounds and boost morale. He offered Midshipman Magra a full pardon, noting "no cause has been found for any action." Remembering the limbo that had caused Magra's alleged violation, Cook sought to maintain the frantic solidarity of the hours atop Endeavour Reef by ordering all food and vegetables to be split equally, without regard to status. "Whatever refreshment we got that would bear division I caused to be equally divided among the whole company. The meanest person in the ship had an equal share with myself or anyone on board, and this is the method every commander of a ship on such a voyage as this ought ever to observe."

Endeavour sailed on August 3, her stores replenished with turtle meat and other Australian delicacies. After weaving her way carefully outside the confines of the Great Barrier Reef, she reentered the known world at the uppermost tip of Australia, sailing west through the Strait of Torres. Luis Vaez de Torres, a Spanish navigator, had charted the passage in 1606.

The channel was about eighty miles wide. Navigation, although possible, was extremely dangerous due to a raging current and gauntlet of small islands. *Endeavour* weaved through the tricky currents cautiously. Cook seemed oblivious to the nail-biting tension. He even felt confident enough at one point to name an island off the port beam after Banks. But the crew was far more skittish. After Endeavour Reef the entire crew was on guard for potential shipwreck.

Endeavour survived the strait. Cook put ashore on New Guinea to see if it was worth exploring for a short time. But in a mood to return home, and knowing that the Spanish had already claimed the territory (calling it Nuevo Guinea because the locals reminded them of West Africans), Cook spent little time on the tropical equatorial island. Humidity and a swampy coastal area choked with mosquitoes drove him back out to sea. New Guinea had nothing *Endeavour* needed.

Cook nursed his damaged vessel through the Timor Sea. She was so beaten down by two years on the ocean that Cook wrote, "Many of our sails are now so bad that they will hardly stand the least puff of wind." He happily made port in the Dutch bastion of Batavia, on Java, on October 11. For the first time since Rio de Janeiro, almost two years prior, *Endeavour* was anchored in a proper port. Cook promptly apologized to the Dutch for not offering a greeting, explaining he didn't have enough cannon to perform the salute properly.

Of all the Asian ports in use by Europeans, Batavia was undoubtedly the busiest. Situated near the strait between the islands of Sumatra and Java, Batavia was a trader's dream, equidistant between Capetown and China, with easy access to India and Ceylon. The

Dutch East India Company's warehouses dominated the skyline, with shipments being channeled from Europe to Asia and vice versa. In short, Batavia was bustling.

Batavia also stood as a prime example of European civilizations in-sinuating themselves into, then slowly taking control of, an indige-nous population and their natural resources. A Hindu king granted Portuguese traders permission to build a fort on the ruins of the for-mer city Taruma in the early sixteenth century. In 1527, Fatillah, a Muslim warlord trying to protect his trade routes from Portuguese intrusion, conquered the fort. Fatillah gave it the new name Jayakarta.

A century later Dutch traders captured Jayakarta and renamed it Batavia. They rebuilt the settlement to resemble a Dutch city with canals and a walled fortress, but a humid climate and the fort's loca-tion in a low-lying swamp meant a high death rate. In the early 1800s the city expanded as the Dutch began moving to the south, where the ground was higher and less prone to breed disease.

Batavia became the primary outpost of the Dutch East India Com-pany. Several nations had East India company charters, including Britain.

Incorporated from a number of smaller companies by the States General of the Netherlands in 1602, the Dutch East India Company had a monopoly extending from the Cape of Good Hope eastward to the Strait of Magellan, with sovereign rights in whatever territory it might acquire. At the peak of its power, in 1669, the Dutch company had forty warships, one hundred fifty merchant ships, and ten thou-sand soldiers. Between 1602 and 1696 the annual dividends that the company paid were never less than 12 percent and sometimes as high as 63 percent. The charter of the company was renewed every twenty years, in return for financial concessions to the Dutch gov-ernment. The company was a government unto itself, able to pass legislation, issue currency, negotiate treaties, wage war, and extract justice. And though the company was in decline when *Endeavour* sailed into Batavia, it was still a multinational monster, with power extending into Japan, India, and China. That power would eventually extend across the centuries—the recent introduction of coffee as a Javanese cash crop would alter the island's economy for centuries to come. Java and coffee would become synonymous, thanks to the Dutch East India Company.

In addition to the lack of a salute, there was a measure of impudence in having *Endeavour* overhauled in Batavia: Cook had not only discovered but had surveyed a shoreline the Dutch had been unable to document for centuries. Though Cook forbade his men from talking about their voyage—Cook would only tell Dutch officials that *Endeavour* was an English vessel, bound for England—*Endeavour*'s tattered condition certainly fueled speculation about her voyage. No doubt, any rumors were later confirmed by the People, telling tales of their fantastic journey in seaside bars.

That Tasman had finished his journeys—and, ultimately, his career—in the same tropical crossroads was not lost on Cook. The display of pride was a small way of enjoying *Endeavour*'s slow return to civilization. Cook sent word to London on a vessel headed that way, assuring his Admiralty masters all was well. Then he gathered news of the world from the scores of ships floating in port as he began a few days away from the rigors of command. In one development that could have implications for his naval career, he learned that tensions between Britain and the American colonies had gotten much worse.

To the People, however, none of that mattered. Batavia was a liberty port, with fresh food and exotic women and oceanfront taverns. The crew had looked forward to Batavia with the same eagerness they'd once felt toward Tahiti and planned to make *Endeavour*'s repair stop a time of rip-roaring celebration.

The People weren't ashore a week, however, before a savage blow was dealt the entire crew. Malaria and dysentery attacked one and all. The Dutch were to blame, having let their canals go to seed and stagnate when they'd pushed inland. Mosquitoes bred easily in the standing water. Cook's men, who had known nothing but fresh air and clean water since leaving England, had no resistance to disease, for no disease beyond the social had infested their ranks in two years.

Banks was one of the first to fall ill, and Solander soon followed. Showing that Endeavour's voyage had changed him drastically (if only for the length of the voyage), Banks rose from his sickbed to take care of his friend and fellow botanist. Due to Endeavour's poor condition, the time in Batavia was to be lengthy, so Banks quickly arranged for a house in the country where the air was fresh and the local river was clean and swift. As soon as both men recovered, Banks recruited two Malay women to provide round-the-clock comfort.

Even the hardy Cook got sick. Concerned, however, about Endeavour's overhaul, he refused to leave Batavia's city limits to convalesce and somehow recovered quickly. One by one, however, the ship's most popular and valuable crew members died. Among those were Robert Molyneaux, the ship's master, and Charles Green, the astronomer and former Yorkshire farm boy with whom Cook had observed the Transit and spent so many hours computing longitude. When Lieutenant Zachary Hicks died and was buried at sea, Cook promoted popular master's mate Charlie Clerke in his stead. Cook liked that Clerke was both efficient and cheerful, if a bit fond of drink.

After ten weeks in Batavia, the unnecessary deaths of six crew, and the desertion of midshipman Patrick Saunders on Christmas Day, Endeavour sailed for England the day after Christmas, 1770. After a brief stop in Cape Town, where Endeavour's logs were transferred to a British merchant vessel for faster transit to England, Endeavour continued her journey home. She was leaking, flew badly torn topgallants, and was so fragile she might have sunk if a major storm had blown her way. Finally, over six months

after leaving Batavia, Cook anchored *Endeavour* at the Downs off
Deal, just north of Dover on the English Channel at 3 P.M. on Sat-
urday, July 12.

Cook's journey was done. A pilot would guide *Endeavour* up the
Thames to Woolwich for refurbishment. She had been to sea for
1,074 days. Though some of her crew had died, none had perished
from scurvy—a first in circumnavigation history. The Transit had
been recorded (how successfully, Cook was anxious to learn). Banks
and Solander had far surpassed any previous botanical cataloging,
making their reputations forever.

First Lieutenant James Cook, the forty-two-year-old upstart, had
pulled off his unlikely circumnavigation. Saying his good-byes to the
crew and his officers with little fanfare, Cook rushed from the ship
to complete the summation of his orders. "Upon your arrival in England you are immediately to repair to this office in order to lay before us a full account of your proceedings in the full course of your
voyage," the Admiralty had commanded three years earlier.

Literal as ever, Cook raced straight to the Admiralty. He accepted
Banks and Solander's offer of a carriage ride inland to Banks's home
on New Burlington Street, off Savile Row, in the heart of London.
The three circumnavigators parted company warmly, having formed
a deep bond in their cramped years sharing *Endeavour's* great cabin.
Then Cook scampered down Regency Street. He could have taken a
carriage the few short miles to Mile End Road, where Elizabeth and
the children waited anxiously. She would have known he was in
port, for the London newspapers were already running preliminary
stories about *Endeavour's* successful return. She had so much to tell
him, including the sad news that four-year-old Elizabeth had died
three months before.

But Cook didn't go home immediately. Nor did he dawdle
through London, absorbing the sights and smells of the city that had
enraptured him as a young man.

He went to the Admiralty.

Cook's face was bronzed from the sun, his uniform was clean but weathered from years at sea, his walk was more splay-legged than ever as his legs adjusted to terra firma on London's cobblestones. Cook was like a young boy eager to brag, giddy with excitement at all he had to share with his higher-ups. He'd followed his orders explicitly, then had the fearlessness not only to discover new lands, but carefully chart them so the next generation of explorers would know the location of safe harbors, freshwater, rocky shoals, coastal currents. He had given friends and allies and the king the gift of posterity, naming thousands of geographic features for these men (and their wives, and their estates). Before Cook, timid Tasman and unlucky Magellan had been the benchmarks of exploration. Now, Cook reflected happily, turning right onto Whitehall, then stepping smartly under the archway guarded by a pair of granite sea horses, he would be the gold standard. No other man had seen as much nor gone as far.

But as he walked across the cobbled courtyard, the man who'd commanded the Pacific and been hailed by chiefs as their better was once again back in London's class society, subordinate to men of wealth and power. Men who owed their eminence to inheritance, not achievement. Cook was again just the boy from Whitby with the thick burr. His domain was no longer those millions of square miles of Pacific, but the narrow four walls at Mile End Road, nothing more.

And for all Cook had accomplished, he was painfully aware that he wasn't even guaranteed another command. After three years of deciding his fate, and that of the People, through navigational decisions and barked commands, Cook was essentially powerless. The dash to the Admiralty was an attempt to convince his masters that he should be given another command—be given, again, that wondrous power in which Cook had quietly reveled. If need be, he was prepared to return to sea immediately.

Only after presenting his drawings and charts to Sir Phillip

Stephens, secretary of the Admiralty, did the gallant lieutenant speed home.

Stephens flipped through the documents, appraising Cook's achievement, for better or worse. What lay before him, he soon realized, was a feat of navigation and discovery unparalleled in human history. He hastened to inform King George III.

PART THREE

First *Resolution*: Farther Than Any Man

CHAPTER 11

Local Hero

August 1771

C ook never expected a hero's welcome. But he was a man of some ego who had guided *Endeavour* around the world, discovered a cure for scurvy, recorded the Transit of Venus, intermingled with several new cultures, charted the entire coastline of New Zealand, discovered and charted eastern Australia, and saved his men from shipwreck (while also discovering the Great Barrier Reef), all the while graciously sharing his great cabin with botanical specimens and the carcasses of fish and birds.

At the very least, Cook must have expected a morsel of recognition. Instead, Banks initiated a publicity campaign taking credit for the entire voyage. London newspapers focused on the brave and gallant Mr. Banks, running endless stories of his exploits and discoveries. The Royal Society lionized Banks. Oxford awarded him an honorary doctorate in civil law. Leading botanist Carl Linnaeus referred to Banks as "immortal" and made a public suggestion that Australia be renamed Banksia. Even King George III visited Banks, eager to hear tales of the bold adventure. "Banks," the *Westminster Gazette* wrote, "should be the botanists' oracle, and they should raise a monument to him more lasting than all the pyramids."

To make matters worse for Cook, his connection with Sandwich had landed him on the wrong side of the increasing political upheaval in America. The fiasco dated to 1764, when John Wilkes, a popular London politician, had sharply attacked George III in print. Sandwich had risen on the floor of Parliament to defend his king. Seeking to show the depravity of Wilkes's character—never mind that the two were longtime drinking buddies and members of the Hellfire Club—Sandwich read aloud a bawdy poem penned by Wilkes entitled "Essay on Women."

For his attack on King George III, Wilkes was convicted of seditious libel, sentenced to prison, and forbidden from taking a parliamentary seat upon his release. "I don't know whether you will die of the pox or the gallows," Sandwich gloated after the verdict.

"That depends, my lord," Wilkes shot back, "whether I embrace your mistress or your politics."

Wilkes emerged the hero. He had become synonymous with the American colonies' quest for personal liberties, a pursuit with which the working-class men and women of London strongly identified. Sandwich's condemnation of Wilkes wasn't just seen as a defense of the crown, but an attack on the concept of personal liberty. London newspapers vilified Sandwich as "Jemmy Twitcher," for a turncoat friend in the play *Beggar's Opera*.

During *Endeavour's* voyage, both Sandwich and Wilkes had enjoyed a political resurrection. Sandwich had resumed control of the Admiralty. Wilkes had been elected to Parliament three times, despite a mandate that he be barred from Parliament for life. Each time, the crown refused to let him take his seat. And each time that happened, riots broke out in London. The cry "Wilkes and liberty!" had come to stand for all that was right in society.

King George III and Lord Sandwich had come to stand for all that was wrong with England. George laid the blame for the controversy at the feet of Parliament's ruling party, the Whigs. To break their power, George formed his own informal party of "King's Friends" in 1770. Both Sandwich and Palliser were members and owed their political appointments to the association. The majority of Royal Navy officers, however, were Whigs. With Sandwich installed as First Lord of the Admiralty, tension between the two groups was exceptionally high. Many Royal Navy officers vowed not to serve under Sandwich if war came. Cook's alignment with Sandwich created a gulf between him and his Royal Navy peers.

Regardless, Cook was the man who had made Banks's "bold adventures" possible. In the weeks following his return to England, Cook remained quietly home at Mile End Road, reacquainting himself with his boys and belatedly grieving the death of his young son and daughter. It must have been strange weaving back into the household fabric. The routine, for instance, was not his to dictate. And instead of a hundred men obeying his every wish immediately, and the shipboard routine rotating around watch duty, Cook was in a household firmly commanded by two women—Elizabeth and Frances Wardale, the cousin who had helped Elizabeth in Cook's absence. While his presence was welcome, and his paternal authority never denied, he had been gone a very long time. The children clearly didn't really know their father anymore, nor were they used to viewing him as the ultimate authority.

James and Nathaniel were still young, seven and six, respectively. Like all young boys, they were prone to being active and loud, especially during the warm summer months. Their commotion, combined with the gin mill next door and the busy thoroughfare just outside his front door, made Cook's home feel extremely loud compared with shipboard life. When things became really chaotic and Cook needed to think, he walked the few miles to Will's Coffee House in Charing Cross, a mile from the Admiralty.

Coffeehouses had been the preferred gathering places for the men of London for almost a century, and Will's was legendary for attracting wits and intellectuals, making it a perfect haven for Cook. The aroma inside was of rich coffee poured from tall Turkish pots, and tobacco from the American colonies, smoked through the long-stemmed clay pipes that were a coffeehouse trademark. The clink of coffee saucers and the din of laughter and conversation only increased Will's fraternal air.

Cook, for all his pride, was powerless to stop Banks from taking credit for the voyage. Cook was at the mercy of politically connected men like Banks to further his career. Not only would it be an act of folly for Cook to speak up about Banks's true role, it would brand Cook as a loose cannon who didn't know his place.

A month after returning home, Cook finally received a reward for his services. He was promoted to commander on August 14, with King George III himself presenting the commission in Cook's lone postvoyage brush with the monarch. The new rank was marked by Sandwich's influence. He had become First Lord of the Admiralty once again in January 1771; and almost simultaneously, Palliser was named comptroller of the navy. Regardless of how it came to be, that day in August marked Cook's ascendance to the title he would carry indelibly into history. He had officially become Captain Cook.

Despite the promotion, Cook seemed destined for a return to anonymity. Cook's next assignment was to command the *Scorpion* and chart the entire coast of England. His career track had veered inexorably away from ships of warfare (the arena where admirals were made) to less glamorous ships of survey and discovery. Compared with all Cook had done before, the *Scorpion* posting was quite a letdown.

Cook was out of touch with Banks most of August, but he might have gotten a small amount of satisfaction knowing not all was perfect in the headstrong botanist's world. Before the journey, he'd been engaged to a Miss Harriet Blosset. He realized it was a sign of his detachment, fear of commitment, and ambivalence about marrying Blosset that in the months leading up to *Endeavour*'s departure he had never once mentioned the journey, hoping to find the perfect moment to spring this great surprise. Alas, that moment had never come. He had gotten very drunk and taken her to the opera his last night in London before joining *Endeavour*, but hadn't worked up the nerve to tell her where he'd be spending the next three years. Finally, the morning after the opera, Banks dispatched a messenger to Miss Blosset's house delivering an engagement ring and a note breaking the news about the grand botanic adventure. It was a coward's farewell, to be sure, and uncharacteristic of the usually forthright Banks.

Miss Harriet Blosset had not taken his disappearance well. Banks had managed to post missives to his sister Sarah from Batavia to allay any fear *Endeavour* was lost. Miss Blosset received no such reassurance. Nor did she receive an immediate call from Banks upon his return. Even his closest friends were calling Banks a cad and a scoundrel for his treatment of the reputable young lady. Before the backlash grew too strong, Banks paid the lovely Harriet five thousand pounds (roughly a million dollars in modern money) for her pain. In return he got his freedom and her eternal silence to the gossipmongers.

But Banks, resilient and cavalier, didn't labor under a broken heart long. Bolstered by his success and the public fawning, he grandly announced he would soon put to sea again to further his study of the South Pacific. On August 26, just six weeks after returning to the hustle-bustle of London, the *Gazeteer and Daily Advertiser* announced, "Mr. Banks is to have two ships from the government to pursue his discoveries in the South Seas, and will sail upon his second voyage in March."

This time he was to be given absolute command, Banks crowed to London newspapers. The Admiralty would give him two vessels instead of one. His entourage of hangers-on, scientists, and a female companion Banks conveniently failed to mention would be almost double that of the previous voyage. He would need them, of course, because the new journey's travels would make *Endeavour's* seem a mere Channel crossing.

And though he was out of the limelight, Sandwich was again the

Machiavellian mastermind, playing Banks for personal gain. Sandwich had privately promised Banks vessels for a new voyage because Banks and King George III had become extremely close since Banks's return. "The Farmer King," as George III was sometimes known, had entertained Banks at Windsor Castle and accepted an invitation to join Banks at his estate. King George III wasn't always a popular king (his carriage was stoned on more than one occasion), but he had enormous political power.

Banks was basking in that power, and Sandwich, seizing the moment to maneuver closer to the king, allied himself with Banks once again to further his own career. The Most Hated Man in England was using that month's Most Popular Man in England to solidify his political resurrection. "Soon after my return from my voyage around the world," Banks told a friend fifty years later of Sandwich's plotting, "I was solicited by Lord Sandwich, the First Lord of the Admiralty, to undertake another voyage of the same nature. I accordingly answered that I was ready and willing."

Sandwich's plans for the voyage were once again focused around the discovery of Antarctica and perpetuating British power. Not only had French explorer de Bougainville given the French an inroad to Antarctica by claiming Tahiti (the perfect Pacific naval base) for France, but also in August 1771 the British were returning the Falklands to Spain. Sandwich, nonplussed by this act of diplomatic kowtowing, was more determined than ever to prove the existence of Antarctica.

Though Cook's circumnavigation of New Zealand had dispelled such a notion for most people—Cook and Banks included—Sandwich still believed Antarctica existed, and that *Endeavour* just hadn't sailed far south enough to find it. He was convinced that if only a vessel and her crew were bold enough to plunge into the high latitudes, Antarctica and all the vast resources she was purported to possess would be found. Whoever went on the next voyage of discovery would have to share that vision. So it was that once Sandwich dangled the promise of another voyage before Banks, the twenty-eight-year-old botanist had a change of heart about the existence of Antarctica. Banks felt he'd been too hasty in denying its existence. "A Southern Continent exists, I surely believe," Banks commented in fall of 1771.

When Cook got news of Banks's new voyage, he dashed off a congratulatory letter from his outpost at Will's Coffee House. Then, anxious to assume command of the new voyage, Cook sent another post to Sandwich. "I do not believe any such thing exists," he said in firm words, before salvaging his career: "unless in a high latitude."

Cook's craving was to go where no man had gone before. He had sailed places, seen places, dispelled theories. But he hadn't gone *everywhere*. He'd rounded the Horn, then pushed *Endeavour* to exactly sixty degrees south latitude, as ordered, then turned around. Likewise, leaving Tahiti he'd dipped to forty degrees south and doodled back northwest. As much as Cook disbelieved the Antarctica theory—and was earning enemies such as Dalrymple as these beliefs leaked from the Admiralty—he had a deeply scientific heart. If something had not been conclusively disproved, then it might possibly exist. And while sixty degrees south was a fierce latitude, a virtual no-man's-land few ships had ever kissed, it was still thirty degrees shy of the bottom of the world. Until Cook guided a ship to those reaches between sixty and ninety degrees south latitude, he would never know for sure. For this reason, and because circumnavigating Great Britain in the name of cartography was the dull alternative, Cook quietly began lobbying the Admiralty to be released from the *Scorpion* and given command of the new journey.

The three years away from home had permanently detached Cook from his family. He loved Elizabeth and the boys with a passion, but time away had rendered him a father in name only. Elizabeth was already pregnant again and due to give birth shortly after Banks's voyage would set sail in March, but Cook was inexorably being pulled away from his family by the distractions of a growing attraction to power, discovery, and the seduction of the sea.

So while the thought of Cook leaving for another long voyage so soon after *Endeavour's* must have been a source of sadness to Elizabeth, it wasn't daunting or even heartbreaking to Cook. In fact, the notion was extremely attractive. He didn't even mind a potential olympiad away from Elizabeth and the boys as long as it meant more discovery. What's more, Cook was unconcerned that Banks assumed he would be in control of the next voyage—the man-child would be dealt with the instant the ships left port, just as on *Endeavour*. Cook was fast learning how to play politics. He and Banks had a symbiotic, parasitic relationship that enabled each to use the other to advance his career.

This is not to say, however, that Cook was above tweaking the botanist while still in London. In the reply to Banks's messenger informing Cook of his impending promotion, Cook subtly let slip that he'd become a player. "You very obliging letter was the first messenger that conveyed to me Lord Sandwich's intentions. Promotion unsolicited to a man of my station in life must convey a satisfaction to the mind that is better conceived than described. I had this morning to wait upon his Lordship," Cook continues, revealing that he had been taken into Sandwich's confidence about the upcoming circumnavigation, "who renewed his promises to me, and in so obliging and polite a manner as convinced me that he approved of the Voyage. The reputation I have required on this account by which I shall receive promotion calls to mind the very great assistance I have received therein from you, which will forever be remembered with most grateful acknowledgements."

Despite the graceful backpedaling at the end, the letter was Cook's first display of one-upmanship to a societal member above his station. Friendship with Sandwich empowered Cook. Though the older man's years of debauchery were catching up with him—one observer noted the formerly handsome Sandwich looked as if he'd been "half-hanged and cut down by mistake"—he was at the height of his powers. Playing both ends against the middle, he built a solid relationship with Cook to bookend his growing alliance with Banks. Sandwich even became a patron of Cook's. His pre-*Endeavour* belief that close proximity to Cook would pay political dividends was proving true.

The confidence to put Banks in his place wasn't the only subtle difference in Cook. Like many men at midlife, career accomplishment suddenly meant more to Cook than time at home. Instead of relaxing with his family, rekindling relationships, he was instead hanging out around the Admiralty like an insecure sea captain, waiting for his chance to lobby hard and successfully for a way out of the house.

In November, Sandwich finally ended the suspense. He offered Cook command of the new search for Antarctica. A relieved and grateful Cook accepted Sandwich's appointment without consulting Elizabeth.

To soften the blow, Cook suggested they take a short trip together. Just the two of them. Whitby would be the destination—a homecoming tour. James Cook and his lovely bride would travel to his childhood haunts. She would meet John Walker and see those North Yorkshire ports she had heard so much about. More important, she would meet seventy-seven-year-old James Cook senior, who had moved from Ayton to live with his daughter Margaret and her fisherman husband in Redcar.

It would be Cook's first trip home in fifteen years. Once again, he would return home in triumph, for the son had usurped the father. Captain Cook. World conqueror, explorer of nations, captain of the Royal Navy who had stood before the king. It was time to return and tell all.

For all his journal-keeping, Cook wrote nothing of this December journey. It was three days north by stagecoach, alongside a woman four months pregnant. John Walker and all of Whitby came out to greet Cook, toasting him and his new voyage, gathering round in the pub to hear long stories of *Endeavour*'s travels. Cook and Walker shared private moments in the Green Room of Walker's Grape Lane home, drinking home-brewed ale and rekindling their friendship.

But of Cook's meeting with his father, it's hard to know what happened, and whether his desire for parental acceptance was met. Whether the dream was fulfilled or whether Cook bitterly discovered the dream for what it truly was: a wish for acceptance. Either way, it was the last time Cook ever saw his father. Cook became different after that trip, more selfish. He had always been detached and reclusive, absorbed in his own thoughts and dreams. But after this trip, Cook became even less aware of others' needs.

It was mid-January 1772 when Cook and Elizabeth returned to London. He immediately dove into final preparations for the voyage. He had selected his two ships, both Whitby colliers: the majestic 462-ton *Marquis of Granby* and her weaker sister, the 340-ton *Marquis of Rockingham*. They were renamed *Drake* and *Raleigh*, respectively.

But there was a problem with those names. The Spanish, touchy as always, had a long memory. To them, Sir Francis Drake and Sir Walter Raleigh were two of the most offensive individuals in the fractured history between the two nations. Raleigh had sacked Spanish settlements in the New World during a 1602 voyage in search of El Dorado. Drake, a relentless abuser of the Spanish, had been aboard a vessel in 1571 that was attacked by the Spanish. From then until his death of dysentery in 1596, Drake had plundered, looted, pillaged, vandalized, harassed, and destroyed Spanish fleets, settlements, and forts, in a theater of operations ranging from England to South America to California.

The Admiralty, having finally soothed Spanish feelings about the Falklands, renamed Cook's ships.

The new names were actually much more appropriate and gallant: *Resolution* and *Adventure*. *Resolution*, Cook's flagship, was being refitted at Deptford. *Adventure* was farther down the Thames at Woolwich alongside the battered *Endeavour*, which was being refitted as a cargo ship. Cook's plan, once both new ships were out of dry dock, provisioned, and crewed, was to leave in March.

In the meantime, Cook and Elizabeth enjoyed the occasional night out, enjoying the budding of Cook's celebrity. At one party, a Dr. Charles Burney asked Cook to compare his voyage with de Bougainville's. As reference, Burney noted a copy of de Bougainville's *Voyage Autour de Monde* on the table before him. "Captain Cook instantly took a pencil from his pocket-book," Burney noted later, "and said that he would trace the route; which he did so in a clear and scientific manner."

That Cook's name was spreading in London society had to do with the coming publication of *Endeavour's* journals. A Dr. John Hawkesworth was combining Banks's and Cook's logs, adding a few adventurous touches of his own, and publishing them as Cook's work (Cook's actual journals weren't published until 1893). The widespread public acclaim that followed was counterbalanced by the unhappy opinion of always disgruntled Alexander Dalrymple. The Scot refused to accept Cook's journal entry that Antarctica didn't exist. He went so far as to claim Cook was a poseur and liar, and even a slacker for failing to push below forty degrees south latitude after circumnavigating New Zealand. If Cook had done so, Dalrymple said to anyone who would listen, he would surely have found Antarctica.

Such sniping made Cook defensive and overpensive. The Burneys' nineteen-year-old daughter, Fanny, making the social rounds with her parents, wrote later of being impressed by Cook's manner, but put off by his intensity and moodiness. "This truly great man seemed to be full of sense and thought; well-mannered and perfectly unpretending; but studiously wrapped up in his own purposes and pursuits; and apparently under a pressure of mental fatigue when called upon to speak, or stimulated to deliberate, upon any other."

The introvert in Cook, so thoroughly acceptable at sea, was an enigma and potential boor in London society. Yet the Burneys were impressed enough with Cook that the good doctor begged Cook to allow his twenty-one-year-old son, an officer who had joined the Royal Navy at age ten, to join *Resolution's* voyage. Eager to curry favor with his new peers, Cook consented. He was pleased that they had approached him instead of Banks, for the majority of men petition-ing to sail on the new journey truly thought Banks was the com-mander. Civilians wrote Banks letters stating that they "panted" to go along.

Banks kept all their letters, especially the ones mentioning his im-pending immortality. He did little to dispel rumors of leadership and slowly selected fifteen people to accompany himself and Solander for their next global lap. In addition to artists, secretaries, and servants, Banks's menagerie included two horn players. To make room aboard *Resolution,* a ship Banks found barely more tolerable than *Endeavour,* Banks demanded of Palliser that modifications be made. He wished apartments prepared on deck. When Palliser refused, Banks went over his head, to Sandwich. The old coconspirator overruled Palliser. Ship's carpenters got to work on Banks's apartments immediately. For the sake of his friendships with Sandwich and Palliser, Cook went along with the orders to modify *Resolution,* but he wasn't happy.

Cook bit his tongue as a new upper "spar" deck was added on top of the existing main deck, the waist was raised, and a roundhouse compartment (which was actually a square room) to house Cook was built above the great cabin. Its roof would be the poop deck. This was necessary because Banks had already determined he would sleep in the captain's quarters and have exclusive use of the great cabin. Cook, again for the sake of peace, acquiesced. Banks's way of thanking Cook was to complain about the cabin's small size.

With all the brouhaha about "Mr. Banks's voyage," *Resolution* be-came a tourist attraction. Spectators gathered to watch preparations. "Scarce a day past on which she was not crowded with strangers who came on board for no purpose other than to see the ship in which Mr. Banks was to sail around the world," Cook noted with amazement.

The March departure date came and went. Banks didn't seem to notice the growing tension between him and Cook. On May 2, Sand-wich even held a dinner party on the nearly completed *Resolution.*

The First Lord, always the political animal, had kept tabs on the renovations. He knew Cook's tight-lipped concerns that the ship was top-heavy and had too great a draft. Sandwich's overruling of Palliser was risky, and if *Resolution* was endangered or weakened by the changes, it would be Sandwich, not Banks, who took the fall. Sandwich decided to wait until the renovations were finished before making a final decision on whether the changes stayed or went.

Cook ordered *Resolution* to sea for trials in mid-May, but the pilot gave up before she was out of the Thames, refusing to take her into the Channel, saying she would capsize under full sail. When Cook sought a second opinion, newly promoted Lieutenant Charlie Clerke—the fun-loving young man who had earned the promotion on *Endeavour*—was eager to offer one. "By God I'll go to sea in a grog tub, if desired, or in the *Resolution* as soon as you please. But I must say I think her by far the most unsafe ship I ever saw or heard of."

That confirmation was all Cook needed. He ordered *Resolution* into the naval dockyard in Sheerness, at the mouth of the Thames. After getting approval from Sandwich, Cook ordered an army of two hundred carpenters and shipwrights to knock down the new spar deck and roundhouse—to level them completely. *Resolution* looked like a Whitby collier again. Banks would not win this battle. Banksia, indeed.

Banks was counting on his social standing to intimidate Cook, not knowing that Cook and Sandwich had become mutual admirers. The same was true of Cook and Palliser, for men of substance seem to find each other. When Cook, Sandwich, and Palliser got together, it was a gathering without pomp or pretense, marked by a casual tone. Cook had told both men of his reservations, as well as his willingness to bend. Now, gambling on those friendships, Cook was provoking a direct confrontation with England's media darling, the one man who could potentially appeal as high as the king himself to have Cook removed in favor of another captain.

On May 28, Cook and Banks finally had their showdown. Cook stood on the quarterdeck, awaiting Banks's imminent arrival. When

Banks came stomping down the dock and saw the changes for himself, he exploded. His tantrum was epic. Spectators said he "swore
and stamped like a mad man." Banks ordered all his entourage off.
Then he had his baggage and personal effects removed. When he ap-
pealed to Sandwich, writing a two-thousand-word letter asking for
an alternate ship, the forty-four-gun ship of the line HMS *Launces-
ton*, the older statesman not only refused the request, but took the
time to draft a written rebuttal in case Banks took his case to the
media. And though the June issue of *Gentlemen's Magazine* editorial-
ized that Cook's action was contrary to King George's wishes, and
lamented that the monarchy had become powerless, Banks had the
good sense to keep his mouth shut. Privately, he felt himself the victim of a conspiracy between Palliser and Sandwich. Conspiracies
were a fine thing as long as Banks was the initiating party. But when
the tables were turned, Banks felt it unfair.

Cook rubbed salt in Banks's wounds. "Sir," he wrote Banks from
Sheerness on the second of June. "Since I am not to have your company on the *Resolution*, I most sincerely wish you success in all your
exploring undertakings."

For his journal, Cook wrote a more candid explanation of all that
had occurred. "Mr. Banks, unfortunate for himself, set out upon too
large a plan. A plan that was incompatible with a scheme of discovery at the Antipodes; had he confined himself to the same plan as he
set out upon the last voyage, attended only to his own pursuits and
not interfered with the choice, direction, or even the ship's things he
was not a competent judge of, he would have found everyone concerned in the expedition ever ready to oblige him, for myself I can
declare it: instead of finding fault with the ship he ought to have
considered that the *Endeavour* Bark was just such another, whose
good qualities gave him the opportunity to acquire that reputation
the public has so liberally and with great justice bestowed upon
him."

As a final attempt to save face, Banks tried to lure the charismatic

Charlie Clerke away from Cook for an alternate voyage to Iceland. Clerke was typically puckish in his reply: "Am exceedingly obliged to you, my good sir," stated the young man who had attached himself to Cook's coattails, "for your kind concern on my account. But have stood too long on this tack to think of putting about."

Redheaded American John Gore accepted Banks's invitation, however, and sailed on Banks's 190-ton charter, the *Sir Lawrence*. The move would harm Gore's career, though he was not particularly concerned. He had a special girl in London, and going away for long periods put a cramp in their relationship. Plus, as an American at a time when the colonies were agitating, Gore's sympathies were suspect. His career security would always be tenuous, at best, and he would certainly never make admiral. Cook, however, would miss Gore's presence on *Resolution*. Gore had been one of the rare men Cook spoke openly with on *Endeavour*.

The important thing to Cook was that arrogant Mr. Banks was finally gone. It was time for Cook and *Resolution* to go to sea. Time for a long sea voyage with one captain holding forth in the great cabin—the great cabin Cook did not have to share with specimens or sleeping botanists. Cook was positively jubilant. No one would be reporting on him or whining about racing back to England as quickly as possible. Cook could do as he pleased. He could sail rings around the Pacific if he wanted—a proposition he was not ruling out.

Lost in all the commotion caused by Banks and his outrageous demands was Elizabeth's giving birth in early June to another boy, George. Cook was present, only the second time he'd been in England for the birth of one of his children. Two weeks after that, on June 21, Cook kissed Elizabeth and their three sons good-bye and took a carriage to Sheerness. He wouldn't come back for three years, in which time his two oldest sons would leave home to attend the new British naval academy. George, just a few weeks old as Cook left to search for Antarctica, would die at four months.

From Sheerness, Cook brought *Resolution* around the bottom of

England to Portsmouth and last-minute provisioning before setting sail. Their send-off was limited to Sandwich and Palliser, who were in Portsmouth inspecting new Admiralty dock facilities. They sailed out on the Admiralty yacht *Augusta* as anchor was weighed.

Endeavour's travels, ironically, have always been depicted as the masterpiece of Cook's voyages. That was hardly the case. *Endeavour's* journey was a mere rehearsal for *Resolution's* unparalleled example of courage. *Endeavour's* journey was a military mission cloaked in scientific disguise, while *Resolution's* was a bold ploy to expand the known parameters of the British Empire. Cook's orders from the Admiralty were simple: Find Antarctica. The subtext, as expressed by First Lord of the Admiralty Sandwich, was just as bold: Don't come home until you do.

So it was that on July 13, 1772, after a year in England, Cook and the other 111 men of *Resolution*, followed by *Adventure* and her 81, set out on what would become the greatest voyage the world had ever known.

CHAPTER 12

Ice

Cook was forty-three when his second circumnavigation got under way aboard *Resolution*. In almost every way, he was still the eager skipper who'd led *Endeavour* to sea four years earlier. His navigational talents, geographic curiosity, leadership skills, attention to detail, fascination with science, desire to reduce shipboard mortality, benevolent attitude toward indigenous peoples, and self-confidence had been elevated to a new level of excellence during that first voyage. Few men, anywhere, possessed this varied quiver of skills so necessary for a career in exploration.

There had, however, been subtle changes in Cook's personality. His patience had grown thin after years of round-the-clock responsibility aboard *Endeavour*. He had become emotionally withdrawn. His constitution was solid and he was still physically fit, but the rigors—fluctuating seas, wild variations in weather, physical confinement, the high level of stress associated with command—of shipboard living and advancing age made him more susceptible to sickness. And his golden dream of visiting the South Pacific was slowly transforming into an obsession with charting every speck of her vast waterways and holding sway over her peoples.

Cook began *Resolution's* journey by sailing due south. He maneuvered straight down the African coastline toward the Cape of Good Hope. By sailing around Africa, then east toward New Zealand, Cook hoped to take advantage of the west-to-east direction of prevailing winds, knowing this would speed him toward the South Pacific quicker. Time was of the essence. With every passing day it seemed another rival was attempting to steal Britain's discoveries and colonial outposts. The French, for instance, were ignoring British claims to Tahiti, saying they were there first. The Spanish were a continual burr. And the Dutch, of course, while focusing more on increasing trade than finding new colonies, were still intrepid sailors. If any of these nations found Antarctica first, England would lose a great number of resources, as well as a good deal of face. Cook needed to push as far south as possible—to the pole itself, if need be—and find the Antarctic continent once and for all. After that, he was free to pursue his secondary—private—goal of ranging across the Pacific in search of new lands.

Because Cook didn't believe Antarctica existed, he was determined to get the polar plunge out of the way as soon as possible. Ever aware of prior explorers' footsteps, Cook's plan was to follow an aggressive version of Tasman's route to the Pacific: down the coast of Africa, refuel at Cape Town; but instead of sailing east to Mauritius, then Australia, Cook would leave Cape Town and angle due south, heading straight for the South Pole. Once the Antarctic myth had been exposed or confirmed, he could wander over to his Pacific kingdom and cross back and forth between New Zealand and Tahiti at will. Cook would be the foreman surveying the farm, the king casing his kingdom.

Cook had one glaring liability he wasn't aware of: *Adventure's* captain, the seemingly capable Tobias Furneaux. Six years younger than Cook, Furneaux came from good stock, with a family heritage dating to the Norman Conquest. He was no James Cook—not a man born with an unquenchable yen for discovery—but neither was he lacking in backbone or experience. Furneaux's background included stints in Jamaica and off the coast of West Africa. When Wallis had circumnavigated on *Dolphin*, Furneaux was a second lieutenant aboard the vessel. This had given him a great deal of command experience, for Wallis had been a sickly man. For long periods during *Dolphin's* travels, Wallis and his first lieutenant had been incapacitated due to one illness or another.

In those moments, Furneaux had assumed control of the ship, displaying skill and judiciousness at the helm. He followed the book, but showed little original thinking. In short, he was a perfect second to Cook. Instead of feuding alongside a competitive captain—a sailing version of Joseph Banks—Cook thought he was sailing into the South Pacific blessed with a second-in-command who would do as ordered each and every time. What Cook didn't yet know was that Furneaux was weak, often lacked courage, and would quietly ignore Cook's orders. Furneaux would break when black and white turned to gray.

The junior officers on both vessels would turn out to be more enterprising. James Burney, son of the social Burneys Cook had met in his London travels, was on board through his parents' beseeching. He had gone to sea as a young man and slowly worked his way up through the ranks. However, to sail aboard *Resolution*, Burney had signed on as a mere able-bodied seaman. He figured that a voyage with Cook was just the sort of high-profile assignment that would ensure career advancement (that hope turned out to be justified; Burney would someday make admiral).

Fifteen-year-old George Vancouver also signed on as able seaman. Vancouver would someday rise to captain and would emulate Cook as an explorer while charting the North American coast.

If Cook faced a personnel problem aboard *Resolution*, it was the father-and-son duo of John Reinhold Forster and his son George. They were natural scientists, brought on board as last-minute replacements for Banks. The Forsters were Polish Prussians who had moved to London to make their fortunes. The son was less painful to be around than the father, but both were self-absorbed, humorless, dogmatic, pompous, and—worst of all—great friends of that frustrated Cook critic Dalrymple. It was through Dalrymple's friendship that the Fellows of the Royal Society had come to know, and recommend, father and son for the voyage after Banks's surprise ouster.

By a vote of Parliament, Reinhold was to receive the ridiculous sum of four thousand pounds for his time at sea (Cook's small military salary meant he would receive less than six hundred pounds for the voyage). Reinhold took this vote more as a sign of importance than the simple governmental agenda item it was and began imagining himself a man of immense influence. Reinhold's favorite shipboard threat to anyone crossing him was that he would report his actions to the king upon *Resolution*'s return. Not only was Cook to find the Forsters immensely irritating, but *Resolution*'s officers and crew took to mimicking, then ignoring, both men.

Reinhold and George would provide many dark hours over the next several years, but Cook was thankful that the supernumerary population was down significantly from *Endeavour*, increasing berth space for his officers. In addition to the Forsters, artist William Hodges and astronomer William Wales rounded out the contingent. Wales's primary function was to look after *Resolution*'s chronometer. Hodges's one affectation was a penchant for neoclassicism, which caused him to draw Polynesians as Greeks and Romans. Though, when he finally drew Cook, Hodges turned the captain's proud profile into a gargoyle's head with a nose extending straight out off the canvas.

The journey to Cape Town was marked by an incident showing Cook's rising reputation. On July 22, a Spanish squadron stopped *Resolution* and *Adventure*. Typically, both vessels would be seized and the crews either pressed or taken ashore. Instead, the ships were immediately released once Cook was recognized. Among the seafaring set at least, his celebrity was now international. Forster, for his part, was unaware of the happening's significance. His journal dwells on his personal sense of embarrassment and impotence at being a Royal Navy vessel boarded by the hated Spaniards.

Throughout the three-month journey south, the People got back into shipboard routine. A third of them had sailed on *Endeavour*. They spent their watch hours cleaning and painting the ship, scrubbing the crowded decks, practicing rifle marksmanship off the side, and fishing with hooks and line issued by Cook. Their off-duty time was spent sewing tattered clothing with needle and thread, carving wood, and playing instruments such as the fiddle or guitar. Dancing and singing substituted for exercise. Cook also instituted a new procedure, the drying of the ship via charcoal fires between decks. This was intended to prevent disease caused by excess dampness, and curb the growth of molds and germs.

Cook force-fed his men antiscorbutics such as malt, raw onions (he'd picked up a thousand bunches in Madeira on July 29), sauerkraut, carrot marmalade, salted cabbage, and condensed beer. He was intent on advancing the scurvy-abatement practices begun on *Endeavour* and was just as dogged in his refusal to let a single sailor die from the scourge. Problem was, Furneaux saw scurvy as a regular part of the sailing life for able seamen (officers typically received fresher, more varied rations than the men, hence few officers suffered this fate) and quietly considered Cook's theories useless mumbo jumbo. The expedition had been just three months at sea when *Resolution* and *Adventure* weighed anchor in Cape Town's Table Bay on October 30, but *Adventure* had already lost several men to "fever," with many others displaying lethargy. *Resolution*'s men, on the other hand, were lively and disease-free. A man had died on *Resolution*, but of stupidity—he had fallen overboard.

Cook pulled Furneaux aside for a word once the vessels were anchored in Cape Town's Table Bay. As they settled into *Resolution*'s great cabin to confer, the obvious division between them was in their old-school/new-school mentalities. Furneaux was a follower who had come to officer's rank after years as an able seaman. The Royal Navy had a way of doing things, he was convinced, and that was simply the way things were done. No matter where in the world, no matter how far from London, this fact of life was unchanging.

Cook, on the other hand, had a more fluid notion of life at sea. Visitors to his ships often commented that discipline seemed lax, but that the men were somehow far more efficient than on other Royal Navy vessels. Morale was higher. The sometimes quirky dietary mandates meant not just greater health on board, but also a sense of well-being that instilled a more positive mental attitude. Finally, as an explorer used to going long months without sighting land, Cook's leadership style was hands-on. He mingled with the men, learned their names and habits, and knew which men worked best through punishment and which worked best through praise. Compared with most Royal Navy captains' "my way or the highway" style of leadership, Cook's was like that of a creature from another planet to Furneaux.

In a passive-aggressive way, Furneaux began a battle of wills with Cook. When Cook gave an order that Furneaux found silly or inconvenient, such as a requirement for diet or that the vessel's holds be cleansed regularly (by having the men remove their bedding topside for airing, then using smoke as a disinfectant in sleeping areas), Furneaux preferred to treat it as a suggestion. Adventure's true function was as a backup vessel in case another Endeavour Reef situation presented itself. But Furneaux hoped that a lifeboat mentality, where the two captains were stuck with each other and had to make the best of a tough situation, would bend Cook's way of thinking toward a more Furneaux-like mind-set.

This underestimation would gravely affect Furneaux's career.

Thus, upon reaching Cape Town, Cook was distressed that Furneaux was ignoring dietary mandates. Giving his fellow commander the benefit of the doubt when Furneaux said the men had died from too much exposure to tropical rain (the same rain falling on Resolution), Cook restated his orders concerning diet and cleanliness. Then Cook moved on to the more pressing matter: the South

Pole. Or, rather, getting lost in searching for it. Upon leaving Cape Town the vessels would push due south. If they became separated for any reason, the ships were to fire their small cannons as a means of attracting each other. If this failed, there would be a rendezvous in Queen Charlotte's Sound. Whichever skipper arrived first was to wait indefinitely for the other.

On November 22, 1772, *Resolution* and *Adventure* sailed from Cape Town. Anxiety permeated both vessels as they prepared to leave the balmy African coast for the Southern Ocean's infamous ferocity. Cook ordered heavy fearnought jackets and trousers issued to ward off the coming cold and wetness.

At forty-seven degrees south latitude Cook entered the antarctic convergence, a zone where northward-moving cold water from the bottom of the world meets with southward-drifting water from the equator. The convergence also marked the entry to the Southern Ocean. Though made up of the southern regions of the Pacific, Atlantic, and Indian Oceans, mariners considered the Southern Ocean an entirely separate body of water due to its lower salt concentration and water temperature. The winds of the Southern Ocean rip along at staggering speeds, channeling northward to the equator in a west-to-east fashion induced by the earth's rotation. Those gales whip the ocean to a fury unseen in other oceans, and sailors who have heard the "freight train" roar of an eighty-foot Southern Ocean wave bearing down on their vessel never forget it.

As Cook plunged farther south, the crew swaddled themselves in the additional clothing. Cook suspended his habit of bathing in unheated seawater because its temperature was far too cold. Likewise, the People's habit of washing clothes by placing them in a bag, then tying the bag to a rope and dragging it behind the ship, was suspended. Not only was the water too cold, but also the chill, damp air meant the clothes would freeze instead of dry.

Within a week, icebergs—"ice islands," as Clerke noted—bobbed off the bow, a fact made all the more fearful because fog thick like pea soup made it impossible to see for any great distance. "Some of them," Cook noted of the ice floes, "are near two miles in circuit and sixty feet high, and yet the sea broke over them. When one reflects on the danger this occasions, the mind is filled with horror, for was a ship to get against the weather side of one of these islands when the sea runs high he would be dashed to pieces in a moment."

Waves began breaking over the deck as gales became a daily fact of life. Normally, orders were given by human voice, passed from one officer to another. But the storms battering *Resolution* drowned out the human voice. Cook resorted to barking commands through a speaking trumpet.

Belowdecks, life was just as harsh. Cook ordered the large windows of his great cabin shuttered with heavy wooden deadlights, depriving the room of fresh air and imbuing a dark, musty feel. The animals acquired as foodstuffs in Cape Town—cows, sheep, chickens, geese, pigs—began freezing to death as their African-raised bodies endured the shocking antarctic cold. It was summer in the Southern Hemisphere, but not like any summer back in England. Snow and mountains of ice and monstrous seas and fog and damp, freezing air lent *Resolution* and *Adventure* the aura of ghost ships plowing through an endless limbo. Crew members had signed on for exploration, but their visions were of the South Seas, Tahitian women. Eating carrot marmalade and raw onions, constantly on the verge of frostbite, living in constant dread of slipping from the icy deck into the black waters—this was like no exploration men had ever heard of. "Fog, sleet, snow, all the rigging covered with ice and the air excessive cold," Cook wrote, trying to pass along a slice of shipboard life. "The crew, however, stand it tolerably well, each being clothed with a fearnought jacket, a pair of trousers of the same, and a large cap made of canvas and baise. These together with an additional glass of brandy every morning enables them to bear the cold without flinching."

And still Cook pushed the vessels south. In mid-January, *Resolu-*

tion and *Adventure* sailed across the antarctic circle, a feat never before accomplished. Instead of the occasional iceberg, pack ice often surrounded both ships, threatening to freeze them inside. Prior to that, scientists had thought salt water incapable of freezing. No longer. Curiously, when Cook lowered boats to explore the consistency of ice floes, he was shocked to discover the water was fresh and incredibly pure (the uppermost sections of the floes contained freshwater because they consisted of rain and snow that had fallen atop pack ice). He ordered chunks calved, then brought on board to replenish water stores. Hygiene was once again enforced. Cook was a firm believer that cleanliness staunched illness, so despite the cold, Cook ordered all clothing washed in casks on deck, and the People's hands scrubbed before dining (especially imperative because paper was a precious commodity aboard ship; the people cleaned their bottoms by using a combination of hands and water, and officers favored pieces of cloth). Bedding was aired. Cook even passed out needles and thread to men appearing especially tattered. The penalty for not complying was flogging.

All this occurred while sailing at a walking pace through seas taller than a house. Since the ships had left Cape Town, whales had been constant companions, coupled with the appearance of penguins as *Resolution* edged toward the bottom of the world. Once again Cook found himself considering the existence of Antarctica. The penguins, Cook figured, were sure signs of land. He meandered carefully through the pack ice, more determined than ever to find it.

Unbeknownst to Cook, *Resolution* and *Adventure* were just fifty miles off the jagged Antarctic coast. *Resolution* and *Adventure* were far into the high latitudes, having reached sixty-seven degrees south. The pack ice, however, was making forward progress increasingly impossible. Though he sensed land was over the horizon, Cook was afraid his vessels would eventually become trapped, then frozen in place (the horrifying fate of Sir Ernest Shackleton, almost 150 years later). On January 18, he gave the order to sail north and to the east,

away from the ice, looking for a more advantageous spot to continue
his southward search. Pushed along by a following wind and sea,
Resolution and *Adventure* clipped along at almost ten knots.

Due to diet, cleanliness, and Cook's sure leadership, the quality of
life was far better aboard *Resolution* than *Adventure*. The men, though
cold, wet, tired, sick, miserable, and bundled in fearnoughts, cheered
themselves by illicitly tapping into the ship's rum casks and nurturing the notion that eventually—someday, hopefully—Cook would
have to run toward the tropics.

On February 8, 1773, one-third of the way between Africa and
Australia, *Adventure* and *Resolution* lost each other in the Southern
Ocean. Not worried, Cook sailed eastward in the general direction of
New Zealand, sticking to high latitudes. He veered as far up as forty-
six degrees south latitude and tiny Crozet Island, just to verify its existence. Then, just when the crew and officers guessed their captain
would continue the path upward into warmer waters (Cook never
shared his plans with anyone else on board), he broke the crew's
hearts by plunging south again. He was determined to divine the location of the antarctic continent he could sense but could not see.
Just as off New Zealand and Australia before, Cook was coasting a
shoreline as he maneuvered into the antarctic latitudes, charting its
boundaries and hidden beauties. But in this case, the shore was a
phantom continent. The coasting was not to show a shoreline's contours, but to prove or disprove conclusively—by careful latitudinal
and longitudinal detective work—that no shoreline existed.

This maneuver frustrated everyone but Cook. The traditional sailing voyage was built upon an assignment—sail to America, chart a
known coastline, deliver supplies to the Falklands. At some point
every voyage was finite. The end could be hundreds of days away,
but it was always out there, a goal to be counted down. The most unpopular voyage—for all the sexual gratification Tahiti offered—was
the circumnavigation. Due to its great length, sailors deserted in
scads before such voyages. They weren't necessarily afraid of the sea,

or even the unknown, so much as being away from a girlfriend or a wife and then coming home to find her in the arms of another man. Once at sea, that fear had to be compartmentalized, those lovers forgotten. Cook was a prime example; he showed robust passion toward Elizabeth in his time home, but ignored women altogether when his ships docked in foreign lands.

Cook was not a captain who heeded traditional time frames on his adventures. He was the archetype of a new discoverer: he didn't care when he got home. The world was shrinking fast and he knew the Admiralty wasn't likely to continue giving him ships and men ad infinitum. Cook had to make the most of every opportunity to find new lands, and to find them quickly, before the French and Spanish and Dutch. It took almost a year to get from England to the Pacific's unknowns; it took another year to get home. Cook thought it a waste of time to cut his journey short by giving the Pacific or Southern Ocean a mere cursory once-over. That had been the paradigm for exploration before Cook. Magellan, Queirós, Tasman, and Drake always seemed as much in a hurry to get home as to explore—but Cook saw things differently. Unlike past explorers, who sailed in linear, math-oriented, left-brain ways, Cook chose to sail the world as if he were wandering in a park on a sunny day.

It was a testimony to Cook's management skills that his men never mutinied, never even considered mutiny. They went about their work with a minimum of grumbling, even on those days when Cook's maddening need to know had them dawdling to all points of the compass. Part of Cook's motivation was self-aggrandizement, for he was showing signs that he wanted to be known as the world's greatest explorer. But another reason was the knee-jerk childhood need to please his superiors. On *Resolution's* voyage, Cook knew how badly Sandwich longed for Antarctica's discovery. There was absolutely no way he was returning to England without scouring the earth for its existence.

Certain that Furneaux and *Adventure* were sailing with all diligence toward the idyllic splendor of their prearranged rendezvous point, Queen Charlotte's Sound, Cook lost track of time. The number of days since the crew had set foot on land ratcheted up past two, then three, then almost four months. Because Cook was following a course to Antarctica never before sailed, land might pop up at any time. This knowledge at least gave the crew a daily sense of hope. The cold and damp air had broken their bodies, with backs strained by hauling ice-encrusted rope, ulcers brought on by the stress of dangerous duty, and joints inflamed by rheumatism. Many suffered bouts of depression from being confined aboard the cramped ship for months at a time.

There were benefits of sailing with a man like Cook, notably that he allowed his men eight hours rest between shifts (compared with the standard four) so they would remain fresh for the duration of the long voyage. Even that perk, however, was moot in the Southern Ocean. In that world of huge waves and rogue ice floes, hypervigilance was the code. In the event of storm or near calamity, all hands were summoned urgently on deck, day or night, then ordered to climb to the uppermost levels of the swaying rigging to take in the topsails. Many reported for duty half-drunk or half-awake, one shoe on and one shoe off, and otherwise fully dressed only because they slept in their clothes. Lashed by winds blowing so hard they could not hear each other, working in darkness so thick they couldn't see each other, and gripping clawlike to the ropes to avoid toppling into the sea, the crew worked to exhaustion. Collapsing into their hammocks' envelopment after the job was done, the People were likely to be summoned back on deck by the mate's cry of "Up every soul nimbly" an hour later for yet another sail adjustment.

Despite their maladies and exhaustion, however, the People performed their duties professionally. *Resolution's* crew was like a fine-tuned machine that always kept one eye out for land. They were proud to be serving with such a famous man. Even the dregs of London society had a palpable sense that history was being made.

Cook kept angling south, searching for a gap in the pack ice. He kept track of his longitudinal position by recording distance traveled on his southerly course. Finally, he gave up. If the Southern Continent existed in this quadrant of the globe, it was an extremely cold place, and not land so much as ice mass. "These seas are not to be navigated without enduring intense cold," he noted. It was the seventeenth of March, and Cook gave the command to set a bearing for Queen Charlotte's Sound. He was at fifty-nine degress south latitude—nine hundred miles due south of Tasmania, but still several hundred miles north of Antarctica. The notion of quitting saddened him, and he wrote a disclaimer in his journal in case higher-ups one day accused him of not trying hard enough. Sailing to Queen Charlotte's Sound was just a breather, he pointed out, not an admission of failure. He would try again in the global quadrant between New Zealand and South America. "If the reader of this journal desires to know my reasons for taking the resolution just mentioned, I desire he will only consider that after cruising four months in these high latitudes it must be natural for me to wish to enjoy some short repose in a harbor where I can procure some refreshment for my people, of which they begin to stand in need of, to this point too great attention could not be paid as the voyage is but in its infancy."

As the air grew warmer, even Cook longed to set foot on land. And when the lookout sighted New Zealand on March 25, Cook opted to find anchorage immediately instead of pushing on up the coast to Cook Strait and Queen Charlotte's Sound. For this reason, Cook found another of the world's most beautiful places, Dusky Sound, nestled into the southwestern corner of New Zealand's fjord land. With steep walls rising from deep, green waters, Dusky Sound offered all the fresh fish, greens, and game *Resolution's* crew ever dreamed of during their endless cold meals in the Southern Ocean. The menu included scallops, duck, seal, oysters, and fish so plentiful that the People gorged morning, noon, and night.

Dusky Sound's only drawbacks were the low clouds and days of rain. Otherwise it was Eden, and even Endeavour Inlet paled in comparison. After the white and gray austerity of the previous four months, the green color and forest aroma of Dusky Sound, plus its plentiful waterfalls, thick forest, and rainbows, felt like sensory overload. Cook noted that Dusky Sound continued inland and sailed deeper and deeper inside until he discovered that Dusky Sound was far more than a large bay. Inlets spidered off in all directions—narrow channels in the rock leading to one secluded anchorage after another. Cook saw prosperity and provisions and peace of mind wherever he looked. When Cook and *Resolution* finally found anchorage deep inside Dusky Sound, he parked his ship in deep water, but so close to the forest that a felled tree doubled as a gangplank. The ship's yards, the horizontal poles on the mast from which the sails hung, tangled in the pine trees.

The crew stepped ashore unsteadily, their sea legs making the world wobble. Cook set them to work making a home, having them pitch tents near a clear, cold stream. Seals were discovered, and hunters sent to kill them for their meat and fat, which would be made into lamp oil. Reinhold Forster, a former minister, found greatest comfort in the silence of the woods, where he no longer had to hear the infernal sailors' swearing. The crew felt the same way about him and his whining.

Despite the rain and soggy texture of the forest ground, Dusky Bay constituted a holiday for *Resolution* and her men. They could sleep without fear of a Southern Ocean grander washing over the decks, or the ship bumbling into an iceberg on a moonless night. Their stomachs were full and duties few. Even the most hardened sailor found himself relaxing, admiring the scenery. "I do think that Dusky Bay, for a set of hungry fellows after a long passage at sea, is as good a place as any I've yet met with," wrote the easygoing Charlie Clerke.

But what of sex? Clerke, a playboy of Joseph Banks's caliber, was a bit disappointed with Maori relations. Or, to be more specific, lack of them. Within days of landing, the crew had spied a few natives, but none hostile. When the opportunity presented itself, Cook sailed the pinnace to three Maori standing on a far shore. They all held spears, but Cook ordered the pinnace pressed close to shore. He stepped up onto the rock where the Maori stood and saw that he wasn't looking at the warriors of a tribe, but the elders of a family—a father and his two wives. Cook bent and touched the man's nose with his own in a typical Maori greeting. Friendship born, the family was dining on board *Resolution* within a few days. In addition to the man and his wives, there was a teenaged daughter and son, and three smaller children. To the regret of the crew, this display of local affection did not include the favors of either woman. And while Clerke referred to the daughter as "one jolly wench," he also wrote with a candor steeped in longing that the Maori "did not seem at all inclined to repay them in the kind Indian women in general trade in, and indeed, the kind that's most welcomed I believe by all men after so long an absence from the sex."

Cook, chaste as always while away from Elizabeth, watched with concealed amusement as Clerke and the other "sportsmen" pursued the daughter. She proved the prototypical worldwide teenager, with the sort of firm flesh that attracted men and the same coquettish indifference that fended them off. "They met with," Cook wrote of his men, "indifferent success."

This pleased Cook. Though his discoveries glorified himself and England, his growing connection with the South Pacific granted him an ever-sterner paternal eye toward the locals. Like a benevolent ruler, he wished them the very best quality of life so long as it didn't infringe upon his own goals. And while not a prig or a religious man or even a man of high morals—more than two decades at sea, and months spent in the world's seedier ports, meant Cook had pretty much seen it all—he didn't like local women prostituting their heritage for the pleasure of his men. What would it do to the dynamic of island family life when, after his vessels had sailed away, local men and women took the time to examine what had happened? How would a father feel to know his daughter had given freely to a man outside marriage—or a number of men? Would the local women reject their men or expect payment now that their bodies had a price? Would the men ostracize the women or feel inferior in their presence for being cowed by the might of English swords and guns?

It pained Cook to think that his idyllic Pacific kingdom was being besmirched, even if it meant less frustration on the part of his men. New Zealand held a special place in his heart, and he wrote: "The women of this country I always looked upon to be more chaste than the generality of Indian women. Whatever favours a few of them might have granted to the crew of *Endeavour* it was generally done in a private manner and without the Maori men seeming to interest themselves in it. We debauch their morals already too prone to vice and we introduce among them wants and perhaps diseases which they never before knew and which serves only to disturb the happy tranquility they and their forefathers have enjoyed. If anyone denies the truth of this assertion let him tell me what the natives of the whole extent of America have gained by the commerce they have had with Europeans."

Cook was changing inside, feeling less a member of England's sphere of influence and more a sun around which lesser planets revolved. Elizabeth was the love of his life. That much was true. And James and Nathaniel were fine boys, with Cook making them honorary members of *Resolution's* crew as they had also been on *Endeavour's* roster (in addition to the fatherly side of Cook figuratively sailing with his boys at his side, the practical side of him was granting them seniority at sea—the ship's crew list was an official Royal Navy document, and the two would be credited these years if they ever joined the navy). But Cook was going native, becoming more emotionally tied to his Pacific kingdom than England. This was where he belonged, a fact he had sensed back in London and which stirred greater as he plunged through the Southern Ocean. This place, New Zealand, made him happier than any other place in the world. It was no wonder Cook chose to let the sportsmen be foiled. Their swordplay was spreading a pox throughout Cook's kingdom.

Sexual disappointment aside, *Resolution's* men reveled in Dusky Sound. Morale remained extremely high, even when men contracted colds and fever from extended hours working in the rain. Even Cook took ill at one point, getting caught in a downpour and contracting rheumatic fever. But, as in Batavia, he pushed himself through the sickness, refusing to take a day off. He felt well enough by mid-May to order the ship back to sea. Cook had stayed six weeks in Dusky Sound. The crew was refreshed and even talking longingly of being under sail again. With Southern Hemisphere winter approaching, the days were getting colder and wetter. The retreat was over. It was time to fetch Furneaux, then take on the Pacific.

Resolution sailed from Dusky Sound on May 11, and was anchored alongside *Adventure* in Queen Charlotte's Sound a little less than two weeks later. *Adventure* was, Cook quickly discovered, a vessel in turmoil. Furneaux was turning out to be an indifferent leader, not knowing when to exert his authority and when to let boys be boys. It was obvious to the crew that Lieutenant Scott, a Scotsman commanding the Royal Marines contingent, ignored and even verbally bullied Furneaux. Having a command undermined in such a manner didn't bode well for a long sea passage still in its infancy.

Indeed, *Adventure* was a ship on a collision course with infamy. Shipboard life needed a certain level of discipline, starting with the captain and trickling down through the officers. Furneaux's junior officers were proof of that. Heavy drinking was tolerated in the Royal Navy, even among officers, so long as a man showed up for his watch and didn't fall asleep. Drunken officers, then, were common, and drunken junior officers were known for their roughhousing and wild antics. But what had happened aboard *Adventure* one night in the Southern Ocean had gone beyond accepted mores.

Late one evening, after consuming all their own liquor, the ship's junior officers had drunkenly sought out *Adventure* astronomer William Bayly, who was known to have a private cache of spirits. Furneaux's first and second lieutenants—the two highest-ranking of-

ficers on board after Furneaux—and surgeon began by knocking on
Bayly's door. When that didn't work, they began pounding so loudly
that every man on the ship must have been awake, including
Furneaux. But Bayly pretended he was asleep and Furneaux was so
intent on being popular with his officers that he pretended to hear
nothing. Finally, the young officers—men of college-fraternity age
but forced to contain their libidos for months at a time—used a hammer and chisel to knock out Bayly's hinges. Though Furneaux's cabin
was right next door, he still didn't break up the rabble until after the
officers had pulled Bayly from bed and begun beating him about the
head and shoulders. Even Mr. Andrews, the surgeon, was so desperate for more alcohol that he was threatening to pound Bayly's head
with a hammer.

Cook would have flogged the men harshly and immediately.
Furneaux did nothing. His command was unraveling. Instead of seeing Adventure's journey as a stepping-stone to higher command upon
his return to London, Furneaux quietly chafed under Cook's direction. His every action underscored by this sense of powerlessness,
Furneaux pulled inward emotionally, abrogating responsibility as he
kept more and more to himself and became oblivious to the growing
pandemonium. He was a man adrift, wishing he were home in London, regretting the moment he'd accepted command of Adventure.

On May 19, Cook summoned Furneaux aboard Resolution in
Queen Charlotte's Sound. They hunkered down in the great cabin to
compare ship's logs. Cook had begun to doubt Furneaux's abilities,
but said nothing. Cook was still junior enough in his head that he
gave Furneaux leeway, no matter how outrageous the man's stupidity. It was up to Furneaux to pull himself together. Hopefully, now
that Resolution and Adventure were a pair again Cook would be able to
watch with a closer eye.

But Cook became enraged as he stared at Adventure's log.
Furneaux's records showed Adventure as a vessel beset by scurvy.
Even in Ship's Cove, where antiscorbutics such as wild celery were

plentiful, Furneaux was ignoring Cook's dietary commands. Furneaux didn't force his men to eat anything beyond whatever menu the ship's cook felt like preparing.

Cook wasn't going to meddle in Furneaux's shipboard discipline about drunken junior officers, but defying the scurvy mandate was another matter entirely. Cook immediately dispatched a messenger to *Resolution* ordering one of his personal cooks be reassigned to *Adventure*. If Furneaux wasn't going to impose diet, Cook's proxy most definitely would.

As the two men closed the logbooks that day, Cook addressed another disturbing issue: Furneaux seemed to be under the impression that *Adventure* and *Resolution* would be spending the winter in Queen Charlotte's Sound.

Furneaux looked at Cook strangely. Weren't they?

Furneaux was sure it would be suicidal—too suicidal even for Cook—to explore the Southern Ocean in winter. Back when Furneaux had first arrived in Queen Charlotte's Sound in mid-March, he'd had *Adventure*'s stores unloaded and temporary housing built onshore. He'd ordered an observatory and scurvy quarantine areas constructed in the middle of the sound on the island of Motuara. Furneaux, sure that Cook had impaled *Resolution* on an ice floe somewhere beyond rescue, had authorized trade between his men and the Maori for fish. Just as Furneaux was impotent to stop his ship's surgeon from stealing liquor with a hammer, he also politely ignored grotesque evidence of Maori cannibalism such as severed heads lying in the fishing canoes alongside the day's catch. Like all traditional skippers, Furneaux was following normal procedure for settling into winter quarters for a time of seasonal "ease and quietness." That his next-door neighbors had a taste for human flesh was something he was willing to overlook.

Then three sudden occurrences jolted Furneaux's tranquillity: an earthquake, a second earthquake, and Cook's May 18 arrival. Amazingly, Cook not only sailed into Ship's Cove looking fat and happy, the captain thought winter quarters were the province of cowards and conventional minds. Furneaux was both. He hadn't counted on Cook's gaining "ease and quietness" through six weeks in Dusky Sound. The restless, plump commander sitting at Furneaux's side in his great cabin, comparing ship's logs, was in no mood to stay put. Queen Charlotte's Sound was drab by comparison to Dusky Sound, and Cook couldn't imagine staying any longer than he had to. Cook wanted to press on, impending winter or not. He strongly suggested Furneaux reload his stripped-down ship—immediately.

When Furneaux protested about the coming weather, Cook told him it wouldn't matter. The two captains and their bold crew would tempt winter. Instead of staying in the Southern Hemisphere they would flirt with her temper by sailing east at forty-six degrees south latitude. But only for a few hundred miles, Cook assured the ashen-faced Furneaux. If no land was found by then, both ships would turn north toward Tahiti.

The mention of Tahiti made Furneaux sit up and take notice (in fact, when crews later heard the news, they were overjoyed at the coming "party of pleasure"). But there was more, Cook told Furneaux. The rest of the plan had three steps.

First, instead of sailing home from Tahiti, both vessels would return to Queen Charlotte's Sound for reprovisioning and whatever refitting the carpenters deemed necessary. Then, summer months upon them, *Resolution* and *Adventure* would sail east plunging below the antarctic circle again. The theory of the Southern Continent below the Indian Ocean had been disproved in Cook's mind, but now he would see if it lurked beneath the Pacific.

Second, instead of going home then, the ships would head back to Tahiti for refreshment. Only if Cook was satisfied he'd seen all the Pacific he'd come to see would they head home.

Third and finally, instead of rounding the Horn and running north for England, *Adventure* and *Resolution* would hug the high latitudes below the Horn, then continue all the way across the South

Atlantic to Africa, where they would cross paths with their out-bound route from England. To shut up forever the Dalrymples of the world, and even to deflate the high hopes of Sandwich, Cook was proposing a circumnavigation at the high latitudes. This would irrefutably prove or disprove the existence of Antarctica.

Furneaux blanched. The timid skipper of *Adventure* saw vivid images of his robust floating platform slowly withering away until she was nothing but a plank. This was no glorious voyage of exploration, this was a tedious voyage of discovery. The miles to be sailed far eclipsed those of any previous sailing expedition. Instead of two years or three, Cook was proposing a four-year expedition. He intended to use New Zealand and Tahiti as bases, returning to them again and again to re-supply his vessels before setting out on another circuit of discovery.

To Furneaux, the worst thing was Cook's enthusiasm. It was un-flagging. Cook looked at the map laid across the great cabin's table and stabbed his forefinger here and here, then drew circles and lines connecting two points and wondered aloud what lay between them. This was his passion, his unquenchable romance. What fun—what adventure—lay in racing back to England? That was a known quantity. There, fops like Banks usurped bold men like Cook. But here, on this blue expanse with no known southern boundary, men like Cook and Furneaux controlled their destiny. Cook was never one for reading the great philosophers, but sailing the monstrous, unending, angry, blue and green and black Pacific imbued him with images of self-determination Plato and Aristotle could never have imagined.

Cook laid out his three-part plan in hypothetical terms, even offering it as a "proposal" to Furneaux. Wearily, suddenly missing his family a great deal and wondering if he would ever see the inside of his home again, Furneaux, in Cook's words, "readily agreed." Not with a smile on his face, nor with a hearty handshake for Cook, but tersely. Implicit was the awareness that if anything happened to Cook or *Resolution*, Furneaux was setting his sails for home right away. Cook knew this. But, like Banks before him, Furneaux was a man of great intellect and ability. For optimal results, Cook needed to manage Furneaux as if he were managing a very smart child, telling him exactly what to do and how to do it, but always reminding him quietly he was a child.

Resolution first, then *Adventure*, sailed single file from Queen Charlotte's Sound on June 7. *Adventure's* men had gotten healthy on the enforced diet. They were strong again, ready for whatever lay ahead, though without the cocky air of *Resolution's* crack crew. The men of *Resolution* were exceptional. They knew it because Cook told them so.

Reinhold Forster, whose constant complaining had become such a source of frustration to Cook that he'd stopped listening, started in again with his unsolicited criticisms as soon the vessels were away. Cook's plan to sail the Southern Ocean was unnecessarily dangerous, Forster fumed. Crazy. Doesn't disprove a single one of Dalrymple's theories. Cook ignored him, or at least pretended to. But mindful that Forster was keeping a journal of his own and was quite likely to seek a publisher upon their return to London, Cook made sure to pencil his rationale for future rebuttal. "It may be thought by some an extraordinary step in me to proceed on discoveries as far south as 46 degrees in the very depth of winter, for it must be owned that this is a season by no means favorable for discoveries. It nevertheless appeared to me necessary that something must be done in order to lessen the work I am upon least I should not be able to finish the discovery of the Southern part of the South Pacific Ocean the ensuing summer. Besides, if I should discover any land in my route to the east I shall be ready to begin with the summer to explore it. Setting aside all these considerations, I have little to fear, having two good ships well provided and healthy crews."

A reluctant Furneaux in tow, Cook sailed south of the fortieth parallel for four weeks. The ocean there is an endless mess, all waves and angst—and even more so in winter. The concept of land is a pipe dream. All the professional sailor can do is hunker down and pray the raging seas don't sink his ship or toss him overboard like a fatal hiccup in seaboard life. *Resolution* was battered and bruised. She suffered gale-related mishaps almost nonstop. Two steersmen almost got bucked overboard by the flailing wheel (the steering wheel on a sailing ship was a momentous beast, with handling a matter of proper balance and upper-body strength), but other than the anticipated foul weather, nothing of great interest occurred.

Finally, on July 17, Cook signaled Furneaux that he was turning north. Within days the weather began to get warmer. The crew sensed the tropical air and began to chatter happily of Tahiti's charms.

The only thing giving Cook pause was the diminishing supply of antiscorbutics. The fresh greens from New Zealand were gone, and Cook reverted to the sauerkraut and beer-extract diet. Word came from *Adventure*, however, on a calm day off Pitcairn Island, that scurvy was once again devastating her crew. Twenty men were ill. Ironically, on July 23, *Adventure's* cook—steward of the disease—had died.

Cook exploded. If a more capable man were available, Furneaux would have been relieved of command. His insubordination bordered on stupidity, for his inability to follow simple orders wasn't just endangering the life of his crew but himself. Cook sent a boat from *Resolution* with a new cook, and with written instructions on exactly which steps had to be taken to cure the outbreak. In addition to dietary changes, Cook insisted on higher standards of hygiene. He noted that on *Resolution*, even when sailing the Southern Ocean, bedding and clothing were regularly washed. Walls and decks of sleeping quarters were scrubbed with vinegar and smoked with "fire balls." Furneaux wasn't as diligent, and his men were paying the price. "They have scarce room to stir," Lieutenant Burney wrote of the men in *Adventure's* cramped, dank hold, "and are depressed at the length of the passage."

Burney also wrote of an anonymous midshipman's grumblings. "Nothing hurts him more than this cruise being mentioned as a part of pleasure," Burney noted of the young officers who signed on for glory and the carnal pleasures of Tahiti. "If, he says, they had put it down to the account of hard services, I would have been content and thought myself well off. But to have it set down under the Article of Refreshment is damned hard."

Discovery, the misinformed were learning, was rough work. Glory was the reward, but that was a long way off. While *Adventure's* men slowly accepted this fate and recuperated under a new diet of spruce beer and malt that many found revolting, Cook pushed for Tahiti. He arrived August 17. His men rejoiced, but Cook was deflated, for the tropical kingdom had been decimated by disease. Thanks not only to Cook's last visit four years prior, but subsequent arrivals of French vessels, the carefree spirit of Tahiti's people had been replaced by a scamming, commerce-driven attitude. They swarmed *Resolution* and *Adventure*, stealing anything not nailed down, even before the ships came close enough to anchor. The villages, once Cook went ashore, were depleted. Fresh fruits and vegetables were fewer. Live-stock, especially pigs, which he'd counted on purchasing as a source of food, were in short supply. Cook's kingdom had changed, forever.

CHAPTER 13

Cannibals

Cook stayed in Tahiti just three weeks before sailing west. Everything about the aborted visit thoroughly depressed him, from the drunkenness of his men to the ménage à trois between the despicable John Edgcumbe of the Royal Marines and local King Maritat and his wife—instigated by the Tahitians. Astronomers Wales and Bayly were robbed. It was as if Europe's corruption had transferred itself to Tahiti. Cook had idealized the South Pacific when he was away from it. He'd even considered it the one place on earth his potential was realized. But he began to feel like a man trapped between two worlds—a starstruck outsider in London, a power-loving outsider in the Pacific. No place on earth was home for James Cook.

One bright spot was being remembered as a friend by Chief Ori, whom Cook had met on *Endeavour's* visit. Not only did the two exchange the warmest pleasantries, but Ori made sure Cook received a large quantity of hogs and other provisions—items Cook had been unable to secure. The Tahitians, it seems, had been plundered one too many times by Europeans and had moved their farms inland.

As *Resolution* sailed with her holds resonating with the grunts of almost three dozen live hogs, Cook was glad to be under way. Clerke, however, was saddened. He said good-bye to his local girlfriends and wrote nostalgically of Tahiti before she'd even disappeared behind the quarterdeck. "I must own that it is with some reluctance I bid adieu to these happy isles where I've spent many very happy days, both in the years '69 and '73. In the first place, you live upon and abound in, the very best of pork and sweetest and most salutary of vegetables. In the next place, the women in general are very handsome and very kind, and the men social and the last degree benevolent, so that I'm sure whenever we get among them we may with very great safety say we've got into a very good neighborhood. In short, in my opinion, they are as pleasant and happy spots as this world contains."

Clerke had a contemplative side, and his preference for Tahiti over New Zealand showed the differences between him and Cook. Clerke liked Tahiti for its pleasures of food and free love, and because he was a laid-back young man who didn't take life too seriously. Cook was his direct opposite, the man who enjoyed New Zealand for its functional nature (perfect for resupplying ships) and because it reminded him so much of his childhood home. While Cook stood over the crew, commanding from a distance, third-in-command Clerke was not above tipping a bottle with them.

Yet the pair were becoming the best of friends, with Cook confiding in Clerke as he had done with Gore on *Endeavour's* travels. Cook enjoyed Clerke because he was his opposite, not despite the fact. This yin and yang combination strolled *Resolution's* bridge, a tensionless duo. Veteran members of the crew appreciated the stability this easy arrangement engendered. Cook was obviously mentoring, as he had been mentored.

Despite the last-minute hog presentation, Cook was forced to return to Queen Charlotte's Sound for reprovision. This disappointed him greatly. Without admitting it aloud or even making much more than a cursory note in his journal, Cook had hoped to immediately set out on the trail of Abel Tasman. This competitive push would match Cook's discovery skills against the Dutchman's. Cook was intent on erasing Tasman from the history books, as if the sloppy and tentative nature of his discovery disqualified him from mention. When historians compared the two, they would see Cook's thoroughness, his commitment. In fact, Cook was setting standards of discovery few explorers would ever attempt to challenge. His purpose was to own the history books forever, to etch his name for eternity on these islands he called a kingdom.

The provisioning issue, however, delayed that hope. On his way back to Ship's Cove, Cook retraced Tasman's path only as far as the Tonga group of islands. This cluster of thirty-five islands lay one thousand miles west of Tahiti, and another one thousand north of New Zealand. The Dutch first discovered Tonga in 1616, then Tasman paid a visit in 1643, naming two islands Amsterdam and Middleburg. No European had returned until Cook arrived October 4, 1773.

Cook received the sort of warm welcome he'd once known in Tahiti, with hundreds of boats paddling out to greet the two vessels. The Tongan welcome was devoid of the frantic looting Cook found so distasteful. As a result he renamed the chain the Friendly Islands. Perhaps as a reaction to the Tahitians' debasement, Cook was quick to praise the Tongans when he went ashore. He thought them more serious, better disciplined, and less prone to theft than their island neighbors. The women were even more selective about sleeping with Europeans, a discretion Cook considered akin to membership in a higher social order.

But he had to admit the Tongans and Tahitians were more alike than different. Despite varying customs, skin tone, morals, and languages, Cook was struck most by the similarity in the people he saw on each cluster of islands. Like the Tahitians, Tongans cultivated taro and yams, gathered fruit and coconuts, fished, and raised pigs. They were expert in canoe building and navigation. They used wood and plant fibers to make fishing nets, ropes, and cloth for clothing. Their houses, built of hardwood posts, were walled with lengths of bamboo and plaited palm leaves and roofed with reed thatch. Metal was unknown before the Europeans, but stone was used for utensils and carved into axes, lance points, and religious figures. Wood carving in intricate geometrical patterns was highly developed on many of the islands. The religion of the Polynesians, still practiced, is a form of animism—worship of animals and natural objects believed to possess supernatural powers. A supreme deity, Io, is also revered. The practice of religion as a moral code is largely conditioned by the system of taboo.

Adding *anthropologist* to his quiver of titles, Cook came to what, for him, was an extraordinary conclusion. "By carefully perusing the voyages of former navigators I find such an affinity in the language, manners and customs of the different islanders that I am led to believe that have had one origin." The thought was not unique—Dalrymple had written as much in one of his books, *Voyages*. The extraordinary element came in the fact that Cook stated it without conclusive evidence. Cook's rigid mind was opening, becoming more flexible—or, perhaps, sloppier. Pondering all this, for it had been a pet theory since *Endeavour*, Cook left Tonga on October 8 and sailed toward the loving arms of Queen Charlotte, *Adventure* in tow. Theories about the origin of Polynesians filled him, though, and he made a mental note to pursue it further on his next swing through the islands.

Furneaux chose the moment to make a last, fateful mistake. It all began when *Resolution* tacked into Cook Strait. A gale blew up just as both ships passed the strait's Cape Farewell entrance. Cook chose to fight the storm and navigate into the shelter of the strait's numerous inlets. Furneaux thought Cook's maneuver risky. *Adventure* had become porous, with water seeping into the hold requiring constant pumping. A sharp storm might wreck her.

Three miles behind *Resolution* when the storm began, Furneaux reefed his sails and let the wind drive *Adventure* north and east rather than fight. *Adventure* was off New Zealand's North Island when the storm abated, tacking into stiff winds and tall seas. When

Furneaux finally fought his way back to the coast, he was forced to find safe harbor and reprovision. "On the 4th of November," Furneaux journalized, giving insight into *Adventure*'s misery, "we again got in shore near Cape Palliser and was visited by a number of the natives in their canoes with a great quantity of crayfish, which we bought off them for nails and Otaheite cloth. The next day it blew hard from WNW, which again blew us off the coast and obliged us to bring to for two days, during which time it blew one continual gale of wind with very heavy squalls of sleet. By this time our decks were very leaky, the people's bed and bedding wet, and we began to despair of ever getting into Charlotte's Sound or joining *Resolution*."

The late-spring squall was so long and severe, it would take until November 25, almost a month, for *Adventure* to regain the strait and enter Queen Charlotte's Sound. To Furneaux's distress and relief, Cook had come and gone, sailing for the antarctic circle four days earlier. He didn't expect Furneaux to follow. "I had several times communicated my thoughts on the subject to Captain Furneaux," Cook journalized of his desire to explore the high latitudes. "At first he seemed not to approve of it, but was inclinable to get to the Cape of Good Hope. Afterwards, he seemed to come to my opinion; I, however . . . cannot guess how Captain Furneaux will act."

Just in case Furneaux chose to follow orders, however, Cook had buried plans for his intended course in a bottle at the base of a tree, then announced their location by carving a message into the trunk: LOOK UNDERNEATH.

Cook's buried message informed Furneaux that *Resolution* would be making a giant loop through the Pacific in search of Antarctica's coast. From Queen Charlotte's Sound he would plunge south into the high latitudes and travel east as far as the tip of South America, then curve up and around with the prevailing winds, sailing north and west all the way back to Queen Charlotte's Sound. Cook didn't want to be hindered by time constraints as he made this ambitious (and potentially suicidal, for Cook was guiding *Resolution* back into the Southern Ocean's pack ice and ship-killing waves) trip, but the note hinted that *Resolution* might end up sometime in March at either Easter Island (just two thousand miles off the lower South American coast) or Tahiti. This being uncertain, Cook did not propose a rendezvous, but hinted at a chance meeting should Furneaux follow his path.

Furneaux was in a quandary. He could tell Cook was impatient, ready to explore with just one vessel. Otherwise he wouldn't have sailed from Ship's Cove without *Adventure*. Cook was also Furneaux's boss, and his reports to the Admiralty at journey's end would determine whether Furneaux rose in rank or prestige.

But Cook had commanded neither meeting nor specific course of action, which gave Furneaux wiggle room. Furneaux decided against sailing to either the Easter Island or Tahiti meeting sites. With *Adventure* and *Resolution* having been at sea for over a year, Furneaux and his undisciplined crew were getting antsy to return to England. The last thing Furneaux wanted to do was sail to a remote island and wait several months for Cook.

Furneaux's plan was to make a beeline from New Zealand across the Pacific to Cape Horn. For the sake of ship's logs and later Admiralty inquisition, he would sail in the high latitudes as a sign that he'd attempted to follow Cook.

However, if *Resolution* and *Adventure* didn't stumble into one another by the time Furneaux arrived at South America, he would consider his search for Cook finished and sail directly to England.

Furneaux didn't relish a journey through the high latitudes, but realized it was necessary. If *Adventure* simply followed the shortest, most unadventurous route back to England—say, traveling across the Pacific at thirty-five degrees south latitude instead of sixty-five degrees south latitude—not only would Cook lambaste Furneaux, but whispers of cowardice would inevitably follow him the rest of his days.

Adventure's leaks were getting worse. Instead of braving the Southern Ocean in a flawed vessel, Furneaux had her hauled ashore, stripped down, and repaired. To his credit, the normally complacent disciplinarian cracked the whip on his crew to do the work with all haste. Summer in the Southern Hemisphere meant he could follow Cook into the Southern Ocean, but only by leaving Queen Charlotte's Sound as soon as possible. On December 17, Furneaux was ready to set sail. As a last act before leaving New Zealand, Furneaux remembered he needed to stock up on antiscorbutics. Cook had made it clear he would tolerate no more scurvy on *Adventure*. And so Furneaux sent *Adventure*'s cutter to a bay on the other side of the sound to collect a last provision of wild celery and "scurvy grass." Indeed, this was the spot Cook had named Grass Cove.

Master's mate John Rowe was in command. Nine other men were on board. The cutter made its way to shore. What should have been an easy afternoon's work stretched into the next day. Furneaux, fearing that they'd been swept onto a rocky stretch of coastline, sent Lieutenant James Burney in the launch to fetch them.

What Burney found that warm December afternoon would stay with him the rest of his life. Wading ashore at Grass Cove, he saw shoes, clothing, two severed hands (one was Rowe's; the other, marked by the tattoo T.H., was obviously Thomas Hill's), and large baskets of cooked human flesh. The head of Furneaux's servant, a black man, lay on the sand. Walking over a small rise, he witnessed the remains of several friends being barbecued. It was "such a shocking scene of carnage and barbarity as can never be mentioned or thought of, but with horror," Burney wrote later. "The heads, hearts and lungs of several of our people were seen lying on the beach, and, at a little distance, the dogs gnawing their entrails."

In a rage, Burney fired musket shots into the crowd of Maori around the campfire. Returning to the beach, he destroyed three canoes in a futile act of vengeance, then, with night falling and fearing for his own safety, he guided the cutter back to *Adventure*.

Furneaux spent a restless night plotting whether to seek revenge or simply leave. Ball from the ship's guns would destroy a village, or at least killed enough men to make the Maori think twice about eating an Englishman again. In the end, Furneaux chose to sail rather than fight. The skipper and his numb crew had no intention of searching for Cook as they sailed into the high latitudes. They just wanted to go home.

Meanwhile, on December 20, Cook was at sixty-six degrees south latitude, the imaginary dotted circle on the globe marking the antarctic circle. Conditions were frigid and harsh. The ship's ropes were so thick with ice that they wouldn't slide through the blocks. The sails were hard as steel, hardly capable of billowing. Sleet deluged the decks, coating the men in their fearnoughts, so that those working had the appearance of mobile snowmen. Cook retreated in the face of the bad weather, crossing back above the antarctic circle on Christmas morning.

Despite the weather, the latitude, and Cook's ambition, Royal Navy Christmas Day tradition called for celebration. Cook hove to in the calmest seas he could find, ordering a double ration of pudding for all hands, then tapped the brandy casks. Sailors reeled belowdecks drunkenly as *Resolution* floated aimlessly through a field of a hundred shining icebergs. Normally, there would have been a bare-chested shipboard boxing competition, but the weather was just too cold.

Over the next two days, as the men struggled with their epic hangovers, the temperature dropped even lower. Icicles hung from men's noses and eyelashes. So much ice choked the rigging that a man's hand was barely wide enough to grasp it. Loose ice floated about the sea, and Cook was preoccupied with dodging it, sailing in a zigzag fashion. Even when he was able to break free from the ice fields into open water, icebergs bobbed everywhere. Clerke counted 250 one day, some as tall as two hundred feet out of the water. At one point, frail wooden *Resolution* sailed so close to one berg that all

hands were called on deck and given spars to push her off the floating mountain.

As 1773 became 1774, Cook was frustrated, increasingly detached
emotionally, and driven to find Antarctica at all costs. When a midshipman drunkenly drew his knife on two other crew members,
Cook took out his wrath on the young man, ordering him brought
belowdecks for a lashing instead of a lesser punishment that might
have boosted crew morale.

Finally, in the early days of January, Cook turned *Resolution*
around. The crew had long ago tired of the fierce weather and glee-
fully took the northward course as a sign that their antarctic days
were behind them. The People were sure Cape Horn, and then England, were their next destinations. But though Cook had flirted
with the antarctic coast, he had never actually seen it. Until he conclusively proved or disproved the existence of Antarctica, Cook
couldn't return to England. He needed to venture south again.

On January 11, much to the crew's horror, Cook ordered *Resolution*
to make a sharp turn toward Antarctica. "All our hopes were blasted
in a minute," a crew member later recalled of their horror as Cook
gave the order. "There was a buzz about the ship and a very severe
mortification for the sailors."

Cook's action came even as stores ran so low he had to cut rations
to two-thirds. If the order to explore the high latitudes while reduc-
ing food wasn't enough to kill the People's morale, the weather and
the cold certainly were. For the Southern Ocean was experiencing
storms the likes of which Cook and his men had never experienced.
Seas ran so high that cabins on the upper decks were swamped with
freezing water during some storms. Snow blasted *Resolution*, leaving
behind a thin film of white and sleet. Strangely, there were no ice
floes to dodge, so Cook pushed farther and farther south. January 26
found *Resolution* crossing the antarctic circle once again, but this
time farther to the east. To Cook's astonishment and the People's relief, land was sighted the same day.

But the vision turned out to be a mere cloudbank on the far horizon, so a disappointed Cook gave the order to push onward. He would sail so far south in this brave gamble that only two explorers in history have duplicated the feat since (James Weddell on his trip of 1822–24, and James Clark Ross aboard the *Terror* on his 1839–43 voyage. Both men accomplished this in the South Atlantic; only Cook pushed as far south in the Pacific). Cook was astonished at the increasing latitude, but kept his southerly course because no ice yet waited to stop him.

On January 30, 1774, at 4 A.M. in the bright sunshine of the antarctic summer, the sea began to freeze around him. Cook was forced to turn around. Realizing that he would never sail so far south again, Cook ran to the bow, clambered to the very end of the bowsprit, and waved his hat in exultation. His dream had seen a magnificent outcome: Cook had truly gone farther than any man had ever gone.

Though Reinhold Forster journalized that the vista "looked like the wreck of a shattered world, or as poets describe some regions of hell," Cook positively rhapsodized in his journal.

"A little after 4 am," Cook wrote, "we perceived the clouds to the south near the horizon of an unusual snow white brightness which denounced our approach to field ice. Soon after it was seen from the masthead and at 8 o'clock we were close to the edge of it which extended east and west in a straight line far beyond our sight; as appeared by the brightness of the horizon, in the situation we were now in just the southern half of the horizon was enlightened by the reflected rays of the ice to a considerable height. The clouds near the horizon were of a perfect snow whiteness and were difficult to be distinguished from the ice hills whose lofty summits reached the clouds. The outer or northern edge of immense ice field was composed of loose or broken ice so close packed together that nothing could enter it. About a mile in began the firm ice, in one compact solid body and seemed to increase in height as you travel it to the south. In this field we counted ninety-seven ice hills or mountains, many of them vastly large. I will not say it is impossible anywhere to get in among this ice, but I will assert that the bare attempting of it would be a very dangerous enterprise and what I believe no man in my situation would have thought of. I, whose ambition leads me not only farther than any man has gone before me, but as far as I think it possible for man to go, was not sorry at meeting with this interruption, as it in some measure relieved us from the dangers and hardships, inseparable with navigation of the southern polar regions. Since therefore we could not proceed one inch farther south, no other reason need be assigned for our tacking and stretching back to the north, being at the time in the latitude of 71 degrees, 10 minutes south, longitude 106 degrees, 54 minutes."

Cook would revise the journal later, adding his assumption that "the ice extends all the way to the pole or perhaps joins to some land." Strangely, Cook was well inside the boundaries of the Antarctic landmass, but in an indented portion. He had discovered Antarctica without even knowing it.

The journal writings were further evidence of Cook's emotional estrangement from London. He had always carefully concealed his ambition, lest it put more powerful men on the defensive. Now Cook was saying it didn't matter—he was the very best. No other explorer came close. Cook not only knew it but he wasn't shy anymore about saying it.

Cook weighed his next ambitious step. The crew was tired and hungry, water stores were running low, and winter was approaching. Cook gave orders to steer for Tahiti by way of Easter Island. From there, he would pursue Tasman's path through the western Pacific once again, this time wiping the Dutchman from the history books once and for all.

On Sunday, February 6, he wrote of his plans. "Many of those formerly discovered," he noted of the Pacific's islands, "within the Southern Tropic are very imperfectly explored and their situation as imperfectly known. All these things considered, and more especially as I had a good ship, a healthy crew, and no want of stores or provisions, I thought I could do no better than to spend the ensuing winter in the tropics. . . . I next intend to get within the tropics and proceed to the west on a route differing from former navigators, touching at, and setting the situation of, such isles as we may meet with."

Then Cook broke down. His body was emotionally and physically exhausted, and unable to fight off the effects of little food and severe weather. Succumbing to flu and incessant vomiting, Cook took to bed. Unlike at Dusky Sound, there would be no bravery, no attempt to ignore illness. Cook could barely walk, let alone clamber up the gangway to the quarterdeck. There was no fresh meat on board, so Reinhold Forster's beloved dog was butchered. The meat and a soup from the bones were fed to Cook. The protein fortified him, and he slowly regained his strength.

On March 11, Easter Island came over the horizon. Cook had just shown signs of recovery. Some of the men still harbored the pipe dream Cook would fill stores there and then backtrack to the Horn. Morale was at an all-time low. Cook heard and ignored the grumbling, as always keeping his own counsel. His ability to step inside the head of an able seaman and anticipate those fears and worries was slipping. Focus brought selfishness brought myopia brought heartlessness. Men who'd sworn lifelong allegiance to Cook began having a hard time defending his actions.

Cook went ashore to search for stores. Thirteen-mile-long Easter Island sits two thousand miles from the coast of South America. It was first explored by Dutch navigator Jacob Roggeveen on Easter Sunday, 1722. Called Rapa Nui by the locals, the triangular island was formed by three volcanoes now extinct. The island is warm throughout the year due to benevolent trade winds. Unfortunately for Cook and the men of *Resolution*, coming off three hard months on reduced rations, indigenous vegetation consists mainly of grasses, and the prime source of freshwater is rainfall collected from the crater lakes.

Cook was ravenous with hunger and slowly succumbing to even more illness. All he cared for was resupplying food and water—though he still found the energy to explore the odd statues and stones dotting Easter Island's hillsides. Known as megaliths, archaeological and botanical evidence suggests that the island's original South American occupants built them. The ancestors of the Polynesian population Cook found on the island traveled in canoes from the Marquesas Islands, then massacred the original inhabitants. Over six hundred statues were on the island at the time of the invasion. Material for the statues was quarried from the crater called Rano Raraku. The largest of the statues were called *ahus* and were burial platforms that supported rows of statues. *Ahus* were situated with a sea view. Many of the statues on the burial platforms bore cylindrical, brimmed crowns of red tuff, with the largest crown weighing approximately twenty-seven metric tons. Frenzied by the slaughter, eager to put their mark on their new home, the Polynesians had toppled and destroyed almost all of them.

If Cook, his crew, and his ship had been less tattered, he might have lingered to explore the strange and mysterious island. But Cook's fervent desire, that this remote island offer at least freshwater and produce, was meeting a dead end. "Got on board a few casks of water and traded with the natives for some of the produce of the island which appeared in no great plenty and the water so as not to be worth carrying on board, and the ship not in safety determined me to shorten my stay here."

Cook announced they were pushing on to Tahiti. Instead of being thrilled, the People were shattered by the news. Not privy to Cook's plans, they had assumed he would continue eastward, and eventually home, after his plunges beneath the antarctic circle. That was the way things were done. Ships of circumnavigation didn't backtrack or make great loops upon the world's largest body of water. They left England and sailed west until they were home again, or left

England and sailed east until they were home again. The circuit through Tahiti and Tonga was permissible—a little jaunt through paradise was the reason most men had signed on. But for Cook to push all the way from New Zealand to an area of the high southern latitudes roughly due south of Mexico City—and then not continue home—was absurd. Morale plunged. The crew was facing at least another eighteen months at sea.

For the first time in his career, Cook had entirely lost touch with his crew—not lost their respect nor admiration, but that human connection linking all men with one another. His fantastic views on discovery and his Pacific kingdom were making him a crusader for exploration without regard to the well-being of himself or others. He had pushed the limits of exploration so far he had burst out the other side. Not having an example of what to do next, he'd turned inward. It was a crucial turning point. This is when Cook began the self-aggrandizement and myopia that led to his fall.

As if reacting to this fundamental change, Cook got sick again and stayed in bed for three weeks shortly after pushing away from Easter Island. Near oblivious to the hunger and sickness all around him, the low morale, and the lack of motivation, Cook had become an exploring machine. His will was proving stronger than his body, though sickness seemed to make him all the more determined. Cook saw his career's end looming. He was forty-five in 1773—by the time he got home, wrangled another command, and returned to the Pacific, he'd be fifty, far too old by conventional wisdom for such a voyage. *Resolution's* second lap around the Pacific, therefore, was possibly the last chance he would get to prove himself. It was not enough to find big islands such as Tahiti or New Zealand or New South Wales. Cook was on a mission to find the scattered assortment in between, connecting the dots of civilization as he sailed. He was discovering it all.

On April 6, 1774, when Cook stumbled across the Marquesas Islands between Easter Island and Tahiti, there was cause for jubilation.

No explorer since Àlvaro de Mendaña in 1595 had seen the gorgeous black lava peaks rising straight and tall from the sea, or the wondrous greenery of her interior. Cook was cranky and tired as *Resolution* anchored just outside a small harbor. When natives approached the ship in their lateen-sailed canoes, then refused to give anything in return for a gift of nails, he didn't continue merrily on his way. Instead, a surly Cook fired a musket at them. The shot fell short.

Matters improved between *Resolution* and the Marquesans when it was discovered that red feathers were the Marquesans' most valued currency—simple red feathers, such as the crew had discovered in Tonga. With a red feather a sailor could buy almost anything. Trade thus established, Cook had water casks filled ashore. Several pigs were purchased. And in spite of early difficulties, Cook came to see the Marquesans as the most handsome and intelligent race yet encountered.

Clerke, something of a connoisseur, found the Marquesan women the most beautiful in all the South Pacific. They dressed casually, wrapping a narrow strip of cloth around their waists, connected to a revealing length of fabric draped around their shoulders. Clerke, in the midst of his third voyage to the South Pacific (before Cook, one aboard *Dolphin*), was one of the few members of the crew in no hurry to return to London. In addition to sharing Cook's rootless bent, Clerke needed only to look at the bare breasts on display to be certain that no playboy in London's continuum of bodices and ruffles ever had it so good.

In a similar vein, Clerke found time to write about the predisposition of Marquesan men to decorate their penises. "They do not care one farthing for any article of dress that could not in some form be made to contribute to the decorating of that favorite part. I gave one of them one day a stocking—he very deliberately put it on here—I then gave him a medal, which he immediately hung to it—in short let that noble part be well-decorated and fine. They're perfectly happy and totally indifferent about the state of all the rest of the body."

Resolution sailed from the Marquesas on April 12, then dropped anchor in Tahiti again on April 22. Cook had chosen a most inopportune time to return: war. His good friends in Matavai Bay were preparing an invasion. "The vessels of war consisted of 160 large double canoes, very well equipped, manned and armed. Although I am not sure that they had on board either their full complement of fighting men or rowers, I rather think not. The chief and all those on the fighting stages were dressed in their war habits—that is in a vast quantity of cloth, turbans, breastplates and helmets. Some of the latter are of such a length as to great encumber the wearer . . . their vessels were decorated with flags, streamers and other so that the whole made a grand and noble appearance such as was never before seen in this sea. Their implements of war were clubs, pikes, and stones. Besides these vessels of war there were 170 sail of smaller double canoes, all with a little house upon them and rigged with masts and sails, which the others had not. In the war canoes were no sorts of provision whatever. In these 330 canoes I judged there were no less than 7,760 men."

If Cook had found Tahiti debauched and dissipated on his visit the year before, any remaining image of the luscious, serene island was shattered forever as he sailed into Matavai Bay that April day. Despite his fondness for the islands and her light-fingered people, Cook had to admit he'd viewed them in a very one-dimensional fashion—the noble savage—when first meeting them years before. He had seen the women as promiscuous, the men as uncaring, and the whole society as a throwback to a more virtuous time when mankind was closer to nature, childlike. Pure.

Through Cook's years of visitation, he had come to see the Tahitians as a complex people. He'd noted on a prior visit that not all the women were licentious. Indeed, he wrote that just as many women kept their marital vows sacred as women in London, and just as large a proportion turned to prostitution. Where he'd once thought the islands a fertile paradise providing an unlimited supply of produce and pork, he'd found on his last visit that there was a limit. Undeniably, Cook knew European ships were depleting all that was plentiful and pure in Tahiti.

Now he was seeing Tahitian warriors mounting an incredible assault force. On *Endeavour's* journey Cook had been puzzled by Tahiti's multi-tiered leadership system and thought them incapable of organization. Now he was seeing thousands of Tahitian warriors in specially designed canoes preparing to maim and kill. The force was disciplined, prepared, like something out of ancient Sparta. The men were not only aggressive, but also keen for conquest. The peaceful culture and endless bacchanal Cook had admired now seemed to have vanished. It occurred to Cook that not even his crew would be safe if the Tahitians—or any other native culture—rose against them. "They are very sensible to the superiority they have over us in numbers," Cook would write with prescience, "and no one knows what an enraged multitude might do."

Yet *Resolution* anchored amid the frenzy, untouchable. After months of hard sailing, his authority unquestionable, Cook had forgotten that he had once been respectful of and deferential to the Tahitians. He was like a floating deity on Matavai Bay's aquamarine waters, too powerful with his cannon and iron for even ten thousand Tahitian men to overwhelm. If the setting had been ancient Rome, he would have been the detached emperor finding entertainment in gladiators battling to the death. In Cook's mind he ruled the Tahitians and expected unconditional worship. His men would use the women for release. His ships would use Tahitian food and water and even the fresh, clean air as provision and refreshment, before setting out onto the Pacific again.

The anthropologist in Cook wondered if this was how his South Pacific kingdom had once been settled. Warriors in canoes risking open ocean for conquest. The women would come later and the seed would be planted. That mysterious red-feather affectation would be incorporated. In time, his gut emotion would be ruled correct. The Pacific was found to be separated into three separate kingdoms: Polynesia, Melanesia, and Micronesia. The Tahitians, of course, were Polynesian (Greek for "many islands"). They had been established in the Malay Archipelago about the second century B.C. when they were driven eastward by Malayan invaders. By the thirteenth and fourteenth centuries they occupied the territory they now inhabit.

Cook didn't have the time or inclination to follow the lineage that far. But it was from Cook's intellectual outline that future anthropologists would begin their detective work. The burgeoning creative thinker in Cook recorded his observations in his best descriptive prose. He interviewed participants or had them interviewed. He took pains to be specific about a tribe's origin from "the districts of Attahourou and Ahopatea." He counted ships and men—one imagines Cook on the quarterdeck with a journalist's notebook and pencil in hand, dotting the air with his pencil, tallying—and anguishing over word selection. In his spare moments he rewrote, aware that his words would someday be bound and sold to an English public aching to know of his adventures.

As on her prior visit, *Resolution* stayed in Tahiti just three weeks. Beckoned by the southeast trades, and disillusioned by the jaded little island, Cook aimed his ship westward. While his men bade a sad farewell to Matavai Bay, relatively sure Cook had no plans to return again on this cruise, gunner's mate John Marra was overwhelmed with longing. He was leaving behind a special girl and had hoped to make a family in Tahiti. Marra, a pale Irishman, quietly slipped over the side and began swimming for a waiting canoe. Unfortunately he picked a poor moment to desert, because his buddies could clearly see him swimming—a lone man's white arms churning the waters of the bright blue bay. All were quite jealous that Marra had had the nerve to attempt what they wanted to do—but were afraid to. So they made sure Cook found out. Cook dispatched a boat. A lovesick Marra was fished from the sea. Marines sat Marra down and began rowing him back to *Resolution*, but the Irishman leapt overboard. Once again the marines pulled Marra from the bay, but this time less gently. Marra was rowed back to *Resolution*. To the laughter and heckling of his shipmates Marra was paraded before Cook. His motivations, the dripping and bruised Marra explained, were anthropological. He wanted to live among the Tahitians to record their way of life, then return to London on a later vessel and write a book about them. His shipmates all had a good laugh at Marra's story.

Before *Resolution*, Cook had shown constant benevolence to his fellow man. A benevolence born of indifference, but benevolence nonetheless. But command was changing him. His unquestioned authority was making him selfish, mean. So when Marra was brought before him, Cook remarked casually that if only Marra had asked for permission to remain in Tahiti, it would have been granted. But because Marra had attempted desertion, he had lost his chance forever. Then Cook ordered Marra thrown in chains until Tahiti was well over the horizon.

The rub was Cook's jealousy. For all his feelings of omnipotence in the South Pacific, Cook was still emotionally tied to England. He couldn't shake it any more than he could slip out of his skin. His beloved Elizabeth was there. His boys. His mother had died, but his widowed father had to be thought of. And there were the men of the Admiralty—Sandwich, Palliser, Stephens—Cook was so desperate to please. Finally, there was that all-important legacy Cook was keen to put a polish on. While he longed to do just as Marra—on his own terms, though, with a sailing ship for mobility and cannon for power and men to do his bidding—Cook could not realistically dream of staying in his kingdom forever. A very long rope connected him with England, and sooner or later he would be yanked home to the little red-brick house on Mile End Road, from where he would walk to the Admiralty or Deptford or just Will's Coffee House, with its comforting smells of tobacco and thick coffee.

The side of Cook that wished to remain in the South Pacific would always be defeated by reason. The legacy would be destroyed if Cook announced to all hands that *Resolution* wasn't returning to England. He would forever be known around the Admiralty, and eventually in British history, as the discoverer who had lost his mind and been seduced by the islands. To make matters worse, he wouldn't be left alone with his boat and his guns and his kingdom, but would eventually be tracked down by another British ship. Royal Marines would throw him facedown on the sand and clap the chains on. It might even be his own boys, James and Nathaniel, grown and bitter and making good on some vow to their sorrow-filled mother. Then Cook would be thrown in the hold and returned forcibly to England, where he would be hanged as an example to all.

Cook used the power of the pen to voice his frustration. What he saw in Marra was a man no different from himself. "I kept the man in confinement till we were clear of the isles, then dismissed him without any other punishment. For when I considered the situation of the man in life I did not think him so culpable as it may at first appear. He was an Irishman by birth, a good seaman, and had sailed both in the English and Dutch service. I picked him up at Batavia in my return home from my last voyage, and he had remained with me ever since."

Then Cook zeroes in. "I never learned that he had either friends or connection that confine him to any particular part of the world, all nations were alike to him, where can such a man spend his days better than at one of these isles where he can enjoy all the necessaries and some of the luxuries of life in ease and plenty. I know not if he might have obtained my consent if he had applied for it in the proper time."

In this pensive mood, Cook began making plans for his return to England. He was Cinderella, anticipating midnight's tock. Instead of ruminating, however, he decided it was best to make the most of his remaining time.

Cook set off on a five-month wander around the western Pacific, from May to October 1774, always staying below the equator. First stop was Tonga and the Friendly Isles for another peek at the grand people. *Resolution* passed by the island of Tofua and its imposing volcano, belching smoke and rendering the island air gray and sulfur-smelling. Some fifteen years later this imaginary dotted line on the map would be the exact spot of the infamous mutiny on the *Bounty*. Fletcher Christian's original intention was to leap overboard and float on a handmade raft to Tofua, not knowing the natives were warlike and would have killed him instantly. Instead he led the mutiny. Nineteen men, including Bligh, were set adrift in a small boat with few provisions. Following his knowledge of currents and celestial navigation, surviving on rainwater and seagulls and fish, Bligh brought the nineteen to safety. They put ashore at Timor in the Malay Archipelago, 3,618 miles from where they'd been stranded. He and the men who were loyal to him returned to England. In 1808 a settlement at Pitcairn Island in the South Pacific was discovered. The settlement had been established in 1790 by nine of the mutineers along with six male and twelve female Polynesians whom the mutineers had brought from Tahiti.

The connection with Cook would be twofold. First, Bligh would be master on *Resolution*'s fatal second voyage. Second, Cook's old friends Banks and Sandwich would be the driving force behind *Bounty*'s voyage of botanical experimentation. Though Banks didn't sail on *Bounty*, he effectively commissioned it and would call on Sandwich yet again for assistance in making a harebrained scheme reality.

That historical aside was a long time off when *Resolution* sailed past Tofua. Cook was now firmly on Tasman's trail, in that section of the Pacific directly east of the Coral Sea.

At Niue (pronounced "Nee-oo-ay") Island, halfway between Tonga and undiscovered Rarotonga, a native threw a spear at Cook as he searched for stores. The native missed, which didn't stop Cook from renaming the place Savage Island.

If Cook followed a straight line west from Niue, he would stay on Tasman's trail. But where the Dutchman continued past New Guinea, to Batavia, Cook began sailing a counterclockwise turn southeast.

Toward home. His immediate goal was one last visit to Queen Charlotte's Sound—he obviously knew nothing of Furneaux's misadven-
ture—to resupply, but there would be no more westward ho.

Off Tasman's trail, Cook began chasing a more obscure explorer, Fernandes de Queirós. The Portuguese had stumbled across something
called Australia del Espíritu Santo in 1605. This was the principal island in a chain of seventy volcanic islands Cook renamed the New Hebrides. He chose the moniker not only in honor of the rugged Scottish
islands, but to give the islands a British cast and wipe out any record
that an explorer other himself had set foot there on July 21, 1774.

Cook didn't like the place much, though. He thought the people
skinny and noted that most were covered with skin diseases. The air
was hot and oppressive. The land was black and wet, forest-covered.
Rain fell almost constantly, giving the islands and their lively volcanoes
a gloomy tinge. It was as if *Resolution* had sailed into the underworld.

Ironically, the locals believed the white-skinned Cook and his
men all to be ghosts. Though vegetation was everywhere, they offered Cook a token amount of trade. It was more like an offering intended to feed the dead in their long journey through the afterworld
rather than sustenance—a pig, stray greens, a trickle of water.

The misunderstanding came to a head when Cook had some
marines row him ashore. Cook stepped out of the boat alone, carrying greenery from a local tree as a makeshift olive branch. No matter
that the people of New Hebrides had no heritage equating olive
branches with peace, it was the thought that mattered.

A mob carrying clubs, darts, stones, and bows and arrows waited
where sand met jungle. Cook walked to them alone, green branch
extended. He would wow them with his presence, hand over the
green branch and a pocketful of trinkets, and commence trade, with
worship of the new white godhead to follow at a later hour. At least
that was the plan.

Instead, the mob stepped forward to meet the ghost and make sure
it was quite dead. While they were at it, the mob coveted the ghost's

rowboat. Cook, his mind always comparing his actions with those of one explorer or another, thought of Magellan and the way he had stood tall against the men of Cebu and their phallic hardware. Carefully, in a Magellan-like manner, Cook walked backward down the beach. The locals followed. A chief led them. He instructed the mob to form a semi-circle around the boat's bow. Cook ordered the boat away, and even as his men complied, the mob tried to haul it back onshore. Cook grabbed a musket and fired into the crowd. The gun malfunctioned, however, and all that came forth was a mighty click. The New Hebrideans shrugged, looked at Cook as if he were a crazy man with a very silly weapon, and then began advancing again. This "made it absolutely necessary for me to give the orders to fire," and the New Hebrideans retreated up the beach with four of their own dead on the sand.

Cook and his men began rowing frantically back to *Resolution*. The locals began firing darts and bows and arrows. Two of Cook's men were struck, neither seriously. This was Cook's welcome to Melanesia, clearly a region not as conducive to worshiping him as Polynesia.

With the Pacific turning from friendly paradise to hostile battleground, Cook began the turn eastward that would take him home. He stumbled across another island, named it New Caledonia after the Roman word for Scotland; found yet another new island and called it Norfolk, "in honor of that noble family"; then sailed for Queen Charlotte's Sound. He arrived on October 17, on a glorious spring day. Cook stayed for three weeks, glad to see that Furneaux had found the message in the hidden bottle, but disturbed by quiet murmurs of recent cannibalism, eagerly spread by a tribe farther up the sound.

Still ruminating on whether the rumors were true, Cook sailed from Queen Charlotte's Sound on November 10, 1774, bound eastward for Cape Horn, Cape of Good Hope, and London.

CHAPTER 14

The Forbidden Lands

Cook raced across the Pacific. With the prevailing winds behind her, *Resolution* took just five weeks to travel from Queen Charlotte's Sound to the southern coast of Chile. Even Cook was in no mood to explore his Pacific kingdom further or to continue his search for antarctic landfall. "I now gave up all hope of finding any more land in this ocean and came to a resolution to steer directly for the west entrance of the Straits of Magellan, with a view of coasting the out, or south, side of Tierra del Fuego, round Cape Horn to Strait le Maire. I have now done with the Southern Pacific Ocean and flatter myself that no one will think that I have left it unexplored, or that more could have been done in one voyage towards obtaining that end has been done in this," he wrote wearily.

During the trek eastward, Cook had time to ponder the troubling things he'd seen and heard in Queen Charlotte's Sound. The Maori, for starters, behaved strangely—first by hiding from *Resolution*, then by cavorting rather giddily once Cook acted as if nothing was on his mind. There were the rumors of cannibalism. When confronted, the local Maori shook their heads and laughed at their misinformed hosts. No, Cook and his men were told, that was *another* bunch of sailors who were eaten. Not British. Those English shirts and pants seen worn by a few of the natives were a product of trade.

Cook knew better than to disbelieve the cannibalism rumors. Indeed, when John Marra found true love once again—this time with a Maori woman—and wanted to make Queen Charlotte's Sound his new home, Cook had him lashed just for thinking about it. Then Cook grumbled to Clerke that he would have let the fool stay, except he would have been dead and eaten within a week. Cook couldn't let that happen.

But for beloved Queen Charlotte's Sound to feel like hostile territory, especially on the heels of Cook's Melanesia treatment, was too much. It was as if the walls were closing in on Cook and *Resolution*, or that all the Pacific's far-flung peoples had found a way to communicate, warning one another that the white man wasn't a god, but an exploiter and gun-toting killer. Cook and his men had entered a more confrontational stage of their relationship with the Pacific, and Cook didn't like it. His kingdom used to be so placid, so easy to rule. Now his people were revolting.

After *Resolution* was patched up—the pitch and tar were long gone, so the carpenters and caulkers used gunner's chalk and galley fat to plug her leaks—Cook was immediately away. He didn't give Furneaux much thought, except to assume his fellow captain had gone home as quickly as possible. Cook was deeply disappointed with Furneaux and made a vow to himself that if ever there was another voyage, the commander of the second ship would be someone he could trust.

The Pacific sprint did wonders for everyone's morale. The fearnoughts were issued, but were only necessary for a short time. Cook was happy because the rapid crossing meant being in the South Atlantic for the summer. Unlike *Endeavour's* voyage, where months at a time were spent coasting and surveying, fully three-fourths of *Resolution's* travel was spent on open ocean, far from land's sight. The crew had endured so much of the Pacific's rambunctiousness together that it felt almost like home to set foot on land contiguous with the more familiar Atlantic.

Christmas, 1774, was blissful, spent in a bay on Tierra del Fuego eerily reminiscent of Dusky Sound. Food was plentiful, including six dozen plump geese for the Christmas table. The usual drunkenness accompanied the geese, as well as a certain lighthearted awareness that this was surely the crew's last Christmas of this voyage. Cook was his usual reticent self about his plans, but the men were reasonably confident he was as sick of cold weather and icebergs as they were.

December 28 saw *Resolution* officially leave the Pacific and enter the Atlantic. New Year's Eve saw the men provisioning for the South Atlantic push, slaughtering seals, sea lions' and penguins. The carcasses were hauled on board and salted for storage. The sea lions' blubber was stripped away for use as heating oil. Entrails and blood coated the decks, attracting seagulls. And if that wasn't bad enough, the ocean surface was covered with whales, "tainting the whole atmosphere about us with the utmost disagreeable effluvia that can be conceived," Clerke noted. It was a stinking, seagull-infested *Resolution* that sailed from Tierra del Fuego, the air and water around her reeking of rotting sea life and whale flatulence.

Fearnoughts were issued New Year's Day, 1775. Cook wanted to push down to the sixtieth parallel to destroy the last of Dalrymple's theories that Antarctica extended up toward Cape Horn. Dalrymple had drawn a map in 1769 showing something called the Gulf of Saint Sebastian, a vast bay defining the Atlantic portion of the antarctic.

Dalrymple had based the map on a pair of land sightings almost a century apart. The first was when London merchant Antoine de la Roche had sworn he saw land immediately to the south of Cape Horn in 1675. A Spanish merchant ship, the *Leon*, saw more land thereabouts in 1756. Both were actual sightings, not theory. Dalrymple believed they were the opposite shoulders of Saint Sebastian. Cook believed no such Gulf existed, and that the land was probably the Falklands and some other island not yet discovered.

Cook was right. After three days of sailing in gale-force wind, he was at the exact spot where the western point of Saint Sebastian should have jutted. Continuing east, he metaphorically ran aground on the gulf's eastern point. On the fourteenth, however, land was sighted. A surprised Cook coasted, noted sand beaches, ice cliffs climbing from the sea, and penguins and petrels and seals. Inland, he spied snow-covered mountains that were "savage and horrible. Not a tree or shrub was to be seen, no not even big enough to make a tooth pick."

This barren land was Georgia Island. Cook named it in honor of his king, though Reinhold Forster liked to pretend it was actually for his son George. This is where Ernest Shackleton would one day arrive after his epic open-boat crossing of the South Atlantic. Like Bligh before him, Shackleton's faith in eventual success despite overwhelming odds stands as a mark of navigational greatness. An Irishman by birth and Englishman by choice, Shackleton had been trying to become the first man to cross Antarctica. His Imperial Trans-Antarctic Expedition sailed from Europe for the South Atlantic on the eve of World War I. His vessel, *Endurance*, became surrounded by drifting pack ice. As Cook had feared might happen to *Resolution* and *Endeavour*, the ice closed around Shackleton's wooden vessel and crushed it. The expedition was stranded. Shackleton deemed the situation "not merely desperate but impossible."

Then he did a most amazing thing. In an open lifeboat, Shackleton set out across the South Atlantic for Georgia Island (renamed as South Georgia Island). Unlike Bligh, however, who was saved when his boat washed up on tropical shores, Shackleton's journey was only half done when his boat kissed South Georgia. Ahead, to civilization, he still faced a trek across that savage interior Cook shuddered to lay eyes on.

Without knowing it, Cook was not only drawing the world's people together, but connecting himself with explorers before and after him: Magellan, Queirós, Tasman, Bligh, Weddell, Ross, Shackleton, Steger. He learned from them, others learned from him, and so the world became known. This gave Cook's accomplishments a sort of timelessness.

As *Resolution* pressed on, Cook still insisted on regular cleaning above and below decks. His journal often included notes such as "cleaned and smoked the sloop betwixt decks," and "got everything up from betwixt decks in order to clean and air the sloop."

Hugging the sixty degrees south latitude, *Resolution* discovered another island group before reaching Capetown. Cook named it for his patron, Sandwich, whom he would see in just a few months. Nothing makes a patron more proud than to have an island chain named in his favor (except maybe discovering precious riches on an island chain named in his favor). Sailing east from Sandwich Land until he crossed over his outbound path, Cook settled in to write his definitive take on the Southern Continent controversy. The closer he got to England, the more insecure he got about his place in history. Having learned his lesson with Banks on the *Endeavour* voyage, Cook was taking pains to outline his own publicity campaign. This time around there would be no doubt that Cook was the great explorer.

The problem facing Cook as his seventy-thousand-mile odyssey (equivalent to almost three times around the world) came to an end was how it would be remembered. It was not so much a voyage of discovery as antidiscovery—Cook the wandering scientist exploding forever the myth of the Southern Continent. Although Cook had, ironically, found Antarctica, this voyage would be remembered for finding nothing. His insecure side—not an insignificant portion— feared his antidiscovery would somehow be construed as cowardice, that people would say he hadn't pushed far enough south, despite the ice. Instead of ranking *Resolution*'s voyage as the greatest of all time, Cook fretted that it would be remembered as a boondoggle, an absurd waste of men and money and time that did nothing to advance England's colonization plans or even man's understanding of his globe.

During February 1775, as *Resolution* sniffed Cape Town, Cook sat in the great cabin, preoccupied. Journal open before him, he struggled to find the words that would give meaning to *Resolution's* voyage. He decided the typical, terse prose of a captain's log would not be enough; he would need a prosaic summary of his travels, his accomplishments, and his hopes for posterity. Cook's strategy for career advancement had always been achievement wrapped in humility. Ego and a relentless pursuit of his dream were never brought out for the world to see. But as Cook summed up *Resolution's* days, he felt the time had come to bring these vanities into the light.

"It is however true that the greatest part of this Southern Continent (supposing there is one) must lay within the Polar Circle where the sea is so pestered with ice, that the land is thereby inaccessible. The risk one runs in exploring a coast in these unknown and icy seas is so very great, that I can be bold to say, that no man will ever venture father than I have done and that the lands which may lie to the south will never be explored. Thick fogs, snow storms, intense cold, and every other thing that can render navigation dangerous one has to encounter, and these difficulties are heightened by the unexpressable horrid aspect of the country, a country doomed by nature never once to feel the warmth of the sun rays, but to lie ever buried under everlasting snow and ice. The ports which may be on the coast are in a manner wholly filled up with frozen snow of a vast thickness. But if any should so far be open as to admit a ship in, it is even dangerous to go in, for she runs the risk of being fixed there forever, or coming out in an ice island. The islands and floats of ice on the coast, the great falls from the ice cliffs in the port, or a heavy storm attended with a sharp frost would prove equally fatal. After such an explanation as this reader must not expect to find me much farther to the south. It is however not for want of inclination but other reasons. It would have been rashness in me to have risked all which had been done in the voyage, in finding out and exploring a coast which when done would have answered no end whatever, or been of the least use either to navigation or geography or indeed any other science."

Two things made this writing so touching, and neither had to do with Cook's bent toward self-aggrandization. First were Cook's descriptions of the lands and ices of the Southern Ocean, which were more lethal and unmanageable in his mind than the reefs and coral of his Pacific kingdom. Cook was afraid of the Southern Ocean's obstacles. The sea was too harsh in the high latitudes, her lands too unforgiving. She was a true opponent, worthy of his skill and capable of defeating him. Every landfall was viewed through the eyes of failure—as if shipwreck were inevitable. Men of the sea would rot on land like that, slowly starving despite their best efforts at efficiency and survival. Maybe they would end up eating each other or maybe they would just freeze to death once the fearnoughts turned threadbare. When Cook wrote that a land was "horrid," it wasn't a throwaway remark. His premonition that a ship might make it into the ice, then get stuck forever, foreshadowed Shackleton.

Unlike polar explorers who would someday use Cook's findings to step ashore on these foreboding lands, Cook never developed an affection for the ice. He never spent his idle moments enthralled with the hollows and daggers and spires nature carves with wind and water and freezing temperatures, never looked beyond the grotesque tidal wave a calving glacier produces, or saw icebergs as anything other than bobbing ship crushers.

The second remarkable thing about Cook's writing was aimed at the Admiralty. By saying he didn't think it was worth their time sending men and ships south again, Cook was betraying his greatest insecurity—that he'd missed something. Cook feared that a more intrepid man would find an unfrozen passage to the pole. Cook would then be irrelevant, erased from the history books just as he had erased Tasman. Shackleton would make such an attempt in the early twentieth century. He would never reach the South Pole. After his harrowing journey he would return to the South Atlantic for a thirty-thousand-mile journey of exploration along the antarctic shore. He would die before its conclusion.

Before ending the journal, Cook reread what he had written. The words seemed so trite compared with the hardships and joys of the previous thirty-two months. But they would have to do. Cook could only hope that the Admiralty saw the voyage—so epic in his mind—in the same light. He was once again entering the competitive fray of the Royal Navy's command pool. Which vessel you were assigned next depended upon recent accomplishment. Cook hoped he had accomplished enough to warrant some sort of command.

Cook closed the log, gave the order for all logs on board to be collected from whoever might be keeping one—lieutenants, petty officers, and maybe a literate seaman jotting thoughts on the endpaper of his personal Bible—so that sensitive military information wouldn't be compromised. Cook had the lot bundled with his own. In Cape Town a British vessel would be found to transport them home. *Resolution* would stay in port to have her frayed rigging replaced and her jury-rigged hull recaulked. Then she would follow the journals to London.

Land was sighted that evening.

CHAPTER 15

Homeward Bound

A s *Resolution* made for Cape Town with all haste, a Dutch East Indiaman came alongside. Cook was eager for news of the world and dispatched a boat. Word came back that *Adventure* had sailed through a year earlier. Her men were scurvy-infested, almost too weak from lack of fresh provisions to run the ship. Cape Town had revived the lot, and Furneaux was able to make it home by July 14. All this Cook was relieved to hear. However, a great bit of sailors' gossip had spread through the international array of vessels and men during *Adventure's* stay in Cape Town's Table Bay: cannibalism. "One of her boat's crew had been murdered and eaten by the people of New Zealand," the Dutch East Indiaman reported.

Cook was furious. Beginning yet another journal for the push home from Cape Town, he lashed out at incompetent Furneaux. Surely the fine men and women of Cook's Pacific kingdom were somehow blameless. "I shall make no reflection on this melancholy affair until I hear more about it. I must, however, observe in favour of the New Zealanders, that I have always found them of a brave, noble, open and benevolent disposition, but they are a people who will never put up with an insult if they have an opportunity to resent it."

Cook would deal further with Furneaux in London. Whatever tarnish the alleged cannibalism had bestowed upon the voyage, he would make sure it extended only to the well-meaning but courage-deficient captain.

Then Cook turned to the matter at hand: namely, living the good life in Cape Town. Cook enjoyed a drink as much as any sailor. And like all international sailors, Cape Town had a special place in Cook's heart, but never so much as when *Resolution* arrived on March 21. It had been over two years since he and the men had been part of Western civilization.

Cape Town was a boisterous, impeccably maintained city, and a fine way to reenter the Western world. Founded in 1652 by Jan van Riebeeck as a supply base for the Dutch East India Company, Cape Town was the oldest settlement of European origin in South Africa. Table Bay's large natural harbor made it an ideal military fortress, but the Dutch figured they were so far off the beaten path that trade would take precedence over confrontation. They were right, for a time. For over a century beginning in 1652, ships and sailors of all nations took advantage of her strategic location. The local economy thrived from the continual infusion of capital from sailors too long at sea, money and lust burning holes in their pockets.

However, as early as 1688, the mighty Dutch East India Company began to suffer from the ascension of the British navy. With that new might, the British began cutting into Dutch trade. Cape Town endured a political seesaw for the next hundred years. Finally, in 1780, the British decided Cape Town was a strategic asset (five years after Cook's visit with *Resolution*). They simply went in and made it the king's property. A year later, however, the French arrived with a garrison to provide "assistance" to the Dutch, and the British were forcibly expelled. Tensions between England and France, always a shade less than lukewarm, heightened. With their own East India

Company to think of—in India, of all places—the British successfully reoccupied Cape Town in 1795 and made it a British protectorate. In 1799, the Dutch East India Company's century and a half's empire (the first time in world history a commercial, rather than political, entity would effectively control the world) ended. Financial mismanagement, a decline in trade, and a new French-backed government at home would drive the East India Company to bankruptcy.

All that was in the future when Cook landed in 1775, on *Resolution's* first voyage. As long as trade was king—and it was when *Resolution* docked—there was a freewheeling international flavor to Cape Town. Like Batavia, Cook's last international port, the docks were choked with sailors and ships of all nations.

Cook was to stay five weeks. *Resolution* had proven a much more durable ship than *Endeavour*, but she was frayed and tired. Her sails and rigging were in tatters. The rudder was frayed and deemed unfit to last the voyage to England. This vital piece of *Resolution* would be unhung, then taken ashore for repair. The time in port was further lengthened by a lack of caulkers to patch the ship's increasing leaks. Even with the aid of Baron Plettenberg, Cape Town's governor, only four capable men could be found.

The officers stayed with a friend of Cook's, local merchant Christoffel Brand. The People were scattered throughout the port, a tad too eager for dissipation after all that fresh sea air and regimentation. Grog was imbibed, and it wasn't uncommon to see *Resolution's* People sleeping it off on the side of the road.

A letter was waiting from Furneaux. He admitted that men had died of cannibals, and for that reason Furneaux had gone straight home. Cook set the letter aside and decided to delay action on Tobias Furneaux and the *Adventure* until arriving in London, for a much more intriguing opportunity had presented itself, that of interviewing a fellow explorer. Julien Marie Crozet—French, forty-five—had been second-in-command of an expedition led by Marion-Dufresne.

Cook invited him for dinner aboard *Resolution*. Cook needed to hear what other men were doing, though whether to allay his fears of being overshadowed or to gloat in success was unclear. All he knew was that it felt good to speak with another man of his rank and mind-set, a man who knew the worries of command and the hunger to fill in all the colors on the map. Such opportunities didn't come along often. It didn't even matter that Crozet was French, for theirs was a brotherhood beyond borders.

Crozet's ship had left the Cape in March 1772, just eight months before *Resolution* sailed from Table Bay. Dufresne's mission was to return a displaced Polynesian from de Bougainville's voyage. It was a common occurrence to pick a Tahitian and bring him back to European society, where the noble savage was viewed with great curiosity. Cook found the act despicable and distracting—though Furneaux had insisted on carrying a young man, Omai, back on *Adventure*.

Crozet told a chilling tale of his time with Dufresne. After making landfall in New Zealand, Dufresne had taken a party ashore to investigate. Cannibals attacked. Dufresne was eaten, along with several of his men. Crozet escaped, guiding his vessel north to the Philippines, then home via Mauritius.

To Cook's surprise, Crozet then told of islands deep in the Indian Ocean recently discovered by the French explorer Kerguélen. Crozet brought forth a new world map produced by the French, and Cook saw clearly he had bypassed these Kerguelen Islands by mere miles.

And, Crozet went on, the Spaniards had reinserted themselves in the game of international exploration. They'd sent ships to Tahiti and discovered new islands. The thought of Spanish vessels laying claim to Cook's domain filled him with indignation, but he said nothing. Cook's temper was soothed when Crozet allowed that he didn't believe a word the Spaniards said. He and Cook laughed loud and hard at that one. All in all, it was a great evening, one of the best Cook had known on the entire voyage. It was nice to be known internationally.

"Probably more authentic accounts may be got here after," he wrote once Crozet had been rowed back to his East Indiaman. "But it will hardly be necessary to resume the subject unless all discoveries, both ancient and modern, are laid down in a chart and then an explanatory memoir will be necessary and such a chart I intend to construct when I have time and the necessary materials."

Cook not only intended to write other explorers off the map and append his names and routes throughout the world, he intended to make the map himself. The loner who had already learned a hard lesson through Banks's crowing (after *Endeavour*) would not dare leave his legacy to anyone else. Ego and greed were clouding his once pure quest for discovery further and further.

Cook corralled his crew and sailed from the Cape on April 27. He put in at Saint Helena for supplies and was delighted to find that the island's governor was John Skottowe of Great Ayton—the son of Thomas Skottowe, Cook's father's former employer and the man who'd paid Cook's tuition at the local school some forty years prior.

Cook put to sea again after a five-day visit. After years at sea, in lands where cannons were wielded only as instruments of war, Cook proudly saluted Saint Helena's garrison with thirteen guns as he departed. To his surprise, not only was the salute returned, but a Spanish frigate and Dutch East Indiaman in the harbor saluted as well. Cook's international reputation was becoming legend. What man, standing on the deck of a vessel completing one of the world's most ambitious achievements, would not stand and reflect that he had begun life as a simple farmhand? Or wish that his wife or father might be standing at his side, if only for that brief instant of repute?

Emboldened and refreshed, Cook couldn't resist one last bit of exploration, no matter that the crew were dying to get back to England. Just before crossing the equator, he ordered *Resolution* pointed due west. His plan was to sail clear across the Atlantic to investigate a small island, just for the sake of curiosity. Known as Fernando de

Noronha, the island was located off the Brazilian coast. Cook had always wanted to take a look and fix its position accurately. Not caring whether the crew minded a two-week detour after three years at sea, he cranked his vessel west until the island was clear in his sights. Surprisingly, the Portuguese flag flew from a large fort on a mountain overlooking the ocean. Even more surprisingly, the fort fired cannon at *Resolution*. Cook quickly gave the command to veer away, though not before taking careful longitude calculations for his planned world map.

On July 30 Cook made landfall in England. *Resolution* had been gone three years and seventeen days.

Instead of sailing *Resolution* around the Channel and up the Thames, he anchored in Spithead, England, then took a carriage to London. As on *Endeavour*, Cook rushed to his Admiralty masters for a pat on the back and words of a job well done. His return was cause for great excitement, and he was immediately pulled into a lengthy, closed-door meeting with the Admiralty lords (except Sandwich, who was yachting with his mistress) on his voyage. "Two o'clock Monday," an Admiralty observer wrote in a missive to Joseph Banks, "this moment Captain Cook is arrived. I have not yet had an opportunity of conversing with him, as he is still in the boardroom giving an account of himself and company. He looks as well as ever. By and by, I shall be able to say a little more."

The observer was Daniel Solander, of the *Endeavour* voyage. Not only was Cook glad to see Banks's compatriate once the meeting ended, but passed word that he was eager to settle his differences with the botanist.

Cook told Solander this in a hurry, rushing from the Admiralty to see Elizabeth. He explained that he would write the sentiments himself, but the lords had kept him a long time, and he was anxious to be home.

Then Cook traveled by carriage from the opulence of the Admiralty to his quaint home on Mile End. His homecoming was typically passionate—within weeks Elizabeth learned she was pregnant once again.

As for the fame Cook privately craved, the second time was the charm. The journals had come before Cook, and word had already spread through London of his unparalleled voyage. All of England— indeed, all of Europe—was soon in love with the world's greatest explorer, Captain James Cook.

PART FOUR

Last Resolution

CHAPTER 16

Fame

Summer 1775

One of Cook's first orders of business upon returning was to explore the fate of Furneaux and *Adventure*. While the younger skipper had been intractable and insubordinate, he was nonetheless under Cook's command. His actions reflected on Cook. Thankfully, the news was all good. Furneaux and *Adventure* had gotten home on July 14, 1774. Theirs was the first eastward circumnavigation in history.

Furneaux was welcomed home grandly, but soon grilled by an Admiralty vexed by the cannibal incident. Because he had allowed his men to be cooked and eaten, Furneaux's tour of duty with Cook did not equate to glory or career advancement. He was given a year's furlough after returning, then quietly given command of a frigate, *Syren*, shuttling up and down the North American coastline as part of the war with the colonies.

If Furneaux managed one remarkable self-redemption aboard *Adventure* after his separation from Cook, it was to stay the southern course instead of fleeing directly home from Queen Charlotte's Sound. Furneaux passed several hundred miles beneath South

America, then continued at the high latitudes until he was due south of Cape Town. Only then did Furneaux give in to his discomfort and flee to England.

Sandwich had been busy in Cook's absence. On the social front, young Omai, the Tahitian man Furneaux had brought back to England aboard *Adventure*, lived at Hinchingbrooke, Sandwich's estate, through much of the autumn and winter of 1774. He was teaching Sandwich and Banks the Polynesian language. As if the Tahitian were a doll, Banks had dressed him in the latest London fashions. Sandwich was so taken with jovial Omai that when the young man moved to London to be with Banks, even hardened Sandwich found himself lonely. "I am grown so used to him and have so sincere a friendship for him that I am quite depressed at him leaving me."

But while Omai was taking London society by storm, walking around town in English tweed and even gaining an audience with King George III, he had been in London for a very long year when *Resolution* docked. Omai was growing homesick. Sandwich, humanitarian that he was, told the world he was planning a new voyage of exploration that would return Omai to Tahiti.

It was not the only voyage Sandwich had sponsored in Cook's absence. Captain Constantine Phipps had sailed east through the arctic with two ships in search of a passage to the Orient. From the Channel to the North Sea to the Norwegian Sea, Phipps had sailed north along the coast of Norway. Entering the Barents Sea, he turned east for China, but was almost immediately stalled in thick ice off Spitzbergen. Phipps hacked the ships loose before they could be crushed, then sailed home. Unlike Banks on *Endeavour*, or Cook with *Resolution*, Phipps received little fanfare. However, his voyages learned many things of a scientific nature, including—as Cook had discovered—that seawater freezes quite nicely. This repudiated one of Banks's pet theories, that only freshwater freezes. As freshwater comes only from land, Banks had asserted that a continent of some sort had to be nearby wherever ice was sighted.

Perhaps the most novel characteristic of Phipps's voyage was how it was presented to the world. Phipps's journals were published with appendixes of his vast scientific discoveries. This was the first time a captain's journal was published in a scholarly manner. Previously, as with Dampier, they were presented as action-packed travel writing. Phipps's journal not only changed that, but allowed Cook a forum to right a few wrongs. For when Cook's *Endeavour* journals had been published by Hawkesworth, it was with many additions. Hawkesworth had combined Cook's journal with Banks's, Solander's, and even Wallis's. When Cook was shown the final version in Cape Town he was incensed. The writing bore little parallel to his actual journey, and because Banks was a more engaging writer, Banks came off as *Endeavour's* leader and the voyage's hero in that blatant fabrication. Because of Phipps, Cook's *Resolution* journal would be written by Cook and Cook alone. His editor would be the Reverend John Douglas, canon of Windsor. Cook's writing would only be changed to make the book more literary, not to embellish. Douglas, Cook noted, should only make changes, so the book would be "unexceptionable to the nicest readers. In short, my desire is that nothing indecent may appear in the whole book and you cannot oblige me more than by pointing out whatever may appear to you as such."

Sandwich, hoping to bank political currency, was the driving force behind the journal's publication. He used his influence to ensure that Cook's was the only *Resolution* account in print. When Reinhold Forster tried to write a competitive journal, Sandwich effectively shut the Prussian down.

Sandwich had done one more momentous thing in Cook's absence: led the Admiralty into war. The timing was fortuitous, he thought, because peace had been wrecking his navy. Sandwich had proposed to King George III a radical revamp of the military docks in Deptford and Woolwich. For this reform, he needed a perfect window of opportunity—during prolonged peace the cost would have been prohibitive and deemed unnecessary, yet sudden war would prevent the work from being finished in time. The peace, of course, had already stretched too long. Despite a decade of squabbles in America, England hadn't truly been at war since the Seven Years' War ended in 1763. What troubled Sandwich most about this was that myopic forces in Parliament had been clamoring that money previously allocated to the Admiralty be spent on nonmilitary line items. By 1775, Lord North, the prime minister, was even openly challenging Sandwich to reduce the Admiralty budget.

Ever the political mongoose, Sandwich dragged his heels and bought more time. As always, his senses were perfect. Call it luck, call it prescience, but somehow he timed the dock completion and war's outbreak in America just right and was on a tour of the dock facilities with Banks, Solander, Phipps, and Miss Martha Ray (his mistress) when word reached him of Cook's arrival.

Sandwich hastened to arrange a celebration dinner. Solander happily complied. Omai was there, as were a host of others. Banks, however, a little proud and a little embarrassed by his actions three years prior, did not come to dinner. He missed quite a party. Laying eyes on Cook for the first time since their Admiralty meeting on the date of his homecoming, Solander told Cook that the captain not only looked healthy, but he looked even healthier than before sailing from London. For Cook, for whom advancing age was becoming a career issue, the compliment must have been enjoyable.

The evening was spent with Sandwich and Cook in mutual admiration. Much of their conversation excluded the rest of the dinner party. The two men were close in age, with Cook just a decade younger. Sandwich was getting older, feeling out of place in government as the other legislators grew younger. Lord North, for instance, was still a boy at Eton when Sandwich had served his first term as Lord of the Admiralty in the late 1740s. The new breed respected

Sandwich for his crocodile stealth, but otherwise kept their political distance.

Sandwich had graciously supported Elizabeth and the boys in Cook's absence. He knew Cook would listen without judging, caring little for world and English politics unless they interfered with exploration. It was clear Cook owed Sandwich a great debt. But Sandwich's debt was equally large, and he would never forget his political comeback was due to this wonderful man from North Yorkshire whom he had once misjudged as a rube.

Over dinner, Sandwich described the gist of war with the American colonies, which had broken out in April 1775, while Cook was in Table Bay. An organization of John Wilkes's followers, the Society of Supporters of the Bill of Rights, provided a model for subsequent radical reform movements. The Americans had held something called the First Continental Congress in 1774. The purpose was to address Britain's heavy-handedness, especially in trade and taxation. America's long shoreline, so ripe for smuggling, had made collection of customs duties daunting, so the British had responded by levying taxes on everything from molasses to stamps to make up the difference. The colonists had rebelled for almost a decade, though without seeking independence from Britain. If they were going to pay taxes, the colonists noted, they wanted parliamentary representation. The British refused. The treasonous Congress was an exploration of how the American colonies should go about separating from Britain.

Sandwich, as always mouthing the king's words, demanded the colonists be crushed. They were mongrels, Germans and Irish and "the uncouth spawn of British prison transports," as one London newspaper called them. Forcibly subjugating them would set an example to every British colony that the crown was not to be trifled with. In Sandwich's mind, the colonists were no better than the hated French.

Sandwich had other information for Cook, regarding Alexander Dalrymple. The disagreeable little man had bypassed Sandwich and gone directly to Lord North for a new voyage. At his own expense,

Dalrymple wanted to be dropped off on the South Atlantic island discovered by the Spanish aboard *Leon* in 1756. He would grow food there, set up a whaling base, and cultivate a seal rookery for meat. More important, Dalrymple would use this as a base for exploring Antarctica. Lord North had agreed heartily.

When Cook explained about Georgia Island—the very same land the Spanish had cited in 1756—and how it had no connection to a Southern Continent, Sandwich thought it was the funniest thing he'd heard in a long time. The voyage would surely be canceled. It would serve Dalrymple right for meddling with Sandwich's authority (this came to pass: Lord North would eventually let the issue of Dalrymple's voyage quietly drop).

By the time the night ended, Cook had requested a quiet command onshore. In the past seven years he had been at sea all but a year. He had canvassed the Pacific and not only discovered or visited each of her major island chains, but had slowly discovered that even paradise can be foul and cruel. He didn't really know his wife or surviving sons and had been gone during each of his other three children's deaths. At forty-six, Cook was only a few years older but light years more jaded and weathered than the idealistic young version of himself who had charted Newfoundland, then taken command of *Endeavour*. More than anything, Cook wanted to retire and remain in one place awhile. He was tired of the sea and tired of trying to quiet that critical parent inside—his father, still alive back in Great Ayton and inside Cook's head.

What Cook had in mind, as a means of easing into retirement, was command of the Royal Naval Hospital at Greenwich. Sandwich agreed.

First, however, there was the matter of yet another promotion. On August 9, 1775, Sandwich made Cook commander of the seventy-four-gun battleship *Kent* for a day. Experience commanding a warship was a prerequisite for the rank of post-captain—exploring new worlds wasn't good enough. The command was taken away the next day, but the rank stayed. King George III formally presented Cook with his new rank at Saint James Palace.

Then, much to his relief, the new post captain was effectively taken off sea duty.

Orders came through August 10 for Cook to report to Greenwich Hospital. At a relatively lavish salary of 230 pounds annually (placing Cook in the upper 5 percent of British wage earners, or about the same level as titled gentry) with free quarters for himself and his family if he so wished, Cook was to command the senior officers' retirement village. James Cook, England's Great Explorer, was being put out to pasture at his own request. He would spend spare time in his garden at home, attend his many social invitations with Elizabeth, work on his conceived map, and pursue intellectual growth through reading and his contacts at the Royal Society.

But after the excitement of life at sea, that was all easier said than done. At first Cook handled the tedium of life inside a drafty waterfront hospital. In good times and bad, in balmy weather and antarctic gales, the one constant in Cook's life since the day he'd signed on as a seaman in Whitby had been that he loved his job. What he did for a living filled him with meaning and more than a little wonder. At forty-six, he was now leaving it all behind for a boring, unprestigious desk job, answering the complaints of officers too poor to afford a proper retirement home or too infirm to burden their families.

Starting in the fall of 1775, when Cook took command of Greenwich, the Admiralty had Cook right where they wanted him. They had been more than glad to honor Cook's request for the hospital leadership. For starters, Cook had gallantly served Britannia. Command of the sailors' retirement home was a compliment, a safe way to ease into his own retirement. It was time, in the Admiralty's estimation, for the man to stay home and leave global exploring to younger men.

That was the official version. The Admiralty was also rife with whispered rumors about Cook—that he was exhausted from the demands of command, unable to make clear decisions. Armchair

sailors within the Admiralty noted with disdain Cook's informal nature and diffidence toward military fashion. While never inappropri-
ately casual, Cook's uniforms—like their owner—had spent long years
at sea and lacked the starch and sheen of those of wealthier men
who'd built careers without leaving London.

Those armchair sailors looked down their noses at Cook and his
lack of pedigree, disregarding his accomplishments. They grumbled
that he had gone native during those long voyages, enjoying the status of god and king lavished on him by South Sea islanders so much
that Cook was truly beginning to consider himself a deity. There was
no evidence to support their suppositions, just peeks into ship's journals and envy that a commoner had risen to such a prestigious rank.
The air was thin at the top, and once a man began to enjoy that sort
of adulation, there was no telling what sort of moral and emotional
breakdown might ensue.

Cook's boredom at Greenwich required an adjustment, but it was
palatable. Unlike former Greenwich governors, Cook had no peers
in the hospital. None of the officers were his friends, nor were their
experiences at sea aboard warships or merchant ships comparable
with his independent voyages of discovery. Cook felt the distance,
and though maintaining quarters in the hospital, he shuttled home
nightly to Elizabeth at Mile End Road. They socialized occasionally
in some of the higher London circles. The Royal Society had elected
him a Fellow, for his distinguished work on scurvy and the Transit.
Cook wasn't a rich man, but he was comfortable enough to reside on
a cautious budget at Mile End Road after his retirement. Finally,
though he could watch vessels sailing up and down the Thames
from his Greenwich office, Cook was letting the ocean out of his
system.

CHAPTER 17

The Call of Adventure

I n the fall of 1775, Cook received crushing news: there would be a second voyage of *Resolution*, and Charlie Clerke was being considered for commander. Sailing first to Tahiti, Clerke would drop Omai back home, then sail north to Alaska to search for a Northwest Passage through either the arctic or Canada. There would be two vessels. With the war in the American colonies building a wall between Britain and America that might ever prevent the normalization of trade relations again, King George III and the Admiralty were desperately seeking an alternative trading partner to fill the void. It was their hope that a Northwest Passage—a continuous waterway from one side of the North American continent to the other—would allow British vessels to sail more quickly to the Orient, opening up vital new trade routes.

This part of the news wasn't tough to swallow. What floored Cook was that if Clerke found the Northwest Passage, the Admiralty was promising him a stunning twenty-thousand-pound reward (several million dollars today). For all Cook's discoveries, no one had ever made him any such offer. Less than 1 percent of Britain's population earned more than four hundred pounds a year. In fact, only a dozen families in all England earned more than twenty thousand pounds annually, and those all resided in the uppermost levels of Britain's titled gentry.

Even after giving portions of the reward to his officers and crew, Cook could retire to a farm the size of Airyholme and enjoy a comfortable life with Elizabeth. He would be a landowner. With any luck, and through Sandwich's help, he might even procure a knighthood.

But Cook's time was past. "A few months ago the whole southern hemisphere was hardly big enough for me," an unhappy Cook wrote John Walker, still living in Whitby, "and now I am going to be confined within the limits of Greenwich Hospital, which are far too small for an active mind like mine. I must confess, however, it is a fine retreat and a pretty income, but whether I can bring myself to ease into retirement, time will show."

At first, the enjoyment of Cook's fame made losing the Northwest Passage voyage tolerable. James Cook in 1775 was the closest thing England had to a superstar. His every move made the newspapers. He dined with nobility. Publishers begged him to edit his journals quickly for publication. Three different portrait artists, including the legendary Joshua Reynolds, asked him to sit.

Resolution was due to sail in the spring of 1776, and from September to December 1775, Cook tried to ignore *Resolution's* upcoming voyage. He focused on adjusting to the hospital and the fame and the family life. But a midlife crisis ensued as Clerke's new assignment gnawed. There was so much more to discover. And Cook believed himself capable of still more greatness. The quest for greatness was James Cook's touchstone. Ceasing the quest prematurely felt like compromise.

As Christmas faded into the New Year, Cook dwelled on the fact that greatness wasn't likely to happen in the Royal Naval Hospital. He couldn't imagine spending the rest of his naval career in that position, facing day after day of routine, without challenge. Cook missed the deck's sway, the tranquillity of falling asleep in his compact cabin, the lap of water against the hull. Most of all he missed the power.

More than ever, the man who had spent a lifetime searching for a place in the world to call his own knew that place was on board a vessel of discovery. Not ashore in the South Pacific. Not ashore in England. But on the ship itself. "I want to go as far as I think it possible for a man to go." Had he done that? He thought so. But then along came the Northwest Passage with its magnificent bounty and reminder that man could go farther. It was the last undiscovered reach of the world's oceans, or so Cook believed, a sliver of water that would allow easy access to the lucrative Alaskan whaling and seal trade by British ships. That it would involve a trek through ice, Cook's nemesis, was secondary to the money and prestige. There was nothing pure about Cook's motivation, none of the idealism that had made his first two voyages so refreshing.

Most startling was Cook's growing sense of self-importance. It was as if he wanted to be known as the only explorer who'd ever sailed. If Cook could somehow wrangle the Northwest Passage voyage, for instance, he would once again be trying to erase another explorer from the history books, in this case, Spanish explorer Juan de Fuca. In 1592, de Fuca had made preliminary investigations of what he called the Strait of Anian. He reported back to his patrons a land "rich of gold, silver, pearl, and other things," where people dressed in fur. Though he didn't actually sail into Hudson Bay to conclude the journey, de Fuca was quite sure he'd come to the Atlantic. That no other explorer had found the fur people or their riches didn't detract from de Fuca's claims, but gave their rediscovery greater heft. As the Spanish and Russians claimed the Pacific's northern hemisphere as their pond, the British had tried making the same connection from the Atlantic. Either timid commanders or ice had turned back each attempt. The time had come to attempt the passage in the manner of de Fuca—from the Pacific.

And who knew the Pacific better than James Cook? Finding the Northwest Passage would be the greatest discovery of Cook's career.

The thought of another man—even easygoing Charlie Clerke—leading this voyage consumed Cook with proprietary envy.

Without telling a soul, Cook mentally severed himself from the Royal Naval Hospital, Elizabeth, and even the greater needs of the crown. His immediate focus turned in the opposite direction with laserlike intensity: gaining command of *Resolution* again. He ached to walk her decks. But with the voyage less than four months off, he would have to act quickly.

When a very special dinner invitation was extended by Sandwich, Cook plotted ways to make the occasion his return to command. So it was that Cook found himself dining with the three most influential men in the Admiralty on January 9, 1776: Sandwich, Palliser, and Admiralty Secretary Phillip Stephens. Stephens was a relatively new acquaintance of Cook's, but Sandwich and Palliser had made Cook's career—and he theirs. The mutual admiration between these three men gave Cook great confidence as the dinner got under way with wine.

To Cook's delight, he had been invited to the dinner not only because Sandwich enjoyed his company and the tales of radical travel, but also because the Admiralty had finally decided to select a captain for *Resolution*. Sandwich, Palliser, and Stephens considered Cook the perfect adviser. The list of candidates had been narrowed to Charlie Clerke, but the three wanted to know if Cook felt Clerke capable. His maturity was an issue. A quote from Clerke's younger days (that he "is a right good officer. At drinking and whoring he is as good as the best of them") still haunted the man. Since then Clerke had served under Cook on both his circumnavigations. Was Clerke, the Admiralty leaders wanted to know, still as fond of the bottle? Was he serious enough to command a top-secret expedition into hostile waters? Sandwich added that England was under a great cloak of secrecy with war under way.

The wine flowed as Clerke's worth was brought under a bright light. Cook chose his words delicately. On the one hand he didn't want to disdain a friend, especially one who might someday surpass him in rank and wield influence. On the other, there would be no better chance to casually push Clerke into the mud and step over him into command.

Sandwich watched Cook carefully, having seen this man rise from pauper to post captain. Other men thought Cook humble and withdrawn, but Sandwich saw right through him. He knew Cook held himself in high regard and had ambitions equaled by few men. Sandwich, Stephens, and Palliser had planned this dinner to play to Cook's ego, stoke his fires for command. For in reality, Clerke was actually their second choice. The man they truly desired was the man whose explorations had become legendary, James Cook.

Only James Cook had the experience, proven courage, navigation skills, geographical knowledge, and capability of handling indigenous peoples. Equally important to the three, Cook also had a degree of influence, making him a coveted political asset.

Cook possessed one other rare attribute that would play to Sandwich and Palliser's favor: he was a hero. When nations are in trouble, nothing inspires the citizenry like a spectacular achievement—a discovery by one of their own—that strikes a deep communal chord. And on both his voyages Cook had somehow done just that. Mention of his name was heartwarming, a reminder to all commoners of England's greatness. And the opinion of those commoners meant more to Sandwich than that of the disgruntled naval officers, for the commoners' approval gave King George III a greater mandate. With George III's popularity suffering due to the War in the Colonies, Sandwich needed public opinion on his side. At a time when the national population had almost doubled from 15 million to 25 million in less than a century and industry was replacing agriculture, keeping the public happy with the government in power was vital. London, swollen with displaced farm families in search of work, was rife with disease, crime, and squalor. King George III needed a national morale booster.

There was, in the end, a chiliad of reasons why Sandwich and company should have been down on their knees begging Cook's favor, but the game of political one-upmanship meant they would lose face unless Cook was the one doing the begging.

The evening progressed, the banquet was extensive, and the wine continued to flow. Sandwich wanted to know which route Cook suggested to Alaska. Around Africa, came the reply. Much better than fighting the winds off South America.

Then, Cook suggested, warming to the topic, over to New Zealand to harbor at Ship's Cove. Then over to Tahiti, then on to the coast of New Albion (California) and north to the Bering Strait.

Cook felt in his element, speaking of what he knew best. How different from the Royal Naval Hospital. With every syllable and every new glass of wine, Cook's urge to ask—no, demand—command of *Resolution* grew stronger. He reined himself in, didn't want to appear too eager.

Sandwich watched closely, playing to Cook's ego. He pushed a line of questioning that reminded the Great Explorer of all those fabulous places on earth he'd touched. Cook, he knew, was nothing if not guileless. Sandwich knew that he—and all of England—needed Cook. He was a reminder of their glory.

The moment had come. Cook burst to his feet. Eyes a little glassy, burr thicker and lower than usual, he planted himself and eyed each man in turn. He had never been much on grammar or syntax, and the wine didn't helped matters any. "I will myself undertake the direction of this enterprise if I am so commanded," he announced.

It was Sandwich who cheered the loudest. He ordered the glasses filled yet again. A toast to Cook's health and longevity was proposed. Every man felt he had achieved victory, yet on the ride back to Mile End Road it was Cook who felt the greatest relief. Life was much simpler at sea. No tricky political games, no cramped household, no one—not even good friends like Sandwich and Palliser—telling him what to do. On February 10, Cook made it official, writing the Admiralty to formally offer his services. It is likely that Elizabeth, who had thought their days of separation were done, did not treat the news with the same gusto. Yet she must have seen it coming. Even as Cook moped about the twenty thousand pounds and Clerke being given the command, Cook must have shared his ruminations with Elizabeth, his only trusted confidante. Cook wrote the Admiralty:

"Sir, having understood that their Lordships have ordered two ships to be fitted out for the purpose of making further discoveries in the Pacific Ocean, I take the liberty, as their Lordships, when they were pleased to appoint me a captain in Greenwich Hospital, were at the same time pleased also to say, it should not be in prejudice to any further offer which I might make of my service, to submit myself to their directions, if they think fit to appoint me to the command on the said intended voyage; relying, if they condescend to accept this offer, they will on my return, either restore me to my appointment in the Hospital, or procure for me such other mark of the royal favour as their Lordships, upon the review of my past services, shall think me deserving of. I am, sir, your most humble servant, James Cook."

April 1776, Cook decided, was when he would set sail. The public announcement was soon made. Cook left his post at the Royal Naval Hospital and began preparing for the voyage. Elizabeth, alone at Mile End Road now that she no longer needed her young cousin's assistance, steeled herself for another several years without her man.

To soften the impact of stealing his command, Cook put Charlie Clerke in charge of *Discovery*. Clerke's actions would be subservient to Cook's, but it would be his first command and would guarantee his career. The master's mate from *Endeavour* had developed technically and intuitively as a sailor aboard *Resolution*. Just thirty-three, Clerke's sense of duty and honor mirrored Cook's. So whatever their personality differences, Clerke had Cook's respect. And Cook knew Clerke, unlike Furneaux, to be brave and capable, not slacking in leadership.

Clerke was, of course, disappointed over losing the command and potential reward, but soon found himself more consumed with severe legal troubles that threatened his ability to make the voyage at all, let alone command. For shortly after returning home in July, Clerke had guaranteed his brother John's debts. Then Sir John, a captain in the Royal Navy, had sailed for duty in the East Indies with those bills unpaid. Once news got out that Charlie Clerke was about to sail, too, the men owed became fearful they would never see their money. Charlie Clerke was arrested and sent to King's Bench debtors' prison.

Meanwhile, Cook began preparation for the Northwest Passage voyage. Jumping on a ship and sailing away for three years, however, wasn't as simple for Cook as it had once been. His time was precious. By the time Sandwich convinced Cook—or made Cook feel he'd convinced Sandwich—to take the weathered *Resolution* in search of the Northwest Passage, Cook was deeply immersed in a dizzying new social life. On his own he could regularly be seen at the Mitre, a pub frequented by members of the Royal Society. With Elizabeth he attended a great many dinners.

Men of letters and science began to see the onetime rube as their mental equal, lauding him for his bravery and intellect. A sign of Cook's importance was the sudden fascination with him by James Boswell, the observational writer. Boswell traveled in an elite social circle as a member of Samuel Johnson's Literary Club, whose other members included statesman Edmund Burke, artist Sir Joshua Reynolds, and actor David Garrick. Cook and Boswell met at a dinner party. Boswell was Scottish and his thick speech matched Cook's. Born in Edinburgh, Boswell was educated at the universities of Glasgow, Edinburgh, and Utrecht. A lawyer by trade, he devoted himself to writing. His *An Account of Corsica*, published the year *Endeavour* sailed, showed him to be like Cook in his curiosity about other cultures. Though best known for a biography of Samuel Johnson, Boswell would write another epic travelogue, *Journal of a Tour to the Hebrides*.

Because of their predilection for travel and common heritage,

Boswell went out of his way to observe and write about Cook in the most glowing terms. The new post captain was a celebrity, and Boswell's weakness was the cult of fame. "Cook, as Sir John [Pringle] had told me before, was a plain and sensible man with an uncommon attention to veracity. My metaphor was that he had a balance in his mind for truth as nice as scales for weighing a guinea. I talked a good deal with him today, as he was very obliging and communicative. He seemed to have no desire to make people stare, and being a man of good steady moral principles, as I thought, did not try to make theories out of what he had seen to confound virtue and vice."

Boswell rushed to tell the influential Johnson about the encounter. "I have had a feast," Boswell said obsequiously. "I have had a good dinner for I have had a good Cook."

Four days later, Boswell made an appearance all the way out at Mile End. Cook offered him tea. They sat in the garden, where a blackbird sang. The sudden visit was most unusual to Cook, and his deductive mind searched for a motivation. Reading between the lines, Cook deduced that Boswell's traveling bug was the impetus—the writer hoped to sail with *Resolution* for the Northwest Passage and write another travel book.

Cook was pleased with Boswell's attention, as he now spent his days immersed in editing his journals and fancied himself a writer. Cook's new passion for the written word added to the list of mental, physical, and emotional responsibilities already sapping his energy. It was late April when Boswell visited. *Resolution* and her new sister ship, *Discovery*, were overdue to begin the new voyage. The delay was all Cook's fault. He was too busy to be bothered with preparing for the voyage. Unlike on *Endeavour* and the first *Resolution* voyage, Cook was too busy to spend time at the Deptford Yards, overseeing the preparation, especially the refitting, being done on *Resolution*. Despite Sandwich's reforms, the Deptford Yards was still notoriously corrupt. The fleet was far too big for the yards, and the most efficient way to refurbish vessels was to not refurbish them at all—vessels were left to rot in the Thames, and other ships were built to replace them. This voyage would mark the first time Cook had not spent his days looking over laborers' shoulders, making sure—among the myriad tasks—that *Resolution*'s oak planks were replaced and tightly caulked.

Perhaps he felt he could trust the yard, or that he'd become so important and well connected within the navy that Deptford would cease its usual corrupt ways. Regardless, Cook was far too experienced a sailor not to spend his prevoyage time anywhere but at Deptford, keeping an eagle eye on *Resolution*.

For his second-in-command on *Resolution*, Cook selected John Gore, showing no hard feelings about Gore's skipping *Resolution*'s first voyage to journey with Banks. The American was a capable mariner and should have advanced to a command of his own without Cook's help. Gore had a tendency to put female acquaintance over career, but that made no matter to Cook. Gore was one of the rare men Cook confided in, and they had an easy friendship. On a voyage of discovery, where time in cramped ship's quarters far outlasted time on land, good company was vital. With Cook and Gore being roughly the same age—and almost two decades older than the majority of the crew—that fraternity was warming.

Under Gore, as second lieutenant, was James King. This twenty-six-year-old astronomer and sailor was effeminate, unusual for the caustic world of shipboard life, but had such an engaging personality that even hard-core sailors took to him. King had joined the navy at twelve, took time off to attend Oxford—a highly unusual act for a prospective naval officer at the time—but prospered upon his return. Cook took to him like a father to a son.

Cook prided himself as a judge of character, but his absorption in other matters led him to make two questionable choices. As third lieutenant he selected an angry Irishman, John Williamson. This odd choice was surpassed only by his appointment for ship's master, William Bligh. The same man who would someday rise to captain and know mutiny on *Bounty* was just twenty-one. Bligh was arrogant, contemptuous of the People, and always aware that he came from an underprivileged background; only his incredible talent as a surveyor and cartographer exceeded his attitude.

As for *Resolution's* People, a great many had signed on again, men who'd been around the world on *Endeavour* and the first *Resolution*. They came back, most claimed, because Cook was a benevolent genius. He was loath to order a man lashed, unlike many captains. They also bragged about his brilliance in dealing with native people and his unparalleled seamanship. But mostly they signed on because they wanted to go back to Tahiti.

Cook wasn't thinking about Tahiti yet. For all his zeal about one last great voyage to ensure his legacy and tide the Great Explorer over into old age, Cook was preoccupied, bogged down in a list of minutiae. He was consumed with publishing his journals before competitive books from his ship's passengers were released. Cook saw his journal not only as a mark of his accomplishment, but as another potential financial windfall for his old age. In particular, the pesky, pious Forsters—Reinhold and George—were trying to circumvent Sandwich's authority and rush a book into print.

There was also Elizabeth's latest pregnancy. And the portrait sittings. And those high-powered dinners with England's famous and intelligent that Cook had come to enjoy so much. He'd been undervalued all his life, treated like a hayseed. At first it felt uncomfortable when men and women of import finally recognized his measure, invited him and Elizabeth to round out a table. But then he began to revel in—and even expect—the worship they cast upon his achievements. Cook was always the guest of honor. Lords and ladies spoke to him with reverence, hung on his every word, begged him to recount yet another tale of horrific Southern Ocean storms or shipwreck off the Great Barrier Reef or even the antics of those enchanting Tahitian women. Elizabeth took it all in stride, sitting quietly at Cook's elbow as he spoke. But she doted on this man whose greatness only she had foreseen. The passion of their whirlwind courtship had never cooled—indeed, the long years at sea only added to their lust—and she savored his presence. In his best blue uniform, with its elaborate gold braid and buttons and formfitting white pants, he was quite a sight. This was the man for whom she'd left her father's market.

Likewise, Cook, whose mind so often wandered inward to plot and dream, doted on pregnant Elizabeth in his unique, disconnected way.

Cook's greatest worry was Elizabeth's financial security in his absence. His elevated status as he prepared to guide *Resolution* again meant a guarantee of patronage for Elizabeth from Lord Sandwich himself. Cook's heart was much lighter knowing that his family would not see the poorhouse in his absence.

The one thing Cook was not thinking about was *Resolution*. May came and went. Elizabeth gave birth. The boy was named Hugh, after Palliser. And still Cook had neither finished his journal nor stepped aboard *Resolution*. He was tying up loose ends, reveling in his fame. His preoccupation with his journals made him forget his desire to reach Barents by the following June. He also forgot his long-standing connection with the People. The crew had grown tired of waiting for *Resolution* to sail; most had run out of money and were deserting, eager to sign on with other vessels. The notion that they could last months between voyages was preposterous.

Cargo was loaded. In late June, King George III sent a gift of livestock. The animals were brought on board, sharing space belowdecks with the crew. London was humid now, hot. The combination of a hundred sailors and two dozen animals, large and small, in a poorly ventilated space, and their attendant aroma, raised the crew's frustration to a new level. Desertions continued.

Space grew even more precious when Omai brought his possessions on board, among them his suit of arms. New crew were hired.

Finally, the journal was done. Cook delivered it to the publishers. James and Elizabeth—six weeks having passed since little Hugh's birth—enjoyed their trademark last night of flesh on flesh, then Lord Sandwich sent his carriage to fetch Cook. The post captain joined *Resolution* in the Thames on June 25. There had been no sea trials as before the 1772 voyage. Cook felt they weren't necessary, for he'd made few structural changes to *Resolution*.

As Cook began his third and final voyage around the world on a hot summer's day by having a pilot guide *Resolution* down the Thames, he was relieved to finally have the burdens of work and business behind him. He could now focus on being a sailor. Though he planned to do a thorough job, he wasn't in his usual eager-to-explore frame of mind.

After dropping the pilot in Sheerness, Cook sailed down the English Channel to Portsmouth. Hugging the coast, he stopped finally in Plymouth, where the obligatory contingent of Royal Marines came aboard. Their number had climbed from a dozen on prior voyages to more than twenty. As always, their quarters were the buffer between the People and the officers.

Boswell, so eager to sail with Cook, did not make the voyage. There was simply no room.

In the harbor alongside *Resolution* and *Discovery* were sixty-two transports and three warships loaded with mercenaries, all headed to America for war. Yet the Spanish and French spies onshore cared more about the destination of the two former colliers. The Admiralty's official statement was that Cook was sailing for Tahiti to take Omai home; there was nothing about Spanish New Albion or French territories in the South Seas.

The short trip to Plymouth revived Cook's love affair with power. He was not merely the Great Explorer—on the sea he was king. And now he wanted to set sail from Plymouth Sound immediately, as if he could make up the entire self-imposed, three-month delay through sterling navigation and his sheer legend.

Cook waited impatiently for Clerke, still in the King's Bench Prison in Saint George's Fields. When he could wait no more, Cook left a message with *Discovery's* crew that Clerke should "follow me to the Cape of Good Hope without loss of time."

So on July 12, 1776, just eight days after America had signed her declaration of independence and almost four years to the day that he had last sailed from England, Cook set sail. Deckhands clambered up the tar-covered ratlines and then angled out along the yards to unfurl the mainsails. They climbed higher for the topsails, then higher into the crosstrees for the topgallants. Cook paced the quarterdeck in his splayfooted waddle as Bligh cried out orders. Then, into the wind, all 462 tons of *Resolution*, loaded with men and supplies and cows and sheep and chickens and pigs and horses, wallowed down-harbor. Past Plymouth Hoe, then Drake Island. Then Plymouth and all of England were left behind.

Only after *Resolution* made course for Madeira, to fill the hold with thousands of barrels of Madeira's famed fortified wine (mixed with brandy, the wine was famous for both its kick and endurance, making it ideal for long ocean passages), did Cook step into his beloved great cabin. He relaxed and felt a fatigue greater than he'd ever known wash over him. As he took a deep breath, Cook was overwhelmed with his responsibilities. His compulsive need to touch every last island and passage, to do it better than any other discoverer preceding him, to rename all those previously named islands so people would know they were the property of James Cook—it was all becoming exhausting. When would it end? he wondered. How much would be enough? Could he settle back at Mile End or Greenwich Hospital, or would some deep rumination about lands he'd missed along the way gnaw at him like unfinished business, waking him in the dead of night or driving him to boorishness?

Resolution would wait for Charlie Clerke and *Discovery* at Cape

Town, then push on for Tahiti to drop off Omai. On the way, Cook intended to find those islands of which Crozet had spoken. The ones found by the French explorer Kerguélen. Cook would find them, just to say he had been there—just to plant the flag and give them a proper English name. James Cook was going to go farther than any other man could go, even if it killed him.

And it just might. For *Resolution* was already leaking.

In her deepest bowels, where stone was piled for ballast and casks of wine were packed tightly and stowaway ship's cats huddled to pounce on stowaway ship's rats, the cold, gray Atlantic seeped between her planks in thin rivers. And while the problem lay with the Deptford Yards, the blame rested with Cook. His ship was sinking because he hadn't done his job properly. A man who fancied himself a legend had replaced the meticulous able-bodied seaman.

Under these conditions, strain plaguing both his ship and his mind, Cook sailed over the horizon from England for the last time.

CHAPTER 18

Rum, Sodomy, and the Lash

Cook's behavior had descended into the realm Freudians know as the id. This force is bent on anarchy and amorality; its only function is guaranteeing the survival of its host. To this end the id is laserlike in its focus and tenacity. Existentialists claim that denial of the id leads to perversion of human nature. Moralists claim an unharnessed id is a perversion unto itself, a preference for evil over man's singular ability to show reason and compassion.

Cook was proving moralists correct. Discovery had become an ego boost. The fascination, the eagerness, was nowhere to be seen. Closing in on fifty, Cook was jaded by his years of nonstop travel. He was cranky and no longer gazed to the horizon with fascination. His previously always-workmanlike exploration habits were now taking on the air of drudgery. Obligation.

By contrast, a freed Clerke was reveling in his first command. He commanded *Discovery* with the attention to detail, diet, and cleanliness of a man who'd spent years under Cook's shadow. His crew numbered seventy. He caught up with Cook in Cape Town on November 10, three weeks after his mentor had arrived. "Captain

Clerke," Cook wrote, "informed me that he sailed from Plymouth on the 1st of August, and should have been here with us a week sooner, if the late gale of wind had not blown him off the coast. Upon the whole, he was seven days longer in his passage from England than we had been. He had the misfortune to lose one of his Marines by falling overboard; but there had been no other mortality against his people, and they now arrived well and healthy."

Cook, meanwhile, wrote a letter to Sandwich before leaving Table Bay in late November 1776. He had come across two French East India ships, one of which was homeward bound, and he wanted to pass along a missive before entering the great void of the Indian and Pacific Oceans. The voice was informal and randy, closer to Sandwich's than Cook's, and a far cry from the supplicant of Cook's early days. Cook knew that several years would pass before the two would communicate again and wanted to pass along a thanks while it was still relevant. Through a great deal of hard work and lobbying, Sandwich had been responsible for freeing Clerke from debtors' prison, and Cook was deeply grateful. "Your very obliging favor I received by Captain Clerke. We are now ready to proceed on our voyage, and nothing is wanting but a few females of our own species to make the *Resolution* a complete ark. For I have added considerably to the number of animals I took on board in England. Omai consented with raptures to give up his cabin to make room for four horses."

Cook then added a bawdy coda, pointing out how the sheep on board had been subjected to overtures by the local Dutchmen. The London conversations between Sandwich and Cook had obviously centered around more than just sailing, though Cook the farm boy could hardly have been faulted for flaunting his knowledge of animal husbandry with gentleman farmer Sandwich. Cook had his own personal sheep on board *Resolution* for the second voyage, but despite his coming years at sea, his track record of fidelity makes it likely that the sheep was just being fattened for a good meal.

Still, sodomy as conversation was a departure for Cook. Whether to hide his roots from London society or to bury Airyholme in his past, Cook had always refrained from acting less than the sophisticate. It was as if he had hidden his true self from everyone but Elizabeth and had required an achievement on the astounding scale of *Resolution's* 1772–75 voyage to show his heart to a surrogate father. He had been virtuous—or had, at least, convinced himself that virtue was an avenue to greatness. Sandwich had corrupted Cook, plain and simple, if only because both men were lonely for a friend and ally. In a cleansing way, after a lifetime of self-editing, the letter's candor was yet another tentative symbol Cook had achieved greatness. In an era when commoners and lords didn't exchange such informalities, it seems as though Cook was finally comfortable—that in his mind he had finally arrived.

Cook landed just before Christmas, 1776, on Kerguelen Island and renamed it Island of Desolation. The Kerguelens are a group of three hundred volcanic islands and inlets that lie almost exactly halfway between Africa and Australia. Cook thought them sterile and windswept. Nosing above the southern Indian Ocean's surface, the islands are a jagged home to albatross, ducks, penguins, and fur seals. All are migratory, as the islands have no native animal species. A highly antiscorbutic cabbage curiously found nowhere else on earth is one of the few plants.

Of all the islands, Kerguelen—or Island of Desolation—was the only one of importance due to its size and topography, being a massive one hundred miles long and up to seventy-nine miles wide. Fjords crease the mountainous terrain.

After the crew gathered cabbage and slaughtered every penguin they could get their hands on, Cook left the Island of Desolation behind. Unbeknownst to Cook, the island's next visitors would be another French fleet. In 1893 these commas on the map, thousands of miles from nowhere, would become a French protectorate. The name would revert to Kerguelen.

The Cook of *Endeavour*, or even the early days of *Resolution's* first voyage, would have spent more time on Desolation. But Cook was discovering by rote, tapping his foot on islands to say he'd been there, then pushing on.

After leaving Kerguelen shortly before the New Year, Cook continued toward Queen Charlotte's Sound. *Resolution* and *Discovery's* orders were to replenish stores, then push on for Tahiti. A long push across the Pacific to North America would follow, with the ships picking up the coastline somewhere at forty degrees north latitude. Then they would coast north to Alaska, navigate the treacherous Bering Strait, and turn east for Newfoundland through the Northwest Passage—assuming they found it.

But the Admiralty was taking a lot for granted, not just with Cook but also with his vessel. Despite repairs in Cape Town, *Resolution's* strenuous first voyage and the shoddy work at Deptford had taken a severe toll. Her structure was fatigued. She was limping from port to port, barely surviving storms she once brushed aside. Leaks had been a constant since departing Plymouth, but on January 19, 1777, things got much worse when a sudden squall hit off what is now Tasmania. *Resolution's* fore-topmast and main topgallant mast were toppled. The heavy timber would have crashed down onto the deck, likely puncturing the sort of hole that might have spelled doom, if not for the spider's web of rigging spun about sails and masts and yards. Sailors swarmed below, trying to fix the problem but wary of being crushed if the suspended masts were to fall. It was mass confusion—tangled rope and sail and timber and varnish and men clambering and slipping and straining and barking, even as the sea refused to stop churning. Through it all, Cook struggled to keep *Resolution* true.

The destruction and chaos were a sign that Cook was becoming sloppy, gambling to catch up with his original timetable. The masts had snapped because *Resolution* was carrying too much sail. Cook was never known to make such a mistake. The People, some of whom had been on all three voyages, looked at one another in confusion. The silent understanding on Cook's vessels was that he would put men and ship through awful conditions, but his prudence and seamanship meant no mistakes. The unforgiving, all-powerful Southern Ocean would certainly not tolerate error. Had he made similar navigational errors when *Resolution* was skirting ice floes on her first voyage, Cook would have been dead years earlier.

As usual, Cook didn't share his plans or disappointments with the crew. Instead, he calmly made land at Tasmania's Adventure Bay, located several hundred miles south of the Australian coast. Cook even acted as if the broken masts had yielded a good opportunity, writing in his journal how glad he was "to carry into execution a design I had formed of putting into Adventure Bay to get a little wood and some grass for our cattle, both of which we were in great want of." He also left behind some pigs, deep in the woods, hoping they would evade the Aborigines long enough to breed and populate his South Pacific paradise (they didn't). Like Noah, Cook had sailed from Cape Town with a complement of animals—horses, cows, pigs, sheep, rabbits, and chickens. The cows had died on Desolation, and the rest of the animals had died soon after—save the pigs.

Cook stayed four days in Adventure Bay. Masts fixed, it was on to Queen Charlotte's Sound, anchoring on January 26, 1777.

In the weeks and months that followed, Cook exhibited strange behavior to protect his South Pacific kingdom. He was so torn, so ultimately indecisive about his allegiance to his newfound fame in England or to his beloved Pacific islands, that he alienated both Englishmen and islanders.

Every man on Cook's crew, for example, knew what had happened at Grass Cove in Queen Charlotte's Sound a few years prior. They not only sympathized with their fellow Englishmen who had been eaten, they had no problem imagining themselves being eaten. The brotherhood of the sea called for some sort of naval justice to make things right. Yet Cook did nothing. While his crew expected vengeance, Cook instead showed amusement.

The name of the Maori who had led the slaughter and cooking of *Adventure's* sailors in Grass Cove was Kahura, Cook learned. Instead of giving in to the crew's cries for vengeance, Cook allowed the ship's artist to spend time onshore with the man to paint his portrait. Even as this took place, and Cook talked aloud of his admiration for Kahura, he and the crew were aware that this same portrait would be included in the official ship's accounts of the voyage. Kahura's portrait would definitely return to London with *Resolution*. For all Cook knew, it would someday hang in the National Gallery.

Not punishing the Maori was Cook thumbing his nose at London, thumbing his nose at his profession, thumbing his nose at anyone and everyone who had ever crossed him. After all, Furneaux hadn't been punished for disregarding Cook's orders. He'd even been given another, though lesser, command. Hence, for all these possible reasons, Kahura lived. Cook wrote, "I should think no more of it as it was sometime since and done when I was not there. But if they ever made a second attempt of that kind they might rest assured feeling the weight of my resentment."

Cook was beginning to resemble the out-of-touch London poofs he met at parties back home. Instead of being stern and devoted to doing what was best for Britannia or his role as an explorer, he patted the Maori on the head and sent them on their way. They were rebellious children. He was their loving father. A father punishes his children when they do wrong.

By February 27, *Resolution* had replenished at Queen Charlotte's Sound and both vessels had been smoked and caulked. With leaks fixed, Cook set sail for Tonga and Tahiti. Relations between captain and crew were more strained with every passing day, with the People resentful of Cook's refusal to punish the Maori. The tiny ship began to resemble a powder keg, and rage was expressed through petty actions such as theft. It was only a matter of time before minor rebellions would escalate into larger, more confrontational activity. The marine contingent between Cook's quarters and the crew's was becoming necessary for the first time in his career.

On March 15, 1777, things went from bad to worse. In reaction to the small acts of thievery, which had come to include food stores and items from the ship's officers, Cook reduced the crew's salt ration to two-thirds. In addition, when meat was stolen, the entire crew's meat ration the next day would be reduced to two-thirds. Due to the animals that had died on board, meat was exceptionally scarce and valuable. Even Cook's personal sheep had been slaughtered a week out of Queen Charlotte's Sound.

The People banded together. More meat was stolen. Cook reduced rations to two-thirds for the next day. The crew, en masse, refused to eat a single bite of the reduced ration. Veterans of *Endeavour* remarked to newcomers that Cook had once lashed a man for not eating his beef, for Cook thought the protein vital to shipboard health.

The men held their breath, waiting for Cook to take the next action in their power skirmish. He was determined to win. In a rage, Cook declared the People's actions "mutinous" and immediately ordered the reduced ration continued until the thieves were reported. Cook believed that the innocent should not tolerate unlawful action of any sort. By concealing the identity of those who had stolen from ship's stores, they had become party to the act. Hence, their punishment.

The crew refused to eat.

In the end, even as the theft continued, Cook was forced to give in. The battle would be fought another day.

It was a tense *Resolution* that landed on the Tongan island of Nomuka in early May. The chaos only got worse when the Tongan people rowed and swam out to meet the ship. Madness ensued as hundreds of Tongans and sailors crowded the decks, with Tongan women distracting the sailors while Tongan men stole anything that wasn't nailed down. In a loud, sweaty scene, greetings and lusty come-ons and general mayhem were exchanged in Tongan and English. The tropical sun beat down. Cook was powerless to restore order. Indeed, because he thought the Tongans especially smart and his men especially stubborn, Cook had no intention of stepping in until *Resolution* was endangered.

Those sailors and marines with the presence of mind to stop the thieving wrestled items back as best they could. But nothing short of gunfire could stop the insanity.

Then a small army of Tongan thugs invaded the boat. With clubs and fists they beat their fellow islanders. Men, women, and children alike were clubbed in the head, punched in the face, and kicked. Blood washed across *Resolution's* decks in broad pools as the thugs left the vessel to make way for their kings. The local chiefs were to have first dibs on *Resolution's* riches. If anyone was to steal, it would only be after the chiefs had come aboard and carried off needless (to the Tongans) items such as bolts and metallic eyelets. As Cook looked on, the chief's men restored peace and made way for the chiefs by throwing the offenders overboard.

Cook was appalled at the violence, forgetting that Polynesians were just as appalled by the British custom of lashing. But witnessing the carnage opened up a new level of brutality in Cook's mind. He was already predisposed to increasingly more severe discipline, having weathered nearly three months of insolence from his crew. But he didn't want to lose control of his ship entirely by becoming a despot. Instead, he began playing mental games designed to get inside men's heads and wear down their resolve. He began the practice by treating his beloved Tongans maliciously.

For instance, the Tongan chief caught stealing the bolt to a spun-yarn wrench wasn't just lashed, his hands were also tied behind his back and he was brought ashore. Under guard, the chief sat on the beach until the Tongans produced a hog as payment for the bolt. William Anderson, *Resolution's* surgeon's mate, found the action appalling. It was the first time in the history of Cook's voyages that his own men were ashamed of the captain's behavior. Anderson wrote, "I am far from thinking there was any injustice in punishing this man for the theft, as it cannot be determined what might be the consequence if such practices had been permitted. But that he should be confined in a painful posture for some hours after or a ransom demanded after proper punishment for the crime had been inflicted, I believe scarcely will be found consonant with the principles of justice or humanity upon the strictest scrutiny."

Cook's days of benevolent rule and respect for other human beings were long past. In fact, punishment actually seemed to have become entertainment for him. The more outrageous, the better. When the children of his kingdom stepped out of line, they would be punished severely, and in a way that impacted them deeply. Cook was thrilled that chiefs stopped thieving after he'd made an example of the man. "After this," he sniffed happily, "we were not troubled by thieves of rank."

But petty theft by lesser lights continued at an astonishing rate as *Resolution* and *Discovery* lingered without reason for one month, then two, on his "Friendly Isles." Cook lashed a few men, but found that the thieving was unaffected, and that the chiefs were totally unmoved by having their subjects tied to a mainmast and flogged until their backs were bloody. And while the Admiralty forbade giving a sailor more than twelve lashes a day, Cook didn't restrict the number given to a Polynesian. If the man was a property owner, he was also ransomed for hogs and fowl, his limp body dumped on the beach for his family to minister to. Cook mused, however, that "a flogging made no more impression than it would have done upon the main mast." So Clerke and Cook conspired to come up with a fiendish punishment, something that would brand a thief just as surely as the scarlet letter A would brand an adulteress. They decided to shave thieves' heads. Not the whole head, for that wasn't sufficiently embarrassing. Nor was it uncommon. Cook's new practice was to shave half the offender's head. That way Tongans and British alike could spot a thief at a thousand paces. Cook called it a "mark of infamy."

The Tongans didn't take their punishments lightly. Though Cook thought them pliable and ever happy, they were plotting to kill him. The notion that a man could sail into their port, whip their chiefs at will, then sail away unscathed galled them. Perhaps the last straw was Cook's treatment of the son of Finau, a friendly chief. Cook ordered the child thrown in chains for trying to steal Clerke's cat.

Finau was irate and hatched a plan to kill Cook. Cook would be lured to a neighboring island for a massive feast to be held on May 19, 1777. There would be plenty of drinking. During two consecutive days of ceremonial festivities, an army of Tongans would murder Cook and his men.

The plan was sprung. Cook sailed *Resolution* to Lifuka, where a vast Tongan contingent greeted them with hogs, yams, turtles, and fresh water. The crew was brought ashore, where a crowd of hundreds soon surrounded them. A celebration broke out, and displays of wrestling and female boxing began. Cook was awed by the celebration, writing in his journal that the provisions he received "far exceeded any I had received before from an Indian prince."

The next morning Finau stepped forth. He suggested Cook tour the island—a guide would be provided. Cook thought the idea splendid. As Cook walked the trails and beaches of Lifuka, the Tongans back at their village were planning his demise. Cook, his officers, and the marines would spend the evening feasting. On a signal, they would be massacred. In the morning, when the People rowed ashore from the ships to look for their leaders, the Tongans would lead them to the far side of the island, where they would be slaughtered, as well. The ships would then be looted. Some of the Tongan chiefs lobbied for invading the ships at night, instead of walking the crews over to the far side of the island. Finau argued successfully for a daylight slaughter.

When Cook returned from his walk, impressed by the island, Finau suggested casually that he'd love to see the Royal Marines fire their weapons. Would the entire corps be so kind as to come ashore with Cook? Suspecting absolutely nothing, Cook readily agreed.

The feast began that night. Torches surrounded the perimeter of the jungle clearing. The night air was warm and cloudless. Roast pig, cooked sea turtle, and free-flowing kava, the island's most potent potable (made by mashing the root of kava—*Piper methysticum*, a member of the pepper family—then combining it with human spittle) were abundant. Kava is served in a coconut cup called a *bilo*, and drunk in accompaniment to ritual clapping—one clap before drinking and three claps after swallowing.

Cook was the center of attention. He sat among his men, next to a group of chiefs, attired in his best dress uniform and ceremonial white wig. He was lavished with displays of Tongan dancing. One memorable dance had 105 Tongan men writhing to the beat of two hollow-log drums. A "harlequin dance" at the end saw the Tongans surrounding Cook and thrusting and gyrating into his face.

This was when the signal was supposed to be given.

But Finau had rivals of his own, specifically the chiefs who wanted to assault the ships at night instead of during the day. At the last minute those chiefs attempted to change Finau's plan, but the proud chief would have none of it. He forbade his warriors to participate. And so Cook's life was spared. Strangely, Cook never knew of the intrigue. He remained convinced they loved him. Cook, however, did little to return that love, giving one native thirty-six lashes just weeks later, on June 14, and another native forty-eight lashes on June 17. On June 18, Cook barged into a Tongan village and took a group of chiefs hostage for allowing the theft of a turkey cock. They ignored Cook, calmly drinking their kava until the angry white man calmed down and his bird was returned.

On June 23, Cook shot a man as he leapt from the ship after stealing a trinket. Cook had begun keeping a loaded gun handy for just such an occurrence. When a thief successfully escaped the ship, Cook ordered a boat lowered. As his sailors rowed Cook in chase of the swimmer, Cook took target practice with his pistol. When the crew were close enough that shooting the man would no longer be sporting, Cook instructed the men to smash him down with paddles and throw the boat hook at his torso.

Ironically, Cook somehow still regarded himself as the benevolent king of the South Pacific. It was almost as if Cook were suffering from dementia brought on by fatigue, age, and too many years commanding a vessel capable of decimating a native village. Cook was drinking heavily at the time, enjoying long kava sessions with the local chiefs. Paulaho, the ceremonial king of Tonga, had invited Cook to join a kava circle on June 7. Only other chiefs were part of the circle. Cook quickly developed a fondness for kava, and for the deferential treatment he received from the chiefs. Within a month he spent many long hours getting drunk on the local brew.

Still, the thefts continued, and the punishments grew more severe. In a series of punishments Cook didn't write about, but which were vividly recorded in the journals of *Discovery's* master, Thomas Edgar, Tongans were ritually beaten. On June 13, a local man received three dozen lashes for theft. The next day, two men were punished, one with twenty-four lashes, and the other with thirty-six. On June 24, Clerke invited a chief to lunch. When the powerful man stole a tumbler and two wineglasses, Clerke had the master administer sixty lashes. Until that time, chiefs had always been immune from punishment.

When the thefts still continued, Cook had three men taken prisoner on June 28 for throwing stones at a woodcutting detail. One of the men was given three dozen lashes, another four dozen, and the last, six dozen. But that wasn't enough for Cook. The final man—whose back lay open to the bone after seventy-two lashes with the deadly cat-o'-nine-tails—was administered the most inhumane punishment of all before Cook would allow his unconscious body cut down from the mainmast. Cook ordered a nearby seaman to produce a knife, then cut into the victim's biceps, all the way to the bone. Then Cook ordered the seaman to make another cut to the bone, fashioning a cross into the man's arms. All this was done as *Resolution's* crew looked on in horror.

Eventually, the Tongans were rid of Cook. On July 17 he sailed for Tahiti, arriving on August 13. He and his crew spent two peaceful months reuniting with old friends, until another incident of theft on October 8 incited Cook's rage. A pair of goats had vanished. After Cook marched a war party far into the interior, intending to "shoot every soul I met with," he retrieved one goat and cast its robber in chains. The other goat was nowhere to be seen, but Cook was afraid of losing face. "I could not retreat with any tolerable credit, and without giving encouragement to the people of the other islands we had yet to visit to rob us with impunity."

Like Sherman marching on Atlanta, Cook burned everything in sight—houses and war canoes being especially combustible. Despite being Tahitian, Omai was enthusiastic about the destruction and looted the town of Paopao along with Cook's men.

The next morning, Cook found a way to punish beyond a means fitting the crime. He cut one ear off the petty thief and shaved his head.

The only Tahitian who would miss Cook when *Resolution* finally sailed was Omai. This was ironic, because Cook loathed Omai and was angry Furneaux had ever brought him to England. But before leaving the Tahitian, Cook had the men build Omai a house, though it was clear already that Omai's jealous countrymen were planning to pull the nails out one by one for themselves. Under the bright Tahitian sun, where a man sweats just talking, Omai kept his suit of armor handy in case he needed protection. He seemed oblivious to the singular sensation of hot metal on bare skin.

Cook presented Omai with sheep and cattle, then, on November 2, 1777, bade farewell from *Resolution's* quarterdeck. One of the crew wrote of the scene: "Omai hung round the Captain's neck in all the seeming agony of a child trying to melt the heart of a reluctant parent. He twined his arms around him till Captain Cook unable longer to contain himself, broke from him and retired to his cabin to indulge that natural sympathy which he could not resist, leaving Omai to dry up his tears and compose himself on the quarterdeck."

Cook ignored Omai's tears. He was refreshed and eager to push on, though with a heavy heart. "The spirit of desertion," as one crewman wrote, filled Cook's ships after months in the islands. Cook and his men would lose their sense of forward momentum if he tarried much longer. They sailed from Tahiti, then stopped briefly in Bora-Bora as *Resolution* began moving north to the equator, but otherwise Cook and his men were done with the South Pacific.

It was almost the end of 1777 and time to move above the equator for Cook's first real journey of exploration in the Northern Hemisphere. *Resolution* and *Discovery* had been gone from England a year and a half and had not even begun the most difficult part of their job. Cook had a rebellious crew on his hands, a potential five-year voyage, and a growing sadness inside that he'd seen the last of his Pacific kingdom. He would return home by way of the Orient and Batavia, that much was for sure. Tahiti and Tonga and the Marquesas and even his beloved Ship's Cove were in his past forever. As Cook watched Bora-Bora fade over the horizon, it was like closing the favorite chapter of his life. He was no longer king, just a ship's captain aching to earn twenty thousand pounds for finding something most men swore didn't exist.

The rage Cook had directed toward the Tongans and Tahitians had foreshadowed the sadness he knew in leaving them behind. There was simply no way he could ever make a life there.

"Seventeen months had now elapsed since our departure from England," Cook wrote, wary of the unknown North Pacific he was about to lead his vessels into. "With regard to the principal object of my instructions, our voyage was at this time only beginning; and therefore my attention to every circumstance that might contribute to our safety and success was now to be called forth anew."

Shortly after daybreak on December 24, one day after both vessels had crossed into the Northern Hemisphere, they sighted an uninhabited, barren atoll (a ring-shaped coral island surrounding a central lagoon) approximately ten miles long and fifteen miles wide. Bligh was sent to find safe passage through the reef, which he did. Both ships dropped anchor in a shallow lagoon on the lee shore. The People were sent ashore to forage for food and returned not only with ample fresh fish, but also three hundred large sea turtles, weighing between ninety and a hundred pounds apiece. There was much rejoicing, for sea turtles were an incredible delicacy at sea. Christmas Day was spent in the sheltered lagoon, a day full of eating and drinking. Cook named the spot Christmas Island.

The vessels stayed a week, in which time Cook observed an eclipse of the sun. Cook wrote that the island was "light and black, evidently composed of decayed vegetables, the dung of birds and sand." Early Polynesian voyagers had planted coconut palms, but otherwise the island lacked much vegetation. The freshwater was brackish and sparse.

Cook sailed from Christmas Island on January 2, 1778. The frigid North American coast was their next stop. Cook and the men steeled for the change in weather. Two weeks later, though, halfway between Bora-Bora and America, Cook was flabbergasted to see tropical islands off his port bow. It was January 18, 1778. He had stumbled upon Niihau and Kauai, two of the more westerly islands of the Hawaiian group. Despite centuries of Pacific exploration, the existence of such a chain had never been theorized, making Cook's find all the more surprising.

Cook documented the find thoroughly. "At this time we were in some doubt whether or not the land before us was inhabited. Seeing some canoes coming off from the shore towards the ships soon cleared up this doubt. I immediately brought to, in order to give them time to come up. There were three and four men in each and we were agreeably surprised to find them of the same nation as the people of Tahiti and the other islands we had visited. It required by very little address to get them to come alongside, but we could not prevail upon anyone to come on board. They exchanged a few fish they had in the canoes for anything we offered them, but valued nails, or iron above every other thing. The only weapons they had were a few stones in some of the canoes and these they threw overboard when they found they were not really wanted. Seeing no signs of an anchoring place in this part of the island, I bore up for the lee side, and ranged the SE side at the distance of half a league from shore. As soon as we made sail the canoes left us, but others came off from the shore and brought with them roasting pigs and some very fine potatoes, which they exchanged, as the others had done, for whatever we offered them. Several small pigs were got for sixpenny nail or two apiece, so that we again found ourselves in the land of plenty, just as the turtle we had taken on board at the last island was nearly expended. We passed several small villages, some seated upon the seashore and other up in the country. The inhabitants of all them crowded so close to the shore and on the elevated places to view the ships. The land on this side of the island rises in a gentle slope from the sea shore to the foot of the mountains that are in the middle of the island, except in one place, near the east end, where they rise directly from the sea. Here they seemed to be formed of nothing but stone which lay in horizontal stratas. We saw no wood but what was up in the interior part of the island and a few trees about the villages.

"At nine o'clock, being pretty near the shore, I sent three armed boats under the command of Lieutenant Williamson, to look for a landing place and fresh water. I ordered him, that if he found it necessary to land to look for the latter, not to suffer more than one man to go out of the boat.

"As there were some venereal complaints on board both the ships, in order to prevents its being communicated to these people, I have orders that no women, on any account whatever, were to be admitted on board the ships."

The day was a study in contrasts—the earnest, innocent islanders offering all they had to the manic, driven Cook. Little did Cook know that he had stumbled onto one of the most intellectually advanced and warlike Pacific island clusters. For all their innocence, and their eagerness to make Cook welcome, the Hawaiians would not meekly accept lashings like the Tongans or Tahitians.

Kauai is wet and green, covered in jungle rot, deep canyons, and tumbling waterfalls. In fact, the windward summit region of the extinct Kauai volcano is one of the wettest areas on earth. Craggy cliffs called Na Pali, formed by millennia of erosion, define the skyline.

The Hawaiians, or Indians, as Cook called them, were of Polynesian extract. Their legends held that they had traveled by canoe from Raiatea in the Society Islands in roughly A.D. 450—a distance of several thousand miles over open water. They intermarried with the island's first settlers, the small and dark Menehune. Still, they thought of themselves first as citizens of Raiatea, shuttling between Raiatea and the Hawaiian Islands for almost a millennium. Finally, somewhere around the thirteenth century, they developed an independent identity.

The Hawaiians built a society on what could arguably be called the Pacific's most ideal islands. The mountainous terrain, fertile volcanic soil, numerous rivers and streams, and relatively cool latitudes (between twenty and twenty-two north) were effective in producing an active, vibrant culture. Cook's visit, however, with his grand vessels and metal, changed their world forever. "In the course of my several voyages," Cook wrote after he had invited several locals aboard *Resolution*, "I have never before met with the natives of any place so much astonished as these people were upon entering a ship. The wildness of their looks and gestures . . . strongly marking to us that they had never been visited by Europeans."

Like the Tahitians when *Endeavour* had first arrived, the Hawaiians had no history of metallurgy. They took an immediate liking to iron and steel, rejecting beads and other implements of trade in favor of more functional metal objects such as hammers and axes. When these were slow in coming, the Hawaiians proved as adept at theft as their Polynesian brothers and sisters, much to the consternation of Cook.

Things went well between the Hawaiians and Cook's ships for a

few days, with the locals even prostrating themselves in Cook's presence. Within days of their arrival, however, Cook was already killing
Hawaiians. When a crowd of natives onshore who wished to steal
metal overwhelmed Lieutenant Williamson and the crew of a boat
from *Resolution*, he gave the order to fire. One Hawaiian man died
immediately.

Despite the calamity, and oblivious to the tension, Cook stayed
two weeks. Niihau and Kauai were two of Hawaii's leeward, or rainy,
islands, and their lush vegetation allowed Cook to replenish his
stores with a massive quantity of freshwater, pigs, fowls, sweet potatoes, and taro.

Then he hurried north, eager to explore the Alaskan coast during
summer. Setting sail on February 2, 1778, his plan was to travel to
present-day Washington. From there he would coast north to Alaska,
searching coves and inlets along the way for a Northwest Passage.

As in Tahiti, Cook left Hawaii sadly. He was clinging to vestiges of
Polynesia as if clinging to life itself, and he reveled in each day spent
in the tropics. What amazed Cook most about Hawaii was the immensely aquatic nature of the culture. Men, women, and children
were just as adept in the water as on land. Cook, with his inability to
swim, thought those feats almost superhuman. The most amazing
thing was the women who swam while holding their infants:
"Women with infants at the breast to come off in canoes to look at
the ships, and when the surf was so high that they could not land
them in the canoe they used to leap overboard with the child in
their arms and make their way ashore through a surf that looked
dreadful."

Resolution sighted the North American continent on March 7,
1778. The country was heavily forested, pocked by deep inlets much
like Ship's Cove. In fact, the North American coast reminded Cook
so much of New Zealand that he named a section of it after Queen
Charlotte. The ships continued northward, hugging the west coast of
what would become Vancouver Island without realizing that it was

an island, and finally anchored in a deep inlet on its coast. But Cook was so taken with Nootka Sound, as the local Indians called it, that he named the anchorage after his beloved Ship's Cove. And what began as a simple stop for water turned into a stay of four weeks. Cook not only resupplied his vessels, but he replaced much of the masts and rigging of the decaying *Resolution*.

Ship's Cove in Nootka Sound marked the first time since his survey of Newfoundland that Cook had set foot on North American soil. Like the rest of the Pacific Coast of North America, the land was notable for its rocky shoreline and mountainous interior. Cook's affection for the land deeply affected one of his impressionable young crewmen. So much so that, in 1792, George Vancouver, the young midshipman on *Discovery*, would return to those waters and make a circuit of the island's vast coastline, giving it his name.

Cook put to sea again April 26. As *Resolution* and *Discovery* sailed northward up what is now the western Canadian coastline, heading to Alaska, he was amazed at the beauty onshore. "The country," he wrote, "being full of high mountains, whose summits were covered with snow. But the valleys between them, and the grounds on the sea coast, high as well as low, were covered to a considerable breadth with high, straight trees, that formed a beautiful prospect as one vast forest."

Foul weather dogged their attempts at exploration. Squalls and sleet roiled the seas and lowered crew morale. Though miles of sounds and cove rimmed the Canadian coast, the Coast Mountains just inland served as a constant dead-end reminder that none of the entrances led through to a Northwest Passage. However, at approximately sixty degrees north latitude, once the coastline veered northwest into the Gulf of Alaska, Cook's job grew immensely more difficult. The Coast Mountains were behind them, no longer a barrier. Each inlet was deep and seemingly the source of the elusive passage. Problem was, the number of inlets seemed endless. Measured roughly along its perimeter, Alaska's coastline is 5,580 miles long.

However, if all the inlets and islands are taken into account, the total length is 31,383 miles.

Adding to Cook's difficulty were the outrageous tides off the Alaskan coast, often fluctuating twenty feet, producing a brutal current that made coasting difficult. So not only did he have to determine which inlets might lead to the Northwest Passage, and which would not, he had to do so from far offshore. Worst of all, the current—appropriately titled the Alaska Current—was a constant along the entire coastline. From Canada, it flows westward and then, in the eastern Aleutian islands, turns northward to bring warm water along the western coast of Alaska all the way to its northernmost reach, far above the arctic circle, at Point Barrow.

Cook pressed on, despite the growing obstacles.

As with the New Zealand coasting from the *Endeavour* voyage, Cook sailed along this deadly coast without benefit of a map. Explorer Vitus Bering had passed through the same waters but lacked Cook's cartographical skills and produced a rather incomplete rendering. Cook, then, was effectively sailing blind, unsure of hidden hazards.

The deck seams of the *Resolution* began leaking again. Stressed by storms and currents, the masts and rigging were disintegrating less than three months after Cook had replaced them in Nootka Sound. A worried Cook ignored the problems, knowing he needed to use the precious, ice-free summer months to search the Arctic. Stopping for repairs was a luxury he could not afford.

Cook sailed in and out of the wide inlet leading to modern Anchorage without finding his precious Northwest Passage. He continued through the Aleutian Islands and into the Bering Sea. Beyond that lay the Beaufort Sea, then the Arctic Ocean. And, hopefully, the Northwest Passage, although it wouldn't be easy. Cook was entering an area of treacherous sailing, an area that would require him to navigate with the same flawlessness he had shown on his first two voyages—but not, so far, on the third.

Ever so cautiously, Cook nudged *Resolution* and *Discovery* into the Bering Sea ice pack. Somewhere inside lay his Northwest Passage.

At the same moment, in August 1778, on the other side of the North American continent, the Revolutionary War raged on land and sea. The powerful British Royal Navy had deemed Newport, Rhode Island, one of the seven vital ports in America. The Revolutionary War was primarily a naval struggle to protect British trading rights from the Caribbean to Newfoundland. Holding Newport meant holding America. From Newport, British warships could easily sail on the rebel-held port of Boston. Or they could sail in the opposite direction, south and west, to refortify New York, the major British stronghold coveted by General George Washington. And from New York they could leapfrog down to Philadelphia, the Chesapeake, Charleston, and Savannah. As long as the American colonies' naval power was limited to the few privateers and small gunboats under John Paul Jones, Newport was safe.

In spring of 1778, everything changed when the French entered the Revolutionary War on the side of the colonies. Within a month French gunboats were advancing on the American coastline. Under Duc de Choiseul, head of French naval affairs, powerful new ships had been built, and a corps of ten thousand professional gunners trained. The French gunships were heavy, however. When they first tried to wage war in the colonies, the ships ran aground outside New York. Embarrassed, praying the British wouldn't pounce at such an inopportune moment, the French waited for high tide and sailed to safety.

Washington had coordinated the French attack on New York to coincide with a land invasion. Before the French disappeared too far over the horizon, Washington sent word by messenger. He suggested they attack Newport instead.

In an effort to stem the French advance, the British sank ten ships as an offshore blockade, noses touching stems to form a chain like circus elephants. A prison ship recently renamed the *Lord Sandwich* was one of them. As a cargo ship she had carried a load of 574 mercenaries of the Larsborg Du Corps Hessian Brigade to Newport in 1776, then been deemed unseaworthy and converted to a prison ship. Her holds were soon filled with those citizens of Newport who refused to sign a form stating they would fight on the side of the British. Between the summers of 1776 and 1778, she bobbed just offshore in Newport Harbor's choppy waters, with a complement of roughly sixty prisoners at a time.

On August 8, 1778, she was intentionally sunk during the siege of Newport. A thick layer of fine brown silt covers her now.

And while the French were repulsed and Newport stayed in British hands another year, not a single sailor mourned the passing of the *Lord Sandwich*—formerly known as HM Bark *Endeavour*—one of the greatest ships ever to sail the globe.

CHAPTER 19

North

Summer 1778

T he Bering Sea is frozen during the winter, with the ice often extending a thousand miles south of the arctic circle—below even the Alaskan mainland, then out along the Aleutian Islands. In summer the Alaskan coastline thaws. The ice retreats from the Bering Sea altogether, into its more northerly neighbors, the Chukchi Sea, the Beaufort Sea, and the Arctic Ocean, and back above the arctic circle.

Winter comes early in Alaska, and by mid-August 1778, Cook was only halfway up the western coast of Alaska, but already encountering the Arctic ice pack. On August 9, Cook sailed into the Bering Strait, the narrow gap between Alaska and Russia where the Bering Sea ends and the Chukchi Sea begins. Off his starboard bow he sighted a headland and named it Cape Prince of Wales. The Cape, Cook also noted, "is the more remarkable by being the Western extremity of all America hitherto known."

Resolution and *Discovery* ventured carefully into the Chukchi Sea. Cook sailed one hundred, then two hundred miles north without success. All the while, ice threatened to trap him, but the challenge brought out the best in the old navigator. Cook was displaying flashes of sailing brilliance again, maneuvering through ice and fog and summer blizzards and roiling, frigid seas. With swashbuckling confidence, he sailed back and forth between the North American and Asian landmasses, trying to find a gap in the ice.

But with summer edging toward autumn, Cook's chances of finding the Northwest Passage in 1778 were growing dim. He was above seventy degrees north latitude—almost as far into the Northern Hemisphere's high latitudes as he'd ever sailed in the Southern. When he reached latitude seventy degrees, twenty-nine minutes north, the barrier of ice stretched as far as the eye could see. Cook could go no farther. He ordered *Resolution* and *Discovery* to turn around.

It was the twenty-ninth of August. Cook wrote: "The season was not so far advanced and the time when the frost is expected to set in so near at hand, that I did not think it consistent with prudence to make any further attempts to find a passage this year in any direction, so little was the prospect of succeeding. My attention was now directed towards finding some place where we could obtain wood and water, and in considering how I should spend the winter, so as to make some improvement to geography and navigation and at the same time be in a condition to return to the North in further search of a passage the ensuing summer."

Without knowing it, when Cook retreated, he was just fifty miles southwest of the Beaufort Sea, entrance to the Northwest Passage.

Cook sailed south, charting and naming as he went: St. Lawrence Island on September 4, Anderson Island on September 5. The vessels were battered by snow, sleet, rain, and high seas. *Resolution* began leaking again, this time on the starboard side. Her hold had accumulated three feet of standing water—the same amount that had almost sunk *Endeavour* atop her reef—and was battling caulking problems that threatened still more leakage. The sails and standing rigging were thoroughly rotten from daily confrontations with foul weather.

On October 2, Cook landed in the Russian fur trading port of Unalaska for three weeks of repairs. Smack in the middle of the Aleutian Island's hook, Unalaska was the last point of land between Alaska and the Sandwich Islands, almost three thousand miles south.

Unalaska was the perfect spot for an extended stay. It was rich in freshwater, berries, halibut, and salmon. Like Ship's Cove, it was protected inside a deep sound. Cook could have wintered there, then leapt immediately back into Alaskan waters when spring arrived. The danger, however, lay with the crew. They were on the verge of mutiny and didn't have the sort of heavy clothing to survive an Arctic winter. Fearnoughts wouldn't provide much protection, and there wasn't time to manufacture furs into jackets for almost two hundred men. Shelter would have been another problem, as would acquiring food under winter conditions. In the end, any gains from wintering in Unalaska would have been lost through tension, anger, and the likely deaths of many sailors.

Pushing south to the Sandwich Islands was the only guarantee of a restful winter. The distance was almost akin to an Atlantic crossing, but Cook knew it was for the best. He composed a letter to the Admiralty, then gave it to departing Russian trader Jacob Ivanovich to post upon his return to Europe. In it, Cook explained he was leaving to winter in warmer climes, but would resume his search for the Northwest Passage come spring. "But I have little hopes of succeeding," he noted.

The letter was Cook's first since leaving Table Bay two years before. It would also be his last.

On October 22, 1778, Cook prepared to sail from Unalaska. Uncharacteristically, after a brilliant summer navigating the Bering Sea, Cook ran his ship aground on the harbor bottom. Four days later he finally got his stern unstuck and was on his way. The holds of both ships had been recaulked, and the leaks had been fixed. Cook had stocked plenty of fresh water and spruce beer. Some problems had been unfixable, such as rust-eaten pieces of metal and tattered sails, but winter was upon them and Cook needed to be away.

However, he was hardly at sea a full day when tragedy struck *Dis-*

covery. Her main tack broke loose, the wooden yard falling from the mast. One man was killed as it crashed to the deck. The boatswain and three other sailors were severely injured.

The event once again undermined Cook and Clerke's command and was cruelly followed by four days of the worst weather of the voyage. A gale swirled about both ships, casting snow, sleet, and waves from all directions. Cook ran westward in a blizzard to escape, squeezing through a gap in the Aleutians, fearful of running aground on the island's tricky shoals. Clerke followed. The weather cleared. Then another storm hit them, blowing so hard that *Discovery* was stopped dead in the water.

The weather cleared once again, followed by another gale that shredded *Resolution*'s main topsail. All hands were brought on deck to assist in emergency repairs.

Finally, on the morning of November 26, a weary and old Cook sighted the island of Maui at first light. He could see homes and people onshore, and canoes raced out to greet him. But big surf and lack of a sheltered port made him push farther south. He'd noticed a very large island and learned from the natives who'd paddled all the way out to *Resolution* that its name was O'why'he. On November 30 he was off its shores.

CHAPTER 20

Lono

It would be seven weeks before Cook made landfall. In a power play to remind the crew of his authority, Cook coasted around Hawaii, charting its contours, without going ashore. The men began grumbling as they sufferd from a weird juxtaposition of discomforts—rampant venereal disease on the one hand, and the overwhelming urge for copulation on the other.

The People also had a powerful thirst. Stocks of rum aboard the ships were becoming low after two and a half years away from England. To conserve what remained, Cook decided to replace the daily ration to the crew with the beer he had brewed from sugarcane brought aboard by the Hawaiians. None of the sailors, however, would drink it. They'd had quite enough of Cook and his absurd discipline. They wanted to go ashore and were furious he was spending months coasting Hawaii's paradise instead of heading to land. And though Cook was just as tired and irritable, he had decided to find the perfect port—another Ship's Cove, another Unalaska, another Table Bay—before parking for the winter. The threat of mutiny was ignored.

Finally, on January 17, the ships anchored in Kealakekua Bay on the western side of Hawaii. Not only was it the perfect port, a protected deep-water anchorage, but also Cook was being treated to the welcome of his life. The Hawaiian reception was so effusive—more like worship—that Cook would have to have been the world's most humble man to sail past. Ten years prior, he might have. But in January 1779, prideful and emotionally adrift, James Cook found the Hawaiian greeting at Kealakekua Bay just what he needed.

Kealakekua is a crescent-shaped harbor a mile wide, carving out territory a mile inland. The entrance—the convergence points of the crescent—is a half mile wide. The land is rocky but flat. Slowly, the earth tapers upward on both sides of the bay to the rounded backside of the crescent (Kealakekua's distinguishing feature), a plateau several hundred feet above the water. Sheer cliffs drop straight into the bay from the plateau's summit. Kealakekua locals buried their chiefs in these sacred cliffs. They believed that royalty's power resided in their bones. To preserve this power, or *mana*, gravesites were kept secret. Remains were lowered over the side, along with a warrior to inter the body. Once the warrior had finished the job, he was cut loose to fall to his death. The location's secret died with him.

Cook was unaware of this, of course, when he sailed into Kealakekua. Nor did he know that the bay's name meant "pathway of the gods." Or that the Hawaiians had four major deities, Ku, Kane, Kanaloa, and Lono, with Kealakekua Bay considered the sacred home of Kanaloa.

Cook sailed inside the bay. Cook's officers estimated that between twenty-five hundred and thirty-five hundred canoes were paddling toward their ships, and ten thousand people were either jammed in the narrow canoes or swimming alongside. Deluded by grandeur, Cook assumed his kingdom's inhabitants were frantic to glorify their king. He stood tall on the quarterdeck, stoic, but deeply thrilled at the welcome fit for a god. A thin smile was plastered on his usually expressionless face.

Oddly enough, the Hawaiians truly thought Cook was a god—the one thing the farm boy had always ached to be. Through some act of fantastic coincidence, *Resolution* and *Discovery* had sailed into Kealakekua Bay during the annual festival of Makahiki. This was the time of the year for homage to be paid to Lono, the god of plenty. One of Lono's distinguishing symbols was white banners flown from crossbars. *Resolution* and *Discovery* entered the bay with billowing sails spread across the horizontal yards, looking for all the world just like white banners flying from crossbars. The Hawaiian natives, who had never seen white men or such monstrous sailing ships, couldn't believe their good fortune. Not only was it time for Lono's festival, but also for the first time in their history his supremeness was paying a personal visit.

The residents of Kealakekua paddled to the ships frantically, straining to figure out which of the hundreds of sailors crowding the decks was Lono. One man, they noted quickly, stood above all the rest. He didn't crowd the railing, panting at the women, but stood statuelike at the rear of the ship on a raised platform. No head was above Lono's. Instead of ragged clothing, Lono wore a fine blue uniform. He was older than the others, with broad streaks of gray in his dark brown hair.

Their priests were unsure whether Cook was a god or simply a great chief, but the Hawaiians were eager to welcome Lono. So many climbed aboard *Resolution* and *Discovery* that the vessels almost swamped. They stole anything they could, especially iron, eager to have a relic of Lono's visit.

Cook observed the proceedings with bemusement, as if the proper homage was finally being paid. His journal had taken on a brusque tone shortly after the sighting of Hawaii on November 30. Strangely, for the first time in his life he stopped journal entries altogether January 17, the day the ships anchored in Kealakekua Bay. The act was almost heretical. It was as if he had mentally severed himself from his Admiralty masters. He was God. From that day on, Lieutenant King and Lieutenant Phillips of the Royal Marines reported what happened in Kealakekua Bay.

When Cook went ashore, a wand-bearing priest led him through a throng of local people, performing a welcoming ceremony. Cook heard the name Lono mumbled again and again by the locals. The Hawaiian priests had confirmed Cook's deity by then, and the local chiefs deferred nervously to him. Even King Kalniopu, the aging Hawaiian supreme chief, treated Cook as divine and immortal. For the three-week duration of his stay, Cook was treated to feasts and celebrations, as befitting Lono's visit.

The People and officers, however, though considered immortal by the Hawaiians, were not considered gods. Instead, they were earthly helpers to the divine Cook. "They would often say," King wrote of how the Hawaiians referred to Cook, "that the great atua lived with us."

King later added, "It is very clear . . . they regard us as a set of beings infinitely their superiors; should this respect wear away from familiarity, or by length of intercourse, their behavior may change."

That behavior began to change in slight ways almost immediately. Even as the Hawaiians paid homage to Cook, the People's behavior was beginning to grate on them. The sexual appetite of Cook's men, for instance, their insatiable pursuit of the local women, was making their husbands jealous and angry.

It also seemed unusual that divine beings required so much sustenance for their vessels. No matter how many hogs, vegetables, or fruits the Hawaiians offered, the visitors always wanted more. It was true that one of Lono's characteristics was sailing clockwise around the island, collecting the produce of the earth, but the residents of Kealakekua had never given so much. They began to fear they would be left with nothing. "They supposed," wrote King, "we had left our native country on account of the scantiness of provisions and that we had visited them for the sole purpose of filling our bellies."

Finally, on February 1, the Hawaiians received confirmation that

Cook's crew were not immortal. An old seaman named Watman died and was buried ashore. "This, being lost," a Swiss crewman on *Discovery* named Heinrich Zimmerman wrote, "their reverence for us was gone."

Even as the homage to Cook continued, the Hawaiians became angry—and fearless. They began stealing from the ships, especially knives and iron goods. Their deference to the white men was no more. Women were less willing to offer themselves. Lono's season was coming to an end. It was time for him to continue his clockwise progression around the island.

The Hawaiians were ecstatic when Cook announced it was time for him to set sail. The morning of February 4, after Cook had attended a feast in his honor, *Resolution* and *Discovery* departed. Canoes filled the bay as Lono sailed away, many offering lavish gifts of food. A happy Kalniopu bade Cook/Lono farewell.

Cook was in no hurry to return to Alaska and the Northwest Passage. He sailed for the neighboring island of Maui, carrying a few Hawaiian men and women as passengers. The weather became fierce three days later, with severe winds and pounding seas. Several times Cook and his men lowered boats over the side to rescue Hawaiians whose canoes swamped as they paddled out to greet Lono on his journey around the island.

Then *Resolution*'s foremast broke once more. Unable to find a protected anchorage, Cook reluctantly decided to return to Kealakekua Bay to fell a tree and fix the problem.

The gales continued as Cook ordered the ships to reverse course and followed them all the way into Kealakekua. Cook was relieved to finally sail into the bay on February 11, but he and his men were shocked at the change in local attitude. They expected another rousing welcome, but saw not a single canoe. The beaches of Kalniopu's village, Kaawaloa, were deserted.

Finally, Kalniopu paid Cook a visit. He was unhappy that Cook had returned and inquired about the reason. Cook explained about the mast. Kalniopu seemed irritated, but not hostile as he returned to his village. He allowed local men to assist in Cook's repairs, as needed.

As the work got under way, Clerke lashed one Hawaiian forty times for stealing an armorer's tongs. Two days later, in retribution, a Hawaiian mob pelted a British watering party with rocks.

Through a quirk of fate, Cook was stepping ashore from the pinnace as all this occurred. King, in charge of the watering party, apprised Cook of the situation. "He gave orders to me," King wrote, remembering the exact moment when Hawaiian and British relations took a turn for the worse, "that on the first appearance of throwing stones or behaving insolently, to fire ball at the offenders."

Later that afternoon, tensions increased when the armorer's tongs were once again stolen from *Discovery*. The thief raced ashore in a canoe. Cook and King gave chase, but were intentionally misled by locals once they reached shore and asked for directions. The thief got away.

An enraged Cook returned to *Resolution* vowing extreme measures. "I am afraid," Cook said to King, "that these people will oblige me to use some violent measures. For they must not be left to imagine that they have gained an advantage over us."

The next morning, February 14, Cook was greeted with the news that *Discovery*'s cutter had been stolen in the night. Angrily, Cook loaded his shotgun—birdshot in one barrel, solid ball in the other—and ordered the marines to load their muskets with ball. A little before 7 A.M. Cook told King he was going ashore to Kaawaloa to seize a hostage. The hostage would remain on *Resolution* until the cutter was returned. Cook, King later wrote, was "in a hasty, determined, and extremely angry" mood.

Three boats headed to shore: Cook in *Resolution*'s pinnace, the launch filled with marines under Lieutenant John Williamson, and a small cutter under the command of master's mate William Lanyon.

Cook ordered Lanyon to position the cutter at the mouth of the bay so no canoes could escape. The pinnace and launch would proceed to Kalniopu's village. In all, thirteen men descended on the shore. They wove through the underwater rocks forming a barricade to the beach, buffeted by a strong current.

Accompanied by the Marines, Cook leapt from the pinnace in shallow water and stormed toward the village. The ocean bottom was slick and uneven lava. Watched by a throng of natives, Cook walked carefully, making sure not to slip and lose face at such a crucial time. He strode onto the black dirt and white shells marking the water's edge and entered Kaawaloa village. Lieutenant Molesworth Phillips of the marines was at Cook's side, even as the pinnace and launch backed away into the bay. The boats would remain just beyond the submerged rocks protecting the shore, prepared to return instantly if trouble arose.

Old King Kalniopu's thatched house was just fifty yards inland. The king was asleep. With several hundred Hawaiians looking on, Cook sent Phillips under the low doorway to wake the king. When Kalniopu emerged, Cook demanded he accompany the marines back to *Resolution*. As Kalniopu walked to the shore, unworried, his wife yelled to him that he would be killed on the ships. Two other chiefs grabbed Kalniopu by the arm and forcibly attempted to separate him from Cook. Now terrified, the king looked at his fellow chiefs, then at Cook, for an answer.

Meanwhile, the crowd had swelled into the thousands. A handful of the Royal Marines, realizing their guns would be useless with the mob gathered so close, moved thirty yards away from Cook to a rocky outcropping. They would defend their leader from there, having a better field of fire. The rest of the marines, including Phillips, stayed with Cook.

The situation grew dire. King Kalniopu sat down on the ground. Cook attempted to persuade him to follow, while the chiefs insisted he stay. Finally, with the crowd so great that Cook feared for his life, the king was allowed to remain. Covered by the marines, whose muskets were leveled, Cook began retreating to the beach. He walked backward, peripheral vision scanning the entire gauntlet closing around him.

At that very moment news arrived by canoe from the opposite side of the bay, a mile off; Lieutenant King's men had opened fire and killed a senior chieftain, an *al'ii*. The mob was instantly enraged and focused their anger on Cook. An excited warrior taunted Cook with an iron-tipped spear that the men of *Resolution* had presented as a gift. He jabbed at the captain, poking him in the arms and thighs. Never one to take offense lightly, Cook raised his shotgun and fired with intent to wound. The barrel full of birdshot, however, bounced harmlessly off the man's woven-grass shield.

What happened next was Magellan-like, providing one last horrible link between Cook and the great explorers. The emboldened warrior saw fear in Cook's eyes, knew the white man's vulnerability. He jabbed Cook again, harder. Cook fired his second barrel and the shot killed a member of the mob pressing so close. Another warrior plunged his spear into Phillips while all this was going on. The lieutenant managed to raise his musket and shoot the man dead.

The mob erupted. Rocks began to fly, hitting Cook, Phillips, and the marines. The marines fired a volley. Aimed at no one in particular, it succeeded in bringing down six more Hawaiians. *Resolution's* cannon opened fire, raking the shore.

The marines hastily reloaded. Sailors in the pinnace and launch laid down covering fire. Cook called to the pinnace, ordering them to cease fire and come closer to shore. But they paddled away, later swearing Cook was telling them to head back to the ship and save themselves.

That act of turning around to yell instructions proved to be Cook's undoing. The warrior (the angry man's name was Nu'ah) took advantage of Cook's position and stabbed him in the back with an iron dagger. Cook fell immediately, seriously wounded. The mob surged forward and began to stab Cook repeatedly. One by one they took turns shoving daggers into his body. Cook was a blood-covered man crying out in pain. The sharp tips repeatedly punctured his chest and organs. Arteries were severed. He spit up blood. They hit him with their fists, too, punching his handsome face until it was bruised and battered. Blood soaked his hair.

The marines leapt into the sea and swam frantically to the boats, followed by Phillips. The mob ignored them in their frenzy to attack Cook. For ten long minutes his body bobbed at the waterline, stab wounds multiplying by the minute.

"The islanders set up a great shout," King journalized from Phillips's eyewitness account, "and his body was immediately dragged up on shore, and surrounded by the enemy, who snatching the dagger out of each other's hands shared a savage eagerness to have a share in his destruction."

The fatal damage to Cook had been done by the very metal knives Cook had given the Hawaiians. Each Hawaiian warrior, mother, and child had taken a turn thrusting the gift of iron into Cook's lifeless form, then passed it on. Cook was dead long before they halted their slaughter.

Only when the marines were safely away and *Resolution*'s and *Discovery*'s guns had a clear field of fire did the crowd disperse. Salvo after salvo pounded the beach. When it was done, the crowd was gone, as was Cook's mutilated body and those of four dead marines: John Allen, Thomas Fatchett, Theophilus Hinks, and James Thomas.

After dragging Cook's body into a nearby forest of koa trees and brambles, the locals laid it atop a litter. A shift of warriors carried it up the steep lava and clay path winding up from the beach onto the slopes of Mauna Loa. Even as the warriors marched, Clerke had ordered men ashore under a flag of truce to collect

Cook's body, or even just his uniform. They returned empty-handed.

That night, miles inland, Cook's body was placed in an *imu*, a pit three feet deep filled with cooking stones that had been superheated in a mesquite fire. Normally, such a pit was used for roasting pig. Rushes, grasses, and leaves were placed on top of Cook to seal in the heat. Then sand and soil were heaped atop the body to close the unlikely tomb. After six hours of roasting, Cook's muscles and bones had separated, like a luau-ready swine. The bones were pulled from the *imu* in a religious ceremony honoring Cook's great power. He was scalped, and the brain, that wondrous repository of hopes and dreams and world travel—was placed back in the *imu* to be buried with his flesh.

The four most powerful chiefs on the island ate Cook's heart, then split the bones among them as a sacred offering and scattered them about the island, to be placed in special caves for burial.

The next day, as *Resolution* and *Discovery* bobbed at anchor, a warrior wearing Cook's hat paddled his canoe close to the ships and mooned the crew. In the interests of recovering Cook's remains, the man was not fired upon.

Eventually, part of Cook's skull, his arms and hands, and his thighbones were delivered to *Discovery*. Cook's hands had been severed and stuffed with salt for preservation. The scar on Cook's hand from so long ago in Newfoundland served as positive identification. Other returned items included his shotgun barrel and shoes but no uniform. There was nothing else to identify this pile of bones as one of the most powerful men on the face of this earth, or even a mere Royal Navy post captain. Just bones. Hawaiian historical legend claims the bones are still there, hidden high in the caves of Mauna Loa.

Clerke decided to bury Cook in Kealakekua Bay with full military honors. In Cook's honor, it was requested that the Hawaiians withdraw from the bay during the ceremony. They complied.

Cook's remains were placed inside a small coffin. The memorial service was read. Cannonballs weighted Cook's coffin as it was shoved over the side of *Resolution*, surrendered forever to the sea. In the most tragic way possible, James Cook—a brilliant, brave, flawed man—had found a way to stay forever in his Pacific kingdom.

Captain Cook, Hawaii

y quest for Cook ends on the island of Hawaii. I land at Kailua Kona Airport and sweat the moment I step off the plane into the tropics.

Over the course of a year I have seen Cook's world, through thousands of miles of travel, in planes and cars and by boat. I have visited blustery Marton, Great Ayton, Staithes, and Whitby; bustling Cape Town; the manicured lawns of historical Botany Bay and the plaque denoting where Cook and his men came ashore. I have combed for clues of him in Alaska, Canada, and, most powerful of all, the green, idyllic Endeavour Inlet. That quiet patch of New Zealand is still pristine, hard to reach, and awaiting Resolution's return. (Her fate, by some cruel twist of historical irony, is as incredible as Endeavour's—she was sold to the French, rechristened La Liberté, and transformed into a whaler, then ended her days rotting in Newport Harbor. She settled to the bottom just a mile from Endeavour.)

I will likely return to some of these lands, for sheer enchantment and to show my family. And I will make my way to some I have missed. But that will have to wait for another season of life. The true story of Cook will come to a close upon exploring one last destination.

Driving south, I pull into the village of Kailua Kona for lunch. Outrageously, as if Cook and Endeavour have come alive to mark the end of my travels, I'm shocked to see an exact replica of Endeavour bobbing in the harbor. It turns out she is traveling around the world, almost done with a journey that began and will end in Sydney.

If ever a man felt he were looking at a ghost ship, it is I, at this moment. To see Endeavour sailing the world in the twenty-first century would be like some twenty-third-century denizen witnessing an Apollo 15 command module tour the heavens. It's hard to imagine this proud ship's forebear settled at the bottom of Newport Harbor. Every drawing, every architectural blueprint, every model I have ever seen of this epic vessel has come to life before my eyes. But she is in full color instead of black and white, making her seem especially striking. Her decks creak as soft swells rock her. The great cabin's windows face toward the sea, as if Cook were inside at that very moment, haggling with Banks or sipping a port at the end of a long day.

There's a tour later in the day, and I buy a ticket. Then I leave Endeavour and drive south to my final destination on this worldwide journey: Kealakekua Bay. Though a memorial to Cook lies close to where he died, there are no signs pointing the way. (I gather that Cook's death site isn't high on the list of Hawaiian tourist attractions.) When I pass through the town of Captain Cook and see a Captain Cook Street, I know I must be close.

In the midst of my map study, I content myself with the knowledge that if I were searching for Charlie Clerke's final resting place, my task would be much more daunting. After Cook's death, Clerke vowed to continue his mentor's search for the Northwest Passage. Given Clerke's precarious finances, that twenty-thousand-pound reward must have played a significant role. However, when Arctic ice nearly trapped Resolution off the coast of Alaska, Clerke announced, much to the crew's relief, that it was time to go back to England.

But Clerke never made it that far. In August 1779, just six months after Cook's death, Clerke died of the tuberculosis he had contracted during his stint in debtors' prison. At the time, Resolution was sailing into the Russian harbor at Petropavlovsk. Clerke was buried ashore in a tiny churchyard.

Shortly thereafter, news of Cook's death reached England. Sandwich was devastated. "Above all we must keep in mind," he wrote to Banks, "that Cook is no more." Sandwich made good on his vow to patronize Elizabeth and the children and would provide for them the rest of their lives. He also took responsibility for editing Cook's final journals, chairing a committee doing the work Cook would have done alone. Sandwich made Cook's legacy his business and even took to retouching Cook's maps. Sandwich, Hinchingbrooke, and Montagu had been used too often as place names, in Sandwich's estimation. Cook, on the other hand, was barely used at all. He named a large body of water in Alaska the Cook Inlet and replaced many of the Sandwich references with names of members of the royal family. Prince William Sound in Alaska in one of those he renamed.

Sandwich's unhappy and controversial life took another cruel turn in 1779 when his mistress, Martha Ray, was murdered outside Covent Garden. As she stepped from a carriage, a deranged admirer shot her in the head.

Sandwich died January 30, 1792. His lavish lifestyle and largesse meant his last years were consumed with money-related worries, and he had to sell the family manor at Northamptonshire to remain solvent. His lordship's estate was worth just 694 pounds when he died. His last communiqué to his son curiously included a phrase from the hated French, and perhaps a subtle acknowledgment that Sandwich had little optimism for a happy afterlife. "Adieu," he wrote. "Probably forever."

For all his shining accomplishments and genius, Sandwich would be remembered for just one historical factoid. In 1750, a time when dinner was generally served at four in the afternoon, Sandwich often worked (and gambled) late into the night. On one occasion, he raided the kitchen for a midnight snack. By slapping salt beef between two slices of bread, he invented the "sandwich." Regretfully, that would be his only enduring legacy. When Sandwich ceased his tenure as First Lord in 1781, the Admiralty ceased voyages of exploration. The term Sandwich Islands never caught on in Hawaii and fell out of use when it became an American protectorate.

Joseph Banks continued blustery and self-consumed for the rest of his life, only becoming more so with every passing year. He became president of the Royal Society in 1778, and in 1784 he ordered it to strike a gold medal with Cook's likeness. He would remain Royal Society president until his death from complications of gout in April of 1820. He died while living at 32 Soho Square, overlooking a small park, with two male botanists as roommates. Today Banks's former home is the British office of 20th Century Fox. In March 2001, Britain's Natural History Museum in London announced the discovery in their catacombs of fifty fish specimens preserved by Banks on Endeavour. The fish still floated in the same rum Banks placed them in two centuries prior.

Three of Cook's children died young—Joseph in September 1768, Elizabeth in 1771, and George in October 1772—but all would suffer at the hand of fate. On October 3, 1780, three days before Resolution and Discovery reached England after four years and three months at sea, Nathaniel Cook was a midshipman on the Thunderer, a seventy-four-gun frigate in the West Indies. In a famous hurricane off the coast of Jamaica, his ship went down with thirteen other vessels.

Hugh Cook entered Christ's College, Cambridge, with intention of becoming a clergyman. Four months later, he caught fever and died on December 21, 1793. He was just seventeen.

James Cook was thirty in 1793 and promoted commander in the Royal Navy. On January 25, 1794, he was on his way to Portsmouth to join his vessel, Spitfire, a sloop of war. He embarked in an open boat from Poole in bad weather. His body washed up on the Isle of Wight, his pockets empty and his head severely bloodied.

Elizabeth Cook moved from Mile End Road in July 1788 to a house on High Street, Clapham, to live as a guest of her cousin Isaac Smith, who had sailed as a boy on Endeavour and Resolution's first voyage. Smith, *whom Cook had selected to leap ashore first in Australia, rose to rear admiral before retiring to Clapham. Elizabeth Cook remained there forty-seven years. She died in 1835, but not before burning all the letters Cook had written through their years together. Elizabeth took the details of their passionate, intimate love affair to her grave.*

The memorial to Cook at Great St. Andrew's Church, Cambridge, encapsulates the tragedies Elizabeth endured. It reads:

IN MEMORY
of CAPTAIN JAMES COOK, *of the* ROYAL NAVY,
one of the most celebrated Navigators, that this,
or former Ages can boast of; who was killed by
the Natives of Owyhee, in the Pacific Ocean, on the
14th Day of February, 1779; in the 51st Year of his Age.
Of Mr. NATHANIEL COOK, *who was lost with the*
Thunderer Man of War, Captain Boyle Walsingham,
in a most dreadful Hurricane, in October, 1780;
Aged 16 Years.
Of Mr. HUGH COOK, *of Christ's College,* CAMBRIDGE,
who died on the 21st of December, 1793; aged 17 Years.
Of JAMES COOK, Esq; COMMANDER *in the* ROYAL NAVY,
who lost his Life on the 25th of January, 1794; in
going from Poole, to the Spitfire Sloop of War, which
He commanded; in the 31st Year of his Age.
Of ELIZTH COOK, *who died April 9th 1771, Aged 4 Years.*
JOSEPH COOK, *who died Septr 13th 1768, Aged 1 Month.*
GEORGE COOK, *who died Octr 1st 1772, Aged 4 Months.*
All Children of the first mentioned CAPT JAMES COOK *by*
ELIZABETH COOK, *who survived her Husband 56 Years, &*
Departed this life 13th May 1835 at her residence Clapham Surrey
in the 94th Year of her Age. Her remains are deposited
with those of her Sons JAMES & HUGH.
in the middle Aisle of this Church.

James Cook senior outlived his son, but only barely. He died April 1, 1779, at the age of eighty-five.

On a winding, downhill drive named Napoopoo Road, I find the trail Hawaiian warriors used so long ago to carry Cook's body up Mauna Loa. The formal name is the Kaawaloa Trail. Beginning at the thousand-foot level, it gradually descends through the Ekoa Forest to the sea and the remains of Kaawaloa.

The pungent, decaying carcass of a wild pig marks the trailhead. Ferrets and flies attack the exposed ribs. Stepping around them, I follow the clearly marked path for a hundred yards before it disappears into a stand of elephant grass. I press through, trusting the downward slope to point the way. Humidity has me wringing wet after five more minutes' trek. Small black bugs dot my face, bare legs, shirt, and shorts. I lose track of all the spiderwebs I walk through. The soil is alternately muddy and lava. I can imagine the Hawaiian warriors struggling up this steep slope, carrying Cook's bloody litter.

Miles later I stumble out of the jungle at sea level, picking up the trail again as it enters a maze of black lava walls signifying the remains of the ancient village. Vegetation grows through what were once homes and communal areas. The sensation is, again, ghostly. I angle left as the trail enters a corridor between two walls, toward the ocean.

Finally reaching Kealakekua Bay, I dunk my head in the water, then clean my hands and arms. I spy a flat plaque buried beneath the waterline and climb over a fallen tree for a closer look, for I haven't seen mention of this in any guidebooks. "Near this spot," it reads simply, "Captain James Cook Met His Death February 14th, 1779." The incoming tides and slick algae have pushed the plaque from its mount. I heave it square, preserving it from the sea a few days more.

Cook, if attacked anywhere near this spot, would not have been able to run or swim without stumbling. The ocean bottom here is undulating volcanic rock covered by a slick microlayer of marine life. At less than three feet deep, it is too shallow for swimming (if Cook had only known how). Even if the marines had attempted to row back to save Cook, it would have been simple for the crowd of Hawaiians to block their access. It is obvious to me that Cook had been trapped in the perfect killing zone.

Why did Cook chase adventure? And why do men and women who have it all chase adventure, even today? The answer is, because it is their calling. Their gift. Without their wanderings, society would be poorer, more short-sighted, and far more mundane. Cook, a simple man with great dreams, changed the way the world saw itself and inspired future generations of adventurers.

I strip for a swim and half-wade, half-float away from shore. I dive under when the water is deep enough and discover that less than fifty feet from shore, roughly where the pinnace waited for Cook, the ocean bottom drops off like a cliff. The depth changes from six feet to six hundred. The water color changes from a clear blue to a murky gray, then black. Coral blossoms like ten-foot-tall cauliflower jut horizontally from the cliff face. I dive deeper into the darkness, drifting out over the cliff until it feels as if I were flying.

Somewhere down there, on a bottom so deep in the blackness, rests Cook's weighted coffin. For Cook, a man whose mind was constantly divided between sea and land, dying with one foot in the ocean and one foot on land was fitting. To be buried at sea more so.

James Cook and his family paid a horrific cost, but he was the greatest adventurer of all time. There will never be another like him. He went as far as a man could go.